THE CHURCH
WHAT IS IT?

THE CHURCH
WHAT IS IT?

Fair as the moon, clear as the sun,
and terrible as an army with banners
SONG 6:10

THE APOSTOLIC FOUNDATION
OF THE
CHRISTIAN CHURCH

Volume Seven

JOHN METCALFE

THE PUBLISHING TRUST
Church Road, Tylers Green, Penn, Buckinghamshire.

Printed and Published by
John Metcalfe Publishing Trust
Church Road, Tylers Green
Penn, Buckinghamshire

—

—

First Published 1990

—

ISBN 1 870039 23 8

—

CONTENTS

THE CHURCH

And Jesus answered and said unto him, Blessed art thou, Simon Bar-jona: for flesh and blood hath not revealed it unto thee, but my Father which is in heaven. And I say also unto thee, That thou art Peter, and upon this rock I will build my church; and the gates of hell shall not prevail against it.

Matthew 16:17,18

I

What is the Church?

WHAT is the 'church'? To answer this question it is useless to consider what the church has become. It is essential to go back to the beginning, enquiring, What did Christ and the apostles themselves understand by the word 'church', and what was it then? Because whatever has happened since, what it was then is what it should be now: nothing but the original.

Hence, for the answer to the question, What is the church? one must go straight back to its inception.

How? Two sources of information remain to us from those early times. The first appears in the meaning of the word in the original language used by the apostles, that is, the new testament Greek. The second source consists of the sum of the knowledge that may be gleaned from the use of that Greek word in all the passages throughout the new testament.

These two sources are exclusive: there is no other source. And these two sources are infallible: the water from this place is clear as crystal, no pollution exists, it is pure. Here, and here alone, one may drink as from the fountain of the water of life with childlike trust, and with perfect peace.

1. The Word 'Church'

Virtually no language translates the new testament Greek word *ἐκκλησία*, *ekklēsia.* Transliteration—the incorporation into another language of a foreign word, without any attempt at translation—occurs in a few cases such as the French *église*, the Spanish *iglesia*, and the Welsh *eglwys. Ecclesia*, Greek or not, has appeared as such in these—and other—tongues, only slightly modified in the process.

But the English word 'church', together with the Scottish 'kirk', the German 'kirche', the Dutch 'kerk', the Swedish 'kyrka', the Russian 'tserkov', the Finnish 'kirkko', all these, and others still of the same order, neither transliterate nor translate anything at all from the new testament.

Practically, such words mean nothing, yet they have been used to serve as if they had rendered *ecclesia* in their respective tongues.

Scholars, doctors, theologians, schoolmen have laboured long and hard to prove a connection between 'church' or 'kirk' and the Greek *Kurios*, 'Lord'. But they have failed abysmally. There is no connection.

And had they succeeded, somehow implying that the word 'church' was derived from the new testament Greek *Kurios*, 'Lord', what of that? This would still not have translated *ecclesia*: it would have mangled *Kurios*, a different word altogether! And what would be the value in that?

Obviously, one must return to the source, and to the source alone, if one is not to be entangled in the bewildering confusion that has successively accumulated throughout the ages.

The new testament Greek word ἐκκλησία, *ekklēsia*—translated by the word 'church' in the English bible—is in fact a compound word rooted in the simple verb *kaleō*, 'to call'.

Kaleō, 'to call', occurs some one hundred and forty-seven times in the new testament, extending to the words *klētos*, 'called'— occurring eleven times—and *klēsis*, 'calling'—also used eleven times.

This word gives the central meaning to which is joined the preposition *ek*, 'out of', to create the compound (ἐκ- κλησία) ἐκκλησία , *ekklēsia*, literally, *That which is called out*. But how on earth does the word 'church' convey *that* meaning in English?

Far from conveying the meaning of the Greek for the benefit of the English reader, the sense is totally obscured by the substitution of a word having no meaning in itself. This meaningless word is that which, subsequently, has been used to describe a series of 'religious' buildings belonging to a latter-day invented system, endorsed by the State, the very opposite to the *ecclesia* of the new testament.

The imposition of the word 'church' upon the new testament implies that this signifies the same thing as that raised up under the apostles in the new testament. But what passes as the 'church' is not the same thing. It is a very different thing indeed, as the examination of the exclusive and infallible sources shows—and will show—most clearly.

In fact the word 'church', a word lost in antiquity as to any inherent meaning, probably of prehistoric and heathen origin, vaguely superstitious in connotation, pre-dating the Christian era, could hardly be more inappropriate. The translators of the English bible would have been hard put to find a word more calculated completely to obscure and obliterate in English the plain meaning of *ecclesia*, 'that which is called out'.

The word 'church' translates nothing at all, it is transliterated from no language whatever, and is wholly meaningless in itself.

Yet the translators of the successive English versions—because of their vested interest in that religious system which gave them a living, status, and a variety of worldly honours—had no hesitation in putting the word used colloquially to describe their aberrant and worldly corruption from the original, in virtually every place where the word *ecclesia* occurred in the bible. So that their 'church' henceforward must appear to be the same thing as the *ecclesia* of Christ to the ordinary reader of their translations of the new testament.

If this is not what Paul calls 'sleight of men', Eph. 4:14, then what is?

Will they dare to describe this as 'not handling the word of God deceitfully'? as opposed to, 'by manifestation of the truth commending ourselves to every man's conscience in the sight of God', II Cor. 4:2?

And if the truth of the *ecclesia* be not manifest to the conscience of every man, where does this leave us, but stumbling even at the very threshold?

2. The Word 'Calling'

What has been observed from the source of the meaning of *ecclesia*—improperly called 'church' in the English bible—is that it is a word entirely rooted in the concept of 'calling', but calling 'out'. It is 'that which is called out'.

Necessarily therefore the root, *kaleō*, 'to call', together with the branches *klētos*, 'called', and *klēsis*, 'calling', must be considered and summarised, because that is the concept out of which the word *ecclesia* has developed.

This observation is of the essence to the understanding of the word *ecclesia*, 'that which is called out'.

Consider therefore the Call, the Calling, and the Called, in summary, from the new testament:

i. Calling is by grace

That is, 'Calling' is not man's calling upon God, but God's calling to men. As to the men whom he calls, that is his choice, not theirs. He chooses to call them, they do not choose to call him.

Observe: Rom. 9:11, That the purpose of God according to election might stand, not of works, but of him that calleth; and again, Gal. 1:15, It pleased God to call Paul—and that from heaven—by his grace.

Rom. 8:28 speaks of them who are the called according to his purpose; that is, I Cor. 1:2, Called to be saints, whether from the Jews or the Greeks, I Cor. 1:24. Even us, whom he hath called—*he* hath called, mark—not of the Jews only, but of the Gentiles also, Rom. 9:24.

Thus Rom. 9:25. I will call them my people which were not my people: I will call them, notice. Hence, I Cor. 1:9, God is faithful, by whom ye were called. This is of God: Rom. 11:29, for his gifts and calling are without repentance. Thus it appears, II Tim. 1:9, he hath called us: not we have called him. So that it is said, Rom. 9:24, Even us, whom he hath called. Whence, calling is of grace.

ii. Calling is to glory

It is not a calling for this present world, but for the world to come; not for this life, but for a better resurrection. Hence Paul prays, Eph. 1:18, That ye may know what is the hope of his calling: and if hope, therefore it is future.

This calling is for the heavenly glory, Eph. 4:4, Even as ye are called in one hope of your calling. Ye are, therefore, Heb. 3:1, Partakers of the heavenly calling. So Peter tells us, I Pet. 3:9, Ye are thereunto called, that ye should inherit a blessing: and, as we all know, an inheritance is future. So Heb. 9:15, That they which are called might receive the promise of eternal inheritance.

This is called, Phil. 3:14, The high calling of God in Christ Jesus; it is divine and certain, all of grace, and all for glory, as saith Paul, Rom. 8:30, Whom he did predestinate, them he also called: and whom he called, them he also justified: and whom he justified, them he also glorified.

For, I Thess. 2:12, God hath called you unto his kingdom and glory. Whereunto, II Thess. 2:14, he called you by our gospel, to the obtaining of the glory of our Lord Jesus Christ. Or, as Peter puts it, I Pet. 5:10, The God of all grace hath called us unto his eternal glory by Christ Jesus.

iii. Calling is of God

II Tim. 1:9, God hath saved us, and called us with an holy calling, not according to our works, but according to his own purpose and grace. Rom. 9:11, Not of works, but of him that calleth. I Thess. 5:24, Faithful is he that calleth you—not faithful are you that calleth him—who also will do it.

And why not? For, Rom. 8:28, Ye are the called according to his purpose. Not your own purpose: his purpose.

It is he alone, I Pet. 2:9,10, who hath called you out of darkness into his marvellous light: which in time past were not a people, but are now the people of God. It is God who called you unto his kingdom, I Thess. 2:12, and hath he not power to achieve his own end in so doing? Indeed he has, for calling is of God, unto glory. Whereunto, II Thess. 2:14, he called you by our gospel.

Calling is of God, for, John 10:3, He calleth his own sheep —mark that, his own sheep—by name, and leadeth them out: they are called *out*, notice, as in *ek-klēsia.*

This calling is certain, precisely because it is of God, and sure to all the 'sheep' who are thus brought to faith. 'My sheep', John 10:27-30, who 'hear my voice, and follow me.' 'I give unto them eternal life; and they shall never perish, neither shall any man pluck them out of my hand. My Father, which gave them me, is greater than all; and no man is able to pluck them out of my Father's hand. I and my Father are one.'

From which we are to conclude, Calling is of God.

Now, all this underlies *ecclesia*, being implied in the main body of the word. It is 'that which is called' and 'called out'. The *ecclesia* is therefore, by definition, called by grace, called to glory, and called of God.

This calling, which pertains to the *ecclesia*, is first holy: II Tim. 1:9, Called with an holy calling. Next it is heavenly: Heb. 3:1, Partakers of the heavenly calling. Third, it is high: Phil. 3:14, The high calling of God in Christ Jesus. Fourth, it is separate: Mt. 2:15, Out of Egypt have I called my son. Again, it is by the gospel: II Thess. 2:14, Whereunto he called you by our gospel. Sixth, this calling is by the Father to the Son: I Cor. 1:9, God is faithful, by whom ye were called unto the fellowship of his Son. Seventh, it is a calling into a visible unity, Col. 3:15, Ye are called in one body.

All this lies at the root. It may be determined from the meaning of that Greek word—*ekklēsia*—which the translators have failed to translate. Instead, they have inappropriately foisted upon the bible a word—'church'—which means nothing at all to the purpose, but which they and their fathers have used—long after the close of the scriptures—to designate their own religious structure, vastly fallen from the original.

But it is to the original that we must go if we would understand the meaning of the new testament word which they have incorrectly dubbed 'church'. *Ecclesia* is not 'church'. Literally, it is 'that which is called out'. Now, therefore, consider this compound word as such.

3. The Word 'Ecclesia'

The Greek word *ἐκκλησία*, *ekklēsia*, was long in use before being taken up in the new testament, having the general meaning of—according to the lexicographers—'an assembly duly summoned', a sense which went back into the centuries before Christ.

It is in this sense that the word *ecclesia* is used of the 'assembly' at Ephesus, Acts 19:32,39 and 41.

Note that the translators have rendered the same word *ecclesia* as 'assembly' on these three occasions only. Whilst everywhere else they have concealed precisely the same word by the meaningless jargon 'church'!

Little is to be gained from a survey of the use of *ecclesia* in the Greek tongue before the new testament, save to establish the truth of the general meaning, 'a summoned assembly'. This is the meaning taken up by the Holy Ghost and used by Christ and the apostles to describe 'that which is called out' in the new testament by the gospel.

The word *ecclesia* appears in the Septuagint—the Greek translation of the Hebrew old testament scriptures concluded at Alexandria possibly over two centuries before Christ—to signify the congregation or assembly of the children of Israel. That assembly or congregation was the sum of the people of God on earth: God's people Israel in their entirety.

Now, this is the word—with its old testament connotations, as indicated by the Septuagint usage—this is the word, I say, that is taken up *in an entirely new way*, by the revelation of the Holy Ghost, *to indicate an entirely new ecclesia, Christ's ecclesia*, in the new testament.

This is no longer that—earthly and natural—people Israel called out of Egypt as one assembly under the old covenant. Here appears that new testament, heavenly and spiritual people, called out of the world by grace, for glory, by the voice of the Son of God, to be one visible body for his testimony throughout this present age.

The translation of the word *ecclesia* may therefore be rendered 'assembly', or, perhaps better still, 'congregation', but certainly not 'church'. As to 'assembly' or 'congregation', both words at least *translate* 'ecclesia', whereas 'church' translates nothing whatsoever, but only brings everything into confusion.

It is true, however, that some—relatively few—words when translated from one language to another do not find a precise equivalent. The English 'congregation' and 'assembly' are no exception when translating the Greek *ecclesia.* To put this at its simplest, neither English word is derived from a compound the components of which are 'out of' and 'call'.

Yet 'out of' and 'call' were ideas subconsciously imbibed in the minds of Greek speaking users of the word *ecclesia*, and therefore were ideas which would permeate the speakers' awareness of the meaning inherent in Greek usage.

The truth is that the English cannot exactly match such a word. An English phrase would do it, yes: 'That which is called out'. But a word, no.

'Congregation' could be near, provided that it is understood that this is not local or partial but reflects the figure of the entire congregation of God's people Israel travelling with the tabernacle through the wilderness under the old testament. Also provided that the concept of the congregation 'called out' is retained in this unique use of the word *ecclesia* by Christ and his apostles.

Let the right background ideas be retained, and either 'congregation' or 'assembly' would perhaps afford the most suitable English equivalents to the complex word *ecclesia* in the Greek.

So much for the meaning of the word itself. It is now time briefly to turn to those passages in which *ecclesia* appears throughout the new testament.

First, to generalize. The word *ekklēsia—ek* and *kaleō* being borne in mind—occurs one hundred and fifteen times in the new testament. Three times only the translators have rendered the word 'assembly', each time the 'assembly' of Ephesian citizens, Acts 19:32,39 and 41.

In every other instance the translators have substituted a word meaningless in the English, and not equivalent in the least degree to the Greek: the word 'church'.

Of the one hundred and fifteen passages in which the word *ecclesia* appears in the new testament, only three occur in the gospels. All these are to be found in the gospel according to Matthew, and all are spoken by Jesus himself.

In the epistles, the word *ecclesia*, translated 'church', occurs most of all in I Corinthians, with twenty-two references. Provided the three places translated 'assembly' are excluded, the book of Acts comes next, where the word 'church' appears in the English twenty-one times. After this, the book of the Revelation follows with twenty references.

All other books have single figure occurrences, nine in II Corinthians and Ephesians, five in Romans, four in Colossians, three in Matthew, Galatians, I Timothy, and III John. *Ecclesia* occurs twice in Philippians, I Thessalonians, II Thessalonians, and Hebrews. Philemon and James have one occurrence only.

In the English bible, thirty-six times the word *ecclesia* is rendered in the plural, 'churches'. The basic meaning of the word, however, is that of 'the' congregation, namely, that people called out from Egypt in a figure, and from the world in reality, pilgrims and strangers, passing as one body through this present wilderness to the promised land of inheritance in the everlasting glory.

II

The Introduction to the Ecclesia

i. The words of Jesus

MATTHEW is the only one of the four evangelists to record the use of the word translated 'church'. *Ecclesia* occurs three times in this gospel, first in Mt. 16:18, and twice in Mt. 18:17. Each time the word falls from the lips of Jesus himself. It is striking that these are the only references to the *ecclesia* prior to the actual formation of the assembly on the day of Pentecost.

ii. Typified but without precedent

By saying 'My' *ecclesia*, the Lord excludes all that went before. He proposes what is new, and in the future. This is confirmed by the words 'I will build', not 'I have built'.

The exclusively new testament character of the rock upon which Christ will build; the truth that he himself was about to build; the fact that this work had not then begun but was soon to begin: all point to the unique revelation of 'My *ecclesia*'.

It is true that in Acts 7:38 Stephen speaks of Israel as 'the *ecclesia* in the wilderness', just as later in the same book there is reference to an 'assembly' at Ephesus. In both places there is a general use of the word *ecclesia*, first for 'the congregation called out' from Egypt, and then for the Ephesian citizens 'called out to congregate' as an assembly.

This fact does not and cannot contradict the specific use of the word by the Holy Ghost, in which the apostolic usage determines a divinely sanctified meaning that is unique.

There can be no comparison between Israel and the *ecclesia* in the new testament sense, save only that the—once mentioned—'*ecclesia* in the wilderness' was but a pale reflection, a figure of the true, under the types and shadows of the old covenant. Now, however, the true light has come, reality has appeared, and everlasting glory has burst forth with the resurrection of the Son of God.

Henceforward the use of the word *ecclesia* signifies a unique unfolding of the mind and purpose of God in Christ, the revelation of the mystery hidden from ages and generations, a revelation now made manifest according to the commandment of the everlasting God.

The '*ecclesia* in the wilderness' of which Stephen spoke, was the earthly, natural, and worldly shadow of that which was to come. Israel sheltered beneath the blood upon the doorposts and lintels, partook of the passover lamb, and was saved from the judgment of God when the sentence fell on all the firstborn of the land of Ham. The whole congregation was the one assembly, called out of Egypt to go forth through the wilderness to the land of promise.

All passed through the Red sea, all received the living oracles, all were gathered according to God's ordinances about the tabernacle of witness. The congregation was marked out by the signs of the divine presence, 'the assembly in the wilderness with the angel which spake ... in the mount Sina', receiving the tables of the law, a testimony of the righteousness required of man in his pilgrimage through this present world.

Israel was a figure of the true in that the people as one company were led by the pillar of cloud by day, and the pillar of fire by night, eating of the bread from heaven and drinking of that spiritual rock which followed them. As a worldly shadow of the heavenly substance to come they attended the service of the priesthood of Aaron and his sons, and of the Levites, offering sacrifices continually by their hands at the door of the tent of witness.

This was the congregation of the LORD, which in itself comprised all the people of God on earth without exception, gathered into the power and presence of the God of Israel. As to all the world besides, all lay in gross darkness, without God, without covenant, outside the commonwealth of Israel, under condemnation and wrath.

By so much, this was a faint foreshadowing of that spiritual body which was to be called by Christ, 'My *ecclesia*'. The congregation of all Israel thus prefigured that assembly which should be built by the Son of God from the glory after his ascension to the right hand of the Majesty on high.

But with the coming of Christ, 'the assembly in the wilderness', the figure of the true, passed away, for the true light had arisen. Then to earthly, natural and worldly Israel came the word, 'Arise shine, for thy light is come, and the glory of the LORD is risen upon thee.' This glory shone from the heavenly, spiritual, and supernatural fulfilment of all that ever went before. Now it could be said, and that truly, 'Christ our passover is sacrificed for us'. This sacrifice secured eternal redemption, everlasting righteousness, and certain forgiveness for all his people.

Unlike the types and shadows of old, Christ's offering was not a temporal atonement ritually made in a worldly sanctuary on earth, with the blood of beasts being sprinkled by the finger of a corruptible and dying priest upon a decaying gold pattern. For Christ, being raised from the dead, ascended into heaven, sprinkled with his own precious blood the propitiatory made higher than the heavens, thereafter to minister in the power of an endless life, consecrated by the oath of God to an everlasting priesthood, reigning and glorified in the heaven of heavens.

From thence he builds his *ecclesia.* Then this is a congregation already redeemed, and certain to be gathered in the power of the Holy Ghost from heaven. For 'there is one body, and one Spirit, even as ye are called in one hope of your calling; one Lord, one faith, one baptism; one God and Father of all, who is above all, and through all, and in you all.' This unity may be manifest in various assemblies, but what is manifest is *the* assembly: 'My assembly'.

This is that assembly filled with one Spirit, united to one Lord, and indwelt by one God and Father: the one visible holy catholic *ecclesia.* This, 'My *ecclesia*', has been 'delivered from this present evil world', as well as its evil religion. It is not of the world, but has been called out of the world, being a separate body to Christ, who is Head over all things to the assembly, which is his body, the fulness of him which filleth all in all.

This congregation, this *ecclesia*, has passed from death unto life, as through the Red sea, beneath the waters of which 'the world' of Egypt perished—'now is the judgment of this world' —and through the Jordan of death with Christ—'being buried with him by baptism into death.' Risen with Christ out of the waters of death, the entire assembly is brought inwardly in Spirit by faith to sit in heavenly places in Christ Jesus, even upon the heavenly mount Zion in glory.

Christ's *ecclesia* is not gathered as a worldly congregation about an earthly tent of witness, neither does it worship in temples made with hands. The assembly itself is the temple of the living God, an holy temple in the Lord, the very house of God, the *ecclesia* of the living God, the pillar and ground of the truth. This fulfils the word, 'I in them, and thou in me, that they may be made perfect in one; that the world may know that thou hast sent me, and hast loved them, as thou hast loved me.'

This *ecclesia* which Christ builds does not receive—as did the children of Israel in the wilderness—the two tables of stone from mount Sinai. On the contrary, it is an assembly of those dead to the law by the body of Christ, sin no longer having dominion over them, and precisely because of this reason, 'ye are not under the law but under grace'.

For if they which are of the law be heirs, faith is made void, and the promise made of none effect. Why? Because the law worketh wrath. But where no law is, there is no transgression. Therefore it is of faith, that it might be by grace, to the end that the promise might be sure to all the seed.

And it is sure, even to all whom Christ builds into that which he calls 'My assembly'. All who are called out to this assembly are crucified with Christ, buried with him by baptism into death, and thus are enabled to say, 'I through the law am dead to the law, that I might live unto God'. For Christ is the end of the law for righteousness to every one that believeth.

Nevertheless in its time the tabernacle of witness in Israel did testify of better things to come in Christ. But now 'the testimony of Christ is confirmed in you', who are become in Christ the tabernacle of God and the Father. The testimony we receive is not that of the law of commandments graven on tables of stone, but that of the testimony of Christ, the indwelling of the Father, and the witness of the Holy Ghost.

In the new testament *ecclesia*—'My assembly'—the law of Christ is graven on the heart; the law of liberty is inscribed in the mind; the law of faith is impressed upon the soul; the law of love is settled within the affections; the law of kindness is established between the lips; and the law of the spirit of life in Christ Jesus is etched within the character of the new man risen with the Son of God to newness of life.

This is 'My assembly'. In this assembly the fulness of the Holy Ghost testifies abundantly that grace reigns through righteousness unto eternal life by Jesus Christ our Lord.

The congregation of Christ is not led by any outward pillar of cloud or of fire from one place to another in this present world. Rather, being delivered from this present world, this congregation is led to the world to come by the Spirit of the living God: 'For as many as are led by the Spirit of God, they are the sons of God.'

This leading, proper and exclusive to the assembly built by Christ, is spiritual and not carnal; eternal and not temporal; invisible and not tangible; divine and not human; mysterious and not rational; heavenly and not earthly; and it stands by revelation not education.

Under this leading of the Holy Ghost the whole body in every member receives the continuous ministry of the one Priest from heaven, Christ Jesus, the Son of God, who inwardly and spiritually gives of his flesh and of his blood. Nor do the members of this body of Christ come into condemnation. Neither shall they see death. For they have been justified freely by grace alone, and through faith only.

This assembly—unlike that of Israel which foreshadowed the substance of the true—is not served by a fleshly, dying, priesthood, ordained after the law of a carnal commandment. This assembly is served by him who came forth from the Father, and was in the world, and went to the Father, having first laid aside his garments to take a towel, and a bason of water, to wash and dry the feet of all his disciples.

This assembly, which Christ builds, is established upon mercy that endures for ever, and supported by faithfulness established in the very heavens. 'For I have said, Mercy shall be built up for ever: thy faithfulness shalt thou establish in the very heavens.'

Here is a congregation brought through the rent veil by a new and living way, by the blood of Jesus, into the Holiest of all in the heavenly glory. Not simply to attend an outward, earthly, and objective sanctuary, however devoutly, but actually to become the interior sanctuary of the living God, indwelt by Father, Son, and Holy Ghost, God blessed for evermore, Amen.

Christ's congregation or assembly, his *ecclesia*, is a new creation, altogether new, it is the revelation of the mystery, it has a light most precious, it has the glory of God. This assembly is entirely of the new testament, it is heavenly not earthly, of the world to come not of the world that now is, it is divine, spiritual, and supernatural. It is the assembly which answers to the heavenly Jerusalem, to mount Zion, to the bride of the Lamb. It is a holy glorious *ecclesia*, not having spot, or wrinkle, or any such thing.

Within this assembly shines the light, dwells the life, and abides the love of Christ, which passes knowledge, yea, within, all glorious within, the assembly of Christ is filled with all the fulness of God. The fulness of God is instantly and constantly conveyed from heaven to the interior of this united and entire congregation below, by the Holy Ghost, bringing union and communion with the Father and the Son.

This is 'My assembly', and it is unique, and, if foreshadowed, eye had not seen, nor ear heard, neither had it entered into the heart of man to conceive the heavenly glories, the everlasting blessings, the divine mysteries, the spiritual enlargements, the eternal fulness brought in for the Father by the Son of his love. This is that fulness manifest in the united people baptised by one Spirit into one body, the congregation of the living God, the pillar and ground of the truth, the habitation of God through the Spirit: 'My' *ecclesia*.

From which it is to be observed that although the *ecclesia* of Christ had an earthly type, it had no heavenly precedent. This assembly, or congregation, is a heavenly mystery brought in by revelation from on high through the preaching of the gospel of Christ by those sent on his authority for the obedience of faith among all nations.

'Now to him that is of power to stablish you according to my gospel, and the preaching of Jesus Christ, according to the revelation of the mystery, which was kept secret since the world began, but now is made manifest, and by the scriptures of the prophets, according to the commandment of the everlasting God, made known to all nations for the obedience of faith: to God only wise, be glory through Jesus Christ for ever. Amen.'

iii. A great mystery

Hence the assembly, called out by Christ, is a revealed mystery. Never before had there been anything like it. It is a mystery that was hidden, brought to light by the ascension of Christ and the sending down of the Holy Ghost from heaven.

This mystery is made manifest by the baptism of the Spirit: 'For by one Spirit are we all baptised into one body, whether we be Jews or Gentiles, whether we be bond or free; and have all been made to drink into one Spirit.' No matter how graphic the foreshadowing, however vivid the types and figures, how could there have been anything remotely approaching this?

Before the ascension and glorifying of Christ, the *ecclesia* could not have been so much as envisaged: 'This spake he of the Spirit, which they that believe on him should receive: for the Holy Ghost was not yet given; because that Jesus was not yet glorified.' Then, the *ecclesia*, Christ's assembly, was a hidden mystery, divine, heavenly, spiritual: a mystery that could not come to light until wondrously united to Christ on high and formed by the Spirit below, the manifestation of the purpose of God in Christ.

'This is a great mystery', says the apostle Paul, 'but I speak concerning Christ and the *ecclesia*.' By revelation the mystery was made known to the apostle, and it was called 'the mystery of Christ'. And this revelation was of necessity, seeing that 'In other ages it was not made known unto the sons of men, as it is now revealed unto his holy apostles and prophets by the Spirit; that the Gentiles should be fellowheirs, and of the same body, and partakers of his promise in Christ by the gospel.'

Indeed the apostle's ministry was 'to make all'—the elect—'see what is the fellowship of the mystery, which from the beginning of the world hath been hid in God, who created all things by Jesus Christ: to the intent that now'—mark that, now—'unto the principalities and powers in heavenly places might be known by the *ecclesia*'—by 'that which is called out', notice—'the manifold wisdom of God, according to the eternal purpose which he purposed in Christ Jesus our Lord: in whom we have boldness and access with confidence by the faith of him.'

Of this mystery of the assembly he speaks in another place, saying, 'Even the mystery which hath been hid from ages and from generations'—that is, until the time was fulfilled, in which Christ said, On this rock I will build my *ecclesia*—'but now is made manifest to his saints: to whom God would make known what is the riches of the glory of this mystery among the Gentiles; which is Christ in you, the hope of glory.' From which it is evident, no precedent for 'My *ecclesia*' could have existed.

Before the *ecclesia* could come in, God must be glorified; atonement must be made; all righteousness must be fulfilled; the law must be vindicated; justice must be satisfied; the flesh must be condemned; heaven must be opened; the veil must be rent; and the Son of man must be glorified. Then, and only then, could it come to pass that 'Behold, the tabernacle of God is with men, and he will dwell with them, and they shall be his people, and God himself shall be their God.' This shall fulfil what is written, 'That they all may be one; as thou, Father, art in me, and I in thee, that they also may be one in us; that the world may believe that thou hast sent me.'

It is this, by the descent of the Person of the Holy Ghost on the day of Pentecost, that makes manifest Christ's assembly, 'the mystery of God, and of the Father, and of Christ.' It is the revelation of that new, unique work unveiled by the Father and the Son: it is the mystery hidden from ages and generations but which is now made manifest: it is the calling out and uniting together of that people whom Christ calls 'My *ecclesia*'.

iv. Baseless and puerile traditions

This is that *ecclesia* which Christ himself builds, as he says, 'On this rock I will build my assembly'. But which rock? The word 'rock', πέτρα, *petra*, is that from which the name Peter, Πέτρος, *Petros*, or 'a Rock', is derived.

But derivation is not identification. Any more than a rain-drop is the same thing as rain. Or a snowflake as snow. Just so, a rock—or many rocks—may be taken from the elemental nature of rock, yet, whilst being identical in substance, remain different in form.

According to Roman Catholic and Anglican tradition, however, *Petros*, Peter, 'a Rock', and *petra*, 'rock', are identical. So that by this departure from the meaning of plain language, not to say common sense, the ground should be prepared for a more sinister aberration: that the 'church' is built upon Peter's authority, and that this—presumed—authority must be handed down in succession, by no means to be challenged. But we do challenge it. Just as we challenge the false interpretation upon which it rests.

'On this rock', says Christ, 'I will build my *ecclesia*'. Ah, say the Roman and Anglican doctors, the rock refers to Peter. They seek to establish this blatant—and once exploded—error in sundry ways and divers manners. For example, by craftily insinuating this fallacy into the minds of the unwary even as they read holy scripture. How? I will tell you how.

Observe Matthew 16:18. When this place is printed in the King James' Version, and other versions, with a central margin reference, the reader is pointed to the following marginal texts: 'Eph. 2:20; Rev. 21:14'. There is absolutely no authority for these impudent insertions on the part of the 'translators'. There is nothing to translate. No such references exist in the Greek. Only in the crafty minds of clerical 'doctors' centuries later.

This is wresting the scripture with a witness, joining together what God hath put asunder in order to support the unsupportable, namely, their 'apostolic succession' heresy. Why do it? Because this heresy is the basis of their *apartheid* clerical position, and, if so, of the very authority of their respective communions.

But this can neither be proved nor upheld, and the moment these 'doctors' turn from an appeal to the world by way of baseless tradition, to an appeal to the *ecclesia* by way of scripture, they are exposed and undone. Hence they descend to insinuating improper cross-references into holy writ. Why? Because without such crafty schemes to deceive the people, their flimsy arguments—or rather tricks—would dissolve much like to the disappearance of the morning mist before the rays of the rising sun.

Slyly attempting to suggest that Peter himself is the rock on which the *ecclesia* of Christ is built, they slip inappropriate texts into the margin. Observe how craftily they bring forward Ephesians 2:20 into a place where such a text has no reference. What has Ephesians 2:20 to do with Mt. 16:18? Nothing. The ultimate motive of these doctors for such a misapplication lies in their futile effort to support the strange fiction that Peter was 'enthroned' at Rome. This is a presumption on which the entire history of scripture maintains a deafening silence.

Peter at Rome? To establish himself as the first—*first?*—'bishop'? Fabricating a 'cathedra' upon which to become, in their work of fiction, the father of all such as institute a sacramental priesthood as opposed to the apostolic ministry?

Peter the progenitor of every one who plies the trade of sacramentalism as opposed to preaching the gospel? *Peter* the patron saint of those pagan architects who imagine to bring the invisible God—who dwelleth not in temples made with hands—captive within the walls of some idol-house, fabricated with stones, timber, bricks and mortar?

Thus they not only drag poor Peter, willy-nilly, whither he would not—yea, and went not—they make him apostatize from the simplicity of the faith which is in Christ. What? Stealing *Peter's* name to authorize a corrupt system plundered from the old testament, but proliferated into a monstrous parody shocking in its defiance of the authority of Christ? But in truth they cannot do this to Peter—though they steal his name—whatever they may do to themselves, and to all those who put their trust in them.

Let none be deceived: the rotten foundation of this system rests upon the sly manipulation of Mt. 16:18. It stands on the futile attempt to make Peter the rock on which Christ builds his 'church'. The scholars of the Anglican clergy also seek to justify this, inserting the reference 'Ephesians 2:20' into the margin. As though such a text illustrated Christ building his 'church' atop of poor Peter!

The text in Ephesians reads, 'And are built upon the foundation of the apostles and prophets, Jesus Christ himself being the chief corner stone.' These learned doctors utterly stumbled over this stone. Obviously. For the simple reason that the two places which they have joined together—Mt. 16:18 and Eph. 2:20—speak of two entirely different things!

One place speaks of the rock in which the foundation is laid; the other of the foundation which is laid in the rock.

This distinction is illustrated in the parable of the wise and foolish builders, one of whom 'built his house upon a rock', and 'it fell not, for it was founded upon a rock'. Whence it is evident that the foundation of the house was one thing, but the place in which that foundation was laid was another thing.

However, the other builder founded his house upon sand. Both foundations were the same. The houses were the same. But that into which the respective foundation of the houses was sunk was not the same. And it was that, the substance into which each foundation was let down, it was that, I say, that made the difference.

Whence it appears that the sound divine will carefully observe the difference between the foundation upon which the building rests, and the substance into which that foundation was sunk prior to building. A substance, mark, having its existence long before the foundation was contemplated. It is precisely this of which Christ speaks when he says, 'On this rock I will build my *ecclesia*'.

The rock was there before the *ecclesia*, before the foundations, before the existence of any building at all. The rock refers to that predetermined substance into which the foundation was to be let down by the builder when once the time of building should commence.

This is confirmed by the psalmist when he declares 'His foundations are in the holy mountains.' Now, no one supposes that the holy mountains *are* the foundations. Otherwise how could God's foundations be laid in them? If the foundations *were* the mountains, it would follow that the foundations had been founded in themselves. Hardly a stable prospect.

Or ever the building commenced, before the foundations were laid, the holy mountains existed. And every one knows that the nature of mountains is rock. And the parable teaches us, that this was the substance in which the wise man laid his foundation. Which is what Christ refers to when he says, 'On this rock I will build my church'.

Of course all this has nothing whatsoever to do with Ephesians 2:20, which refers to the building itself, and not to the rock in which the foundation of that building was laid.

The last text in the centre-margin references, like Elijah the prophet mocking the priests of Baal, laughs even louder at the calamity of these scripture-wresting Anglican 'doctors', as they strive in vain to enlist its services in their warfare against the building of Christ's *ecclesia*. Not an inch will this or any other text yield, as they labour to force our minds into the blind superstition that the 'church' was founded upon 'Saint' Peter's chair in the Vatican, in connection with which they suppose 'the keys' to be operative.

Consider this second—and last!—text, raked up in their desperation to give credence to their perversion of Mt. 16:18.

The text is Rev. 21:14. 'And the wall of the city had twelve foundations, and in them the names of the twelve apostles of the Lamb.' This is supposed to prove that the 'church' rests upon the authority of Peter's apostolate, 'passed on' to an unbroken series of antichristian popes! Even here they bungle it: quite apart from pope Joan, their series was often broken, sometimes by two rival 'Sees'. Holy See? Dead See!

Rev. 21:14? Oh? Why? Does this text read, 'And the wall of the city had one foundation, and in it the name of Peter, on whom everything rests'? No, it does not. Neither is one apostle distinguished from another, unless it were Paul, the apostle to the Gentiles, who, unlike Peter, actually went to Rome.

Clearly Peter—*Petros*—cannot be the rock—*petra*—referred to in the passage, 'On this rock I will build my church', for then, at least—if Rev. 21:14 applies—Mt. 16:18 must needs read—all else being given: and it is by no means given—'On these twelve rocks I will build my church'. See what a ludicrous situation these people get themselves into, once the light of day illuminates their gloomy habitations.

In any event the *ecclesia* is called, 'The holy city, new Jerusalem', her name being 'The city of our God'. But Rev. 21:14 never mentions the foundations of the *city*—much less the rock upon which those foundations rest!—it mentions the foundations of the *walls* of the city. But the walls are not the 'church': the city is the 'church'. As to the walls, they surround and protect the city. But they are distinct from it.

Besides, if Peter were the rock, or foundation, where are their famous 'Keys of Peter'? Keys, notice, not of Peter at all; not even of the 'church'. Of the kingdom. A very different thing. But where are their keys? Underground? Or, if at the gates, these belong to another covenant; the text speaks of the gates 'having twelve angels, and names written thereon, which are the names of the twelve tribes of the children of Israel': but what has that to do with Peter the apostle?

Or perhaps their keys fit the foundations, not the gates? But since no mention is made of keys in Rev. 21:14, doubtless our learned 'doctors' would be wiser to follow this example of silence, lest their folly appear to all men.

But what are the walls? Why, 'Salvation will God appoint for walls'. And, 'Thou shalt call thy walls Salvation, and thy gates, Praise'. Now the walls of salvation rest upon the apostolic doctrine of the gospel of Christ, as it is written, 'I am not ashamed of the gospel of Christ, for it is the power of God unto salvation to every one that believeth.'

'It' is the power of God unto salvation, the gospel of Christ itself is that power, not the 'priesthood' falsely so-called, not 'sacraments', but the gospel, the apostolic gospel. 'And this is the word which by the gospel is preached unto you.'

Of this mighty salvation by the apostolic doctrine of the gospel, the twelve foundations, having the names of the twelve apostles of the Lamb, serve as a most graphic figure. These are the foundations which support the walls of salvation and the gates of praise, which surround and give entrance to the city, respectively.

These things being so, the question follows of necessity, What then is the rock on which Christ builds his *ecclesia*, or assembly? This must be determined from both text and context, the whole being agreeable with the constant tenor of the new testament. Knowing this first, that no prophecy of the scripture is of any private interpretation, for the prophecy came not in old time by the will of man: but holy men of God spake as they were moved by the Holy Ghost.

Then the interpretation must be by that same Holy Ghost; just as it must be discerned by like holy men of God moved by the Holy Ghost at this present time. For if these things were so of the words and interpretation of the ancient prophets, how much more must they hold good of the words of the Lord Jesus himself, and of the interpretation of the words given by the Holy Ghost from heaven to the apostles of Christ in the new testament?

III

The Foundation of the Ecclesia, Mt. 16:18

1. The Context, Mt. 16:13-20

i. The general context

THE context of Mt. 16:18 commences with the words 'When Jesus came into the coasts of Caesarea Philippi', Mt. 16:13. More than anything else, this marks the end of the immensely significant Galilean ministry, a series of circuits throughout all Galilee, carried out over a considerable period of time.

These extensive preaching, teaching and healing journeys centred upon Capernaum, the city in which Jesus dwelt from the commencement of his public ministry. 'And leaving Nazareth, he came and dwelt in Capernaum, which is upon the sea coast, in the borders of Zabulon and Nephthalim: that it might be fulfilled which was spoken by Esaias the prophet, saying, The land of Zabulon, and the land of Nephthalim, by the way of the sea, beyond Jordan, Galilee of the Gentiles: The people which sat in darkness saw great light; and to them which sat in the region and shadow of death light is sprung up.'

Throughout this great Galilean ministry, with its constant circuits, the Son of man became manifest to all Israel. At this time the 'Sermon on the Mount' was delivered, here Jesus' mighty works were wrought, and during this period much of his doctrine was enunciated: this was the greater part of his public ministry to Israel.

'And great multitudes came unto him, having with them those that were lame, blind, dumb, maimed, and many others, and cast them down at Jesus' feet; and he healed them: insomuch that the multitude wondered, when they saw the dumb to speak, the maimed to be whole, the lame to walk, and the blind to see: and they glorified the God of Israel.' As to his doctrine, 'The people were astonished at his doctrine: for he taught them as one having authority, and not as the scribes.'

These reactions typified the response to the manifestation of the Person, work, and teaching of the Son of man, as he went about all Galilee, departing and returning, again and again, from and to the city of Capernaum.

With what result? Jesus tells us with what result: 'Woe unto thee, Chorazin! woe unto thee, Bethsaida! for if the mighty works, which were done in you, had been done in Tyre and Sidon, they would have repented long ago in sackcloth and ashes. But I say unto you, It shall be more tolerable for Tyre and Sidon at the day of judgment, than for you. And thou, Capernaum, which art exalted unto heaven, shalt be brought down to hell: for if the mighty works, which have been done in thee, had been done in Sodom, it would have remained until this day. But I say unto you, That it shall be more tolerable for the land of Sodom in the day of judgment, than for thee.'

That was the effect of the momentous Galilean ministry which came to its conclusion 'when Jesus came into the coasts of Caesarea Philippi', Mt. 16:13. That is, at the proper commencement of that context which finds its ultimate expression in the words of Jesus 'On this rock I will build my *ecclesia*', Mt. 16:18.

ii. The particular context

The statement 'On this rock I will build my *ecclesia*', was provoked by a series of questions and answers commencing with Jesus' enquiry, 'Whom do men say that I the Son of man am?' 'When Jesus came into the coasts of Caesarea Philippi, he asked his disciples, saying, Whom do men say that I the Son of man am?' Mt. 16:13.

After all the protracted and wonderful Galiliean ministry, marked by unparalleled miracles, unique teaching, attended by such vast multitudes: was there any doubt about it? Yes, there was, for, 'Some say that thou art John the Baptist: some, Elias; and others Jeremias, or one of the prophets.'

John the Baptist? Elias? Jeremias? One of the prophets? Is this all that the multitudes of healed persons can say? All that the great concourse of hearers could conclude? Yes, it was all, and it gave evidence for all time that no amount of outward instruction, no unique dispensation of miraculous healing, could give the slightest saving knowledge of the Person and work of Christ.

2. The Question of the Son of Man

i. The Son of man in the old testament

The question 'Whom do men say that I the Son of man am?' contains within itself the answer which men could not provide. This is the tenth time in Matthew that Jesus refers to himself specifically as the Son of man, a title virtually exclusive to his ministry on earth to the Jews, and to his coming again at the last judgment.

This ministry had been clearly foretold, for, 'The Son of man goeth as it is written of him.' But where was it written?

In more than one place. The prophet Daniel is named son of man: 'Understand, O son of man: for at the time of the end shall be the vision.' From which we conclude that it was written in prophecy of the Son of man that he should be given to understand the mysteries of God; that his ministry should be for a time to come; and that this should appear in the last days: for the vision was for the time of the end.

That is, the ministry of the Son of man would be to Israel at his appearing, declaring the mysteries of the kingdom; and that he should come again at the last day to bring the vision to fulfilment.

In view of such a ministry, revealing the kingdom of God to the Jews, calling them to repentance, bringing to light their wickedness in rejecting the Son of man, and prophesying of his coming again in judgment at the last day, it is no wonder that the psalmist prayed, 'Let thy hand be upon the man of thy right hand, upon the Son of man whom thou madest strong for thyself.'

It is in the book of the prophet Ezekiel that the ministry of the Son of man is most clearly foreshadowed. Here the prophet himself is called 'son of man' no less than ninety-three times, and his ministry itself is made to typify that of the one who was to be rejected of the Jews, of whom Matthew records that 'it is written'.

The commencement of Ezekiel's ministry was in the land of the Gentiles, in the captivity. There he saw visions of heavenly glory, of the cherubim, of the glorious wheels, and of a heavenly Man seated on the throne of the Majesty on high.

Ezekiel saw in the visions of God a glorified Man upon the throne in heaven. Yet his ministry, under the name 'son of man', was to a disobedient people upon the earth. This son of man was sent to prophesy to Jerusalem and Judea. But they would not hear.

They would not receive this ministry, much less did they perceive his vision of the heavenly Man on the throne of the glory. Israel rejected the ministry of Ezekiel, the 'son of man', and the glory departed from the temple at Jerusalem, which was then revealed to be full of secret sin and wickedness.

The son of man prophesied of the destruction of Jerusalem, the ruin of the temple, the captivity and rejection of the people, and the shame and disgrace of Israel's testimony. Nevertheless, there was a spiritual remnant, and to them many encouraging and glorious promises were given and assured.

But, as the book draws to a close, and the prophecy and visions of the son of man are seen to be for the end time, the blessings of the remnant appear not only in terms of Israel, the temple, Jerusalem, and the land, as such, because all these things are extended to encompass a vastly wider scope. Indeed they appear as figures of the true.

The promised blessings for the poor remnant, though given occasion by the earthly prophecies of the son of man, transcend the world and time to soar above to the heavenly Man in the glory. Moreover these exceeding great and precious promises appear at the last in connection not with an earthly but with a heavenly, mystical temple, impossible to conceive in its breadth, length, depth, and height, beyond man's ability to comprehend with the natural senses, Ezekiel chapters 40-44.

Here is revealed a temple not made with hands, a heavenly, glorious temple, to which the departed glory was to return. This was the house of God made higher than the heavens, a temple pertaining to the glorified Man on the heavenly throne, of whom Ezekiel prophesied, and whose ministry he foreshadowed, in the visions of God.

Now, in the ministry of Christ on earth to the Jews, and in their rejection of that ministry, the prophetic role of

Ezekiel as 'son of man' finds its fulfilment. But the prophecy ascends higher, even into the heavenlies, for the revelation of the glorified Man in heaven, shown to Ezekiel, also finds fulfilment in Christ, the Son of God. For it is Christ, risen from the dead, that appears seated on the throne of glory in the ascension, bringing in the mystery of the heavenly temple, that is, of the house of God not made with hands.

This mystery of the house of God, the temple shown in figure to Ezekiel, and the building of it, is that which finds its answer in the words, 'On this rock I will build my *ecclesia*'. Thus the Son of man 'goeth as it is written of him.'

The obvious interpretation of the prophecy is that Ezekiel prefigures the Son of man in his ministry to the Jews on earth. Then who is the separate and distinct Man in the glory of heaven, seen by the prophet from the earth? Here evidently the meaning soars, the prophecy reaches to heights unknown, as the truth becomes clear that the Son of man, and the Man in the glory, are one and the same.

First, in that Christ came as Son of man to the Jews, declaring the kingdom of God. He was rejected and crucified. He was put to death and was buried. So the glory departed from Israel, and the wrath came upon them to the uttermost.

But now is Christ risen from the dead, and is ascended into glory. Not, however, to continue his ministry—which was rejected by the Jews—in the form that it took when he was sent as Son of man to Israel on earth. Now he is to be declared in his proper Person as the Son of God in heaven, his Manhood glorified in the infinite radiance of his divine Sonship. From thence is the ministry of the new testament.

But it was only after the Son of man was rejected that the full glory of his Person was revealed. First he must suffer many things, and be rejected of the elders and chief priests and scribes, and be slain. For the Jews by wicked hands took him, and crucified him, hanging the Son of man upon a tree.

But these murderers, the princes of Israel, and of the world, knew nothing of the true origin and nature of this Son of man whom they crucified. They knew not what they did. Indeed, none of the princes of this world knew, for had they known it, they would not have crucified the Lord of glory.

Nevertheless God raised him from the dead, declaring this same Son of man to be his own beloved Son, the eternal Son of the Father. He was raised from the dead by the glory of the Father, yet raised in Manhood. And it is the revelation of this, of his Person and of his work, by the Holy Ghost from heaven, through the preaching of the gospel, it is the revelation of this, I say, that brings in the *ecclesia* of the living God, the pillar and ground of the truth: 'My *ecclesia*.'

ii. The Son of man and the Jews

Nevertheless, the ministry of the Son of man on earth to the Jews, in the wisdom and counsel of God, of necessity preceded the revelation of the mystery of the Son of God from the ascension.

As to that earthly ministry, when Jesus had completed his vast preaching and teaching circuits throughout all Galilee, having departed for Caesarea Philippi, he asked his disciples, 'Whom do men say that I the Son of man am?' 'And they said, Some say that thou art John the Baptist: some, Elias; and others, Jeremias, or one of the prophets.' Not one said that he was the Son of man. Yet he had said so himself countless times during that Galilean ministry.

So blinded were the Jews by the god of this world, that, in their superstition, they supposed that he was John the Baptist risen again, or some prophet come back from the dead. Not one recalled what he had said—and God had attested—of himself countless times. They had not even mentioned the prophet Ezekiel in their Jewish conjectures. Only Elias, or Jeremias, or 'one of the prophets'. Yet a staggering ninety-three times Ezekiel had been named by the same title, 'son of man'. Then why did not the Jews even mention Ezekiel?

Because the prayer of David had most surely been fulfilled, which said, 'Let their eyes be darkened, that they may not see, and bow down their back alway.' 'According as it is written, God hath given them a spirit of slumber, eyes that they should not see, and ears that they should not hear, unto this day.' And so it has proved in the issue.

None of the Jews knew that Jesus was the Son of man. None of them even knew what 'Son of man' meant. None knew the day of their visitation, and hence none knew the appalling consequences of their obliviousness to his Person, his visitation, and his ministry. Nor do they to this day.

iii. The Son of man and the disciples

Then said Jesus to his own disciples—they being typical of the remnant according to the election of grace—'But whom say ye that I am?'

What will they answer? Will they say, The Son of man? No, they will not. Because above and beyond the manifestation of the Son of man to the Jews, it had been given to the disciples to see by revelation the heavenly wisdom of God in a mystery, even the hidden wisdom, which God had ordained before the world unto their glory.

Simon Peter answered and said, 'Thou art the Christ, the Son of the living God.' 'And Jesus answered and said unto him, Blessed art thou, Simon Bar-jona: for flesh and blood hath not revealed it unto thee, but my Father which is in heaven.' 'And I say unto thee, That thou art Peter, and upon this rock I will build my *ecclesia*; and the gates of hell shall not prevail against it.'

3. The Christ

i. The son of David, the son of Abraham

'Thou art the Christ.' That is, the Anointed. If so, the son of David, the son of Abraham. Yet not any son of these fathers, but the marked out son, the son distinguished by the anointing. Then, the heir. Heir to what? The anointed son of Abraham is heir to the promises.

The first promise to Abraham was that in him, and in his seed, all nations of the earth should be blessed. As to that blessing, it is the blessing of justification by faith, without the deeds of the law. Abraham's son should bring this blessing to all nations by inheritance. 'The scripture, foreseeing that God would justify the heathen through faith, preached before the gospel unto Abraham, saying, In thee shall all nations be blessed.'

Whereby should he know this? By sacrifice. That is, not the sacrifice of beasts themselves, but of the fulfilment of such sacrifices, that is, the sacrifice of the heir. He should, through the eternal Spirit, offer himself without spot to God. This was the sacrifice of the Lamb of God, on behalf of his people. 'For by one offering he hath perfected for ever them that are sanctified.'

The second promise to Abraham, and to his seed—which is Christ—was that of the resurrection from the dead. This promise likewise was a blessing for the nations. 'For the dead shall hear the voice of the Son of God: and they that hear shall live.' Indeed, 'All that are in the graves shall hear his voice, and shall come forth.'

The third promise—to which the first two, justification by faith, and the resurrection from the dead, pertain—was that of the inheritance of the world to come. 'And the LORD said unto Abram, Lift up now thine eyes, and look from the place where thou art northward, and southward, and eastward, and westward: for all the land which thou seest, to thee will I give it, and to thy seed for ever.' This was the promise 'That he should be heir of the world.'

All these promises centre upon the Son of man, Abraham's seed, the Anointed, and upon the blessing of that elect people in him, which thereafter should believe, and confess, 'Thou art the Christ'. By this confession such a people own that these promised blessings were freely given to them in Christ by nothing other than the mere favour of God, and through nothing save the faith of God's elect.

Furthermore, the Anointed was marked out as David's son and heir. That is, heir to the kingdom. For of David's kingdom and dominion—it had been promised—there should be no end.

But since Christ, of the seed of David according to the flesh, was raised from the dead, it follows that the kingdom, which is an everlasting kingdom, pertains not to men alive in the flesh, but to Man risen from the dead. Neither does this kingdom respect an area of land under heaven in Israel, but the entire new heavens and new earth—wherein dwelleth righteousness—for ever to abide in the world to come.

No more does the kingdom pertain to Jerusalem below, but to Jerusalem above, to the heavenly Zion, to the everlasting glory. This kingdom is not for time but for eternity; not for this short passing life but for the everlasting ages; not for this present evil world soon to be dissolved, but for that world without end in glory which shall never pass away.

To this kingdom, and that dominion, belong the people who can say, and that truly, by the revelation of the Father in heaven, 'Thou art the Christ'. Such a people shall speak of the glory of his kingdom, and talk of his power; to make known to the sons of men his mighty acts, and the glorious majesty of his kingdom. His kingdom is an everlasting kingdom, and his dominion endureth throughout all generations.

This is the blessing which all those who believe and confess 'the Christ' inherit and receive from the Anointed. But of this—entailed in the name Messiah, or Christ—how much did Peter or the disciples grasp, when they named him 'the Christ'? Much every way.

They knew, for example, that it was he that should come into the world, John 11:27; that forgiveness of sins was through the Son of man, Mark 2:10; that Jesus was the Son of God, the King of Israel, John 1:49; that Christ was the Lord, who alone had the words of eternal life, John 6:68; and that he, himself, was the resurrection and the life, who should raise the dead at the last day, John 11:24-27.

For it is evident that since Peter confessed Christ by revelation, all this and much more must have been—and must be still—implied, grasped, and confessed in the saying, 'Thou art the Christ', by all who make such a confession.

In principle, and in prophecy, all that was prefigured of Christ, all that was foretold and foreshadowed of him throughout the old testament, must be fulfilled and hence confessed in the new. Then all must have been entailed in Peter's confession. It was not a blind, ignorant confession. It meant something, precisely because 'the Christ' means something. And all, all, that it meant, Peter implied and confessed.

ii. The meaning of 'the Christ'

The name Christ occurs three hundred and eight times in the new testament, being pronounced *Christos* in the Greek. The word means 'Anointed'.

The Hebrew form of 'Anointed' is 'Messiah', which, as a transliteration, occurs twice in the apostolic writings. Hence there are three hundred and ten references to the Anointed, that is, to the Christ, or the Messiah, in the new testament.

The Hebrew word *Mashiach*—'Messiah' in the new testament—occurs thirty-nine times in the old testament, having been rendered 'anointed' thirty-seven times, and 'Messiah' twice.

Jacob's pillar was anointed; Aaron and his sons were anointed; the tabernacle was anointed; the altar, the laver, all that was within the tabernacle, and all the vessels thereof, all were anointed; Saul was anointed; King David was anointed.

All these were anointed with oil in the name of the LORD, by Moses, by Samuel, by the prophets of the LORD. This divinely authorized anointing marked them out, or marked these things out, to be the chosen. Anointed persons and things were separated to the LORD for the use to which he had appointed them, and brought them into being. By the anointing they were marked out before all the people.

But *the* Christ was not anointed with oil. The anointing with oil which went before in the old testament was but a figure for the time then present, in which oil was poured out upon those priests and kings which typified him who was to come. When Christ came into the world, however, he was anointed with the Holy Ghost from heaven, by the authority of the Father. That, Peter's soul knew right well, because it was the witness of John the Baptist, which he had heard and received from the beginning.

John the Baptist testified, saying, 'I saw the Spirit descending from heaven like a dove, and it abode upon him. And I knew him not: but he that sent me to baptise with water, the same said unto me, Upon whom thou shalt see the Spirit descending, and remaining on him, the same is he which baptiseth with the Holy Ghost. And I saw, and bare record that this is the Son of God.' That was the anointing which marked out that he was the Christ, that is, the Anointed, the Son of God.

The very next day Peter was informed by his brother of these things, declaring, 'We have found the Messias, which is, being interpreted, the Christ.' They had found the Anointed. 'Thou art the Christ.'

Christ was to come of the seed of David, and from the town of Bethlehem, Mt. 1:1; Jn. 7:42; Lk. 2:4,11; Acts 2:29,30 and Rom. 1:3. Yet, whilst David's seed, he should be David's Lord, the Son of God, Mt. 22:42-46; Lk. 1:35; Lk. 3:22; Jn. 1:49; Acts 2:25; Acts 13:23 and 33.

Christ should do wondrous works, by which the blind should receive their sight, the lame should walk, the lepers be cleansed, the deaf hear, the dead be raised, and the poor have the gospel preached unto them, Mt. 11:4,5; Jn. 7:31; Lk. 4:18 and 21; Jn. 12:37; Acts 2:22; and Jn. 14:11. Christ should speak as none had ever spoken, Jn. 4:25 and 29; Jn. 1:48; Jn. 7:46; Mt. 7:29; Jn. 6:63 and 68; and Jn. 12:49,50.

Moreover it was written that Christ should suffer, Lk. 24:26 and 46; Mt. 16:21; Acts 3:18; I Pet. 1:11, 2:21 and 5:1. He should forgive sins, I Cor. 15:3; Mk. 2:10; Mt. 26:28; Lk. 7:48,49; and Acts 13:38. And he should be raised from the dead, I Cor. 15:20; Acts 2:30,31 and 32; II Tim. 2:8; I Cor. 15:5, 6, 7, and 8; and Romans 6:9.

Christ should bring in the kingdom of heaven, and of God, first in the heart, then in the world to come, Mt. 4:17; Mt. 13:11; Mk. 12:34; Acts 20:25; Rom. 14:17; and Rev. 11:15.

Furthermore, Christ should be revealed as the light of the world, the light of life, and the glorious light from heaven, Lk. 2:32; Jn. 1:9 and 8:12; Acts 9:3; II Cor. 4:6; and Rev. 1:16.

The Christ should bring in the new testament, Lk. 22:20; Heb. 8:6 and 10-13; Heb. 9:15-17; Heb. 10:16,17; and Heb. 12:24. He should offer up once and for all a perfect sacrifice, Mt. 1:21; Heb. 9:14 and 28; Heb. 10:10; Heb. 13:12; I Pet. 1:18,19; and Rom. 5:8,9. Christ should deliver from the law, Heb. 7:12; Rom. 6:14 and 4:13,14; Rom. 7:4 and 6; Rom. 10:4; Gal. 3:23, 24 and 25; Gal. 5:4 and 6:15,16; and Gal. 2:19. In consequence, he should establish a new priesthood, Heb. 5:5; Heb. 9:11; Heb. 9:24 and 26; Heb. 7:15,16 and 17; Rev. 1:5,6; and I Pet. 2:4,5.

Again, Christ should be made known through preaching, Rom. 10:14,15; Acts 8:5; Rom. 16:25; Gal. 1:16; Acts 9:20; I Cor. 1:23; Acts 10:36; Acts 17:3; and Eph. 3:8. Once more, Christ should indwell his people as their light, life, and hope of glory, Col. 1:27; Eph. 3:17,18 and 19; Jn. 14:18,20 and 23; Jn. 15:5; Jn. 17:21,23 and 26.

Finally, Christ should come again to judge the quick and the dead: to raise the just to everlasting glory, and to condemn the wicked to everlasting damnation, Mt. 25:31-34 with 41,45 and 46; Lk. 17:24 and 26-30; Jn. 5:28,29; I Cor. 15:51,52; I Thess. 4:16,17; Acts 17:31; Rev. 1:7; and Rev. 20:11,12 and 13.

iii. Peter's confession of 'the Christ'

Now all these things were and are true of Christ, and of Christ alone.

They are things which, more or less, in principle, Peter had been taught from his childhood, out of the holy scriptures, set forth in prophecy, pattern, figure, type, shadow, parable, and allegory from Genesis to Malachi. These things had accumulated in the mind of Peter, they had been enhanced under the ministry of John the Baptist, and, above all, concentrated during the two years or more of Jesus' teaching prior to Caesarea Philippi. Suddenly, however, at this point, everything came sharply into focus.

Peter had known in his mind, it was formed in his understanding, stored in his memory, at least in principle, that all these things would be true of the Messiah when he came. Yet somehow, at first, the body of information in the mind of Peter about the Christ, and the Person of Jesus—for all that he owned and followed him—remained two distinct things.

No longer. No more was his learning of the scripture in the understanding one thing, and his vision of the Person of Jesus another. That which had accrued in his mind concerning the Messiah on the one hand, and the Person whom he saw with his eyes—heard with his ears, and handled with his hands—on the other, came together: '*Thou* art the Christ!'

In a blaze of light from heaven, by the direct and interior revelation of the Father, the great truths which Peter had learned to associate with the coming Messiah, and the very Person standing before him, fused together in a way unprecedented: 'Thou—*thou*—art the Christ'.

That was what happened to Peter: And, in the light of it, all Peter's accumulated knowledge lit up that Person, and the Person lit up all that accumulated knowledge. Peter was bathed in the radiance of the revelation from the Father upon the Son. Now, *that* is to be able to say, 'Thou art the Christ'.

iv. The Son of man and Son of God

'The Son of the living God.' This was the revelation from the Father, and out of the fulness of such an immediate divine inshining from heaven to the heart of Peter, his mouth spoke.

Nevertheless, Peter's confession of the Son of God, answering to the sudden illumination of the Father, was provoked by the question asked by Jesus, Mt. 16:13. The question was not, 'Whom do men say that I am?' but, 'Whom do men say that I the *Son of man* am?'

From this enquiry concerning the Son of man, came the revelation of the Son of God. When asked, 'But whom say ye that I am?' Peter did not reply with the answer inherent in Jesus' first question—that is, The *Son of man*. For, as light broke in from above, he cried out in response not to an earthly manifestation, but to a heavenly revelation, 'Thou art the Christ, the Son of the living God.'

From this it is clear that everything in this passage—Mt. 16:13-16—hinges upon the meaning of the terms Son of man and Son of God, respectively. Once this is clearly understood, immediately the passage falls open. It is easily grasped. And since the object of the passage is to show that upon which Christ builds his *ecclesia*, nothing can be of more importance to the understanding of that *ecclesia* than a lucid grasp of the meaning of Jesus' words.

It is an over-simplification to reduce the terms Son of man, and Son of God, as if the one excluded his deity and the other his humanity. During Jesus' earthly ministry it is true that the manifestation of the Son of man veiled—but no more than veiled—the Son of God in his glory. It is equally true that the revelation of the Son of God was only fully unveiled when it shone through his humanity raised from the dead and ascended to glory. But it did not eclipse that humanity.

It was the Son of God who was made of the Seed of David according to the flesh, thence to appear to Israel in his ministry on earth as the Son of man. And it is precisely the same Person who is 'declared to be the Son of God with power, according to the spirit of holiness, by the resurrection from the dead.' If the one term emphasizes his humanity, it is *his* humanity that is emphasized. And if the other term manifests his everlasting deity and eternal Sonship, it is through his risen and glorified manhood that the revelation is made manifest.

Both titles—Son of man, and Son of God—appear in the new testament in terms of the progressive revelation of the divine Person and work of the Son in his manhood. In the first he appears as Son of man on earth; in the second, as Son of God from the glory. This revelation is unfolded according to the way in which Christ is made manifest in the two distinct and consecutive phases of his ministry, the second of which—revealing his divine and eternal Person in risen and ascended manhood—obtains even to this present day.

4. The Ministry of the Son of Man

Consider firstly, the ministry of the Son of man. Consider the proposition that primarily—given the incarnation—this is a title descriptive of Jesus' ministry to the Jews. 'For verily he took not on him the nature of angels; but he took on him the seed of Abraham.'

But if of Abraham, then of the Jews. For it is evident that our Lord sprang out of Judah. Indeed, we ought to remember that Jesus Christ came of the seed of David, and was, according to Paul, a minister of the circumcision for the truth of God, to confirm the promise made unto the fathers. As he himself said, 'I am not sent but unto the lost sheep of the house of Israel.'

This was the ministry of the Son of man, and Son of man was the designation of this ministry.

As to the Gentiles—for the duration of that earthly ministry to the Jews—however humiliating to the flesh, the position is clear: 'It is not meet to take the children's bread, and to cast it unto the dogs.'

Hence, 'Son of man' was a title descriptive of the ministry of Jesus Christ to the circumcision, confining his service to the Jews upon earth. As such, it is not a title to, or ministry respecting, the Gentile nations, although it is the title under which Christ is spoken of as coming again at the end of the age to judge the quick and the dead, beginning at the house of God.

The ministry of Christ as Son of man, whilst everything to do with the Jews in the days of his flesh, was and is—as a ministry—nothing to do with the *ecclesia*. Nor—as a ministry—has it to do with the revelation of the Son of God from heaven by the gospel during this present dispensation of time, a dispensation commencing with the day of Pentecost and continuing till the last day at the end of the age.

This latter is the period during which the words apply 'On this rock I will build my *ecclesia*.' But the title of Son of man—a title indicative and inclusive of a ministry—is nothing to do with it. 'Son of man' was a title exclusive to the house of Israel, in which Christ was denied, forsaken, and rejected of the Jewish nation.

If so, it must follow that the term Son of man will appear primarily in the gospels, particularly Matthew, Mark and Luke.

i. The ministry of the Son of man in Matthew

Matthew refers to the title Son of man thirty-two times, the references applying to two distinct periods, namely, before and after his death.

Matthew declares that the Son of man had not where to lay his head; had power on earth to forgive sins; sent his disciples forth and followed after them throughout the cities of Israel; came eating and drinking; was Lord of the sabbath; was he against whom a word might be forgiven; was he who sowed good seed; yet was still unknown by that name to the Jews despite all the months and months of his Galilean ministry!

Matthew tells us that the Son of man came to seek and to save that which is lost; that he went as it was written of him; that woe was unto that man by whom the Son of man was betrayed; and that the hour was at hand in which the Son of man was betrayed into the hands of sinners.

Matthew records that the Son of man should be betrayed to the chief priests and scribes who should condemn him to death at Jerusalem; that he came not to be ministered unto, but to minister, and to give his life a ransom for many; that he should suffer, being betrayed into the hands of men who should kill him, but that he should rise again; that he should be three days and three nights in the heart of the earth, rising again on the third day.

Matthew also prophesies of the things which should follow thereafter, that the Son of man should fulfil: for he should come again, and that his coming would be in such an hour as men think not.

Men are to watch, for no man knoweth the day, nor the hour, wherein the Son of man cometh; it should be as in the days of Noah, when the flood took them all away.

The glory of his coming should be as the lightning flashing out of the east, shining even unto the west; it should be after certain days of tribulation, the sun being darkened, the moon giving no light, the stars falling, and the powers of heaven being shaken. In those days all the tribes of the earth shall mourn.

The Son of man shall be seen coming in the clouds of heaven with power and great glory, sending forth his angels with a great sound of a trumpet, gathering together his elect from the four winds, from one end of heaven to the other.

The Son of man shall send forth his angels. He shall come in the glory of his Father with all his holy angels, rewarding every man according to his works, being seen coming in his kingdom. Then shall he sit on the throne of his glory, with the apostles upon twelve thrones, judging the twelve tribes of Israel.

For when the Son of man shall come, and all the holy angels with him, then shall he sit upon the throne of his glory, and before him shall be gathered all nations, and he shall separate them one from another, as a shepherd divideth his sheep from the goats. For hereafter shall ye see the Son of man sitting on the right hand of power, and coming in the clouds of heaven.

Now, these are all the passages in Matthew, rendered in sequence, and, observe, all apply either to the earthly ministry of the Son of man, or to his coming again. None is related to the assembly, that is, the *ecclesia*, nor to the present dispensation of time save to end it in judgment.

ii. The ministry of the Son of man in Mark

The gospel according to Mark teaches much the same thing, —though with less copiousness—in the fourteen references to the Son of man found in the second gospel.

Mark records that the Son of man hath power on earth to forgive sins; is Lord of the sabbath; came not to be ministered unto, but to minister, and to give his life a ransom for many.

The Son of man went as it was written of him: but woe to that man by whom he was betrayed; for he was betrayed, and betrayed into the hands of sinners. It was written of him that he must suffer many things, and be set at nought, yea, he must suffer many things, and be rejected of the elders, and the chief priests, and scribes, and be killed, and the third day rise again.

And so it came to pass: for the Son of man was delivered into the hands of men, who killed him, and after he was killed, he rose again on the third day.

Just as is the case in Matthew, Mark passes from those texts which speak of the ministry, culminating in the betrayal, rejection, and slaying of the Son of man by the Jewish nation, and of his resurrection, to his coming again in power and great glory at the last day.

There is no mention of the assembly or *ecclesia* taking the place of Israel in the counsels of God. In Mark there is no mention of the *ecclesia* at all.

Nor is there any hint of the advent of an age-long dispensation of time which should come in between the ascension of Christ and his return. From the ministry of the Son of man recorded in Mark no one could tell of the coming revelation of the hidden mystery, of the descent of the Holy Ghost to bring in the *ecclesia*, or of the calling out of a people from the Gentiles to answer to a new and better testament in a coming dispensation.

From the rejection of the Son of man by the Jews, Mark's testimony passes to the prophecy of his coming again. That is, from that generation, to the last judgment. For whosoever should be ashamed of the Son of man and of his words in that sinful and adulterous generation, of him also should the Son of man be ashamed at his coming again in the glory of his Father with the holy angels.

But when should he come again?

After that tribulation, when the sun should be darkened, the moon should give no light, the stars of the heaven should fall, and the powers of heaven should be shaken; then shall they see the Son of man coming in the clouds with power and great glory.

'Art thou the Christ', asked his murderers 'The Son of the Blessed?' 'I am', said he, 'And ye shall see the Son of man sitting on the right hand of power, and coming in the clouds of heaven.'

But between the ascension of the Son of man, and his coming again with power and great glory, there was to appear a hidden mystery. After his ascension, following the descent of the Person of the Holy Ghost, the declaration of the *Son of God*—then a hidden mystery—was to be made known from the glory by the preaching of the gospel with apostolic power. This was the revelation of the mystery.

This would bring in the *ecclesia*, the assembly of the living God, the pillar and ground of the truth. This would bring in the fellowship of the mystery, a fellowship standing in union and communion with the Father and the Son.

During the ministry of the Son of man on earth, none conceived of this. None knew what God had prepared for them that love him. At that time none knew of this mystery among the Gentiles, which is Christ in you, the hope of glory.

And neither is there much more knowledge of such heavenly and spiritual mysteries in what passes for the 'church' in these present times. The contemporary and professing 'churches' may know of Jesus after the flesh, as did the Jews; they may know of his life on earth, historically followed by his death and resurrection. They may. But they have neither the conception nor the experience of the heavenly revelation of the Son of God from the glory, nor of the *ecclesia* which Christ builds in consequence of the heavenly light of that revelation.

For the assembly of Christ—his congregation—is built upon revelation: revelation from heaven, revelation from the Father, and revelation which creates a tangible reality: the visible, real unity of the Spirit and of the faith on the part of all saints in one body.

From this, the modern profession of Christendom is not only utterly fallen, it is irrevocably fallen, and to it that profession is not merely apathetic, it is downright hostile. It will never revive, reform, or return to what has been lost, save in the futile dreams of those who have an ulterior motive for staying in an apostasy which their own judgment cannot but condemn.

iii. The ministry of the Son of man in Luke

References to the Son of man in Luke are similar to those found in Matthew and Mark, though, as is usually the case with such comparisons, they are generally fuller, and more varied.

These differences are due entirely to the mind of the Spirit in his distinct leading of the respective writers. So spiritual, so sensitive, so submissive were these holy men, that the very words which the Holy Ghost spoke were set down to perfection in each of the four gospels.

The object of the four evangelists was and is to glorify Christ. To this end—in each case—what details were to be included, and what excluded, besides the order in which the details—whether of time, place, speech or action—occurred, was made entirely subservient to that particular doctrinal light in which Christ and his work were to be presented in each gospel respectively.

The fact that unbelieving leaders in religious academic circles ignorantly deride this truth in the name of 'scholarship', means nothing. Long ago these wove a web of evil against the divine authorship of the gospels, overthrowing what faith was left to those 'students' who were foolish enough to submit to them. Inventing fictitious 'sources' to 'explain' the differences between the gospels, scheming up what was tantamount to a fifth gospel, 'Q', to account for the glaring discrepancies in their conjectures, these men set themselves against the Holy Ghost.

Luke refers to the Son of man twenty-six times, telling us that he had power on earth to forgive sins; was Lord of the sabbath; was he on whose account the disciples were blessed when they were hated of men and separated from their company, when they were reproved, and when their name was cast out as evil.

The Son of man was he who came eating and drinking; against whom a word would be forgiven; who came to seek and to save that which was lost, for he did not come to destroy men's lives, but to save them. The Son of man had not where to lay his head. At the last, he went to Jerusalem, where all things concerning him should be accomplished; for he went as was determined of him.

A woe was upon that man by whom the Son of man was betrayed. For he was betrayed: he was betrayed with a kiss, and was delivered into the hands of men. The Son of man must first suffer many things, and be rejected of that generation; indeed, he must suffer many things being rejected of the elders and chief priests, who should slay him; but God would raise him up again on the third day.

When first he rose from the dead, certain women who came to the tomb saw a vision of two men in shining garments, and they were afraid, and bowed down their faces to the earth. But the men said, Why seek ye the living among the dead? He is not here; he is risen: remember how he spake unto you when he was yet in Galilee, saying, The Son of man must be delivered into the hands of sinful men, and be crucified, and the third day rise again?

After the passages relating to the ministry of the Son of man to the Jews, Luke also passes without intermission to the coming again of the Son of man at the last day. This confirms that there is no bearing of the title and ministry of 'Son of man' on the *ecclesia*, the dispensation pertaining to this present age.

The prophetic passages in Luke which concern the coming again of the Son of man to judgment at the end of the age follow immediately after those which record his earthly ministry. Hereafter they should see the Son of man sit on the right hand of the power of God. Then, whosoever had been ashamed of him and of his words, of him should the Son of man be ashamed, appearing in his own glory, and that of his Father, and of the holy angels. For as Jonas was a sign to the Ninevites, so the Son of man should be to that generation. The men of Nineveh would rise up with that generation and condemn it, for they repented at the preaching of Jonah, and, behold, a greater than Jonah was before them.

The Son of man should come at an hour when men thought not; the days would come when they would desire to see one of the days of the Son of man, but they should not see it; it would be too late.

For as the lightning lighteth out of the one part under heaven, shining to the other part under heaven, so would be the Son of man in his day. As the days of Noe so also would be the days of the Son of man: for the flood came and destroyed them all. Likewise as the fire and brimstone rained from heaven, and destroyed all Sodom, so it would be in the day that the Son of man was revealed.

And when he should come, would he find faith in the earth?

There would be signs in the sun, and in the moon, and in the stars; and upon earth distress of nations, with perplexity; the sea and the waves roaring; men's hearts failing them for fear, for looking after those things which shall come upon the earth. For the powers of heaven shall be shaken. Then, then shall they see the Son of man coming in a cloud with power and great glory.

Hence the Son of man cautioned them, whilst yet amidst the Jews on earth, with the following words: Watch ye therefore, and pray always, that ye may be accounted worthy to escape all these things that shall come upon the earth, and to stand before the Son of man. For as a snare shall that day come on all them that dwell on the face of the whole earth.

This concludes the passages from the gospel according to Luke.

iv. The ministry of the Son of man in John

John is, of course, different. It is essential to grasp why he is different.

Out of the four gospels, the last is the exception to the rule. Matthew, Mark and Luke specifically record the ministry of the Son of man to the Jews, emphasizing in turn, that he is the Messiah, the Servant, and the Saviour, each aspect being set respectively against a background of the Kingdom, the Service, and the Grace of God. The entire vision of John is different. Uniquely, John reveals the hitherto undisclosed signs given during the earthly ministry of Jesus. These signs disclose the coming heavenly ministry which the Son of God should exercise when risen from the dead and ascended to glory.

The signs in John foretold—even at that time—the future heavenly dispensation of the revelation of the Son of God, that is, the present age of the *ecclesia*, from the ascension to the return of Christ. John does this in order to make manifest from the life of Jesus the way in which his glory—which should be revealed after his ascension into heaven—was even then being signified and prophetically marked out on earth.

Hence, summarising all the previous chapters, towards the close of the fourth gospel John states, 'These signs are written that ye might believe that Jesus is the Christ, the Son of God', Jn. 20:30,31. Not that ye might believe that Jesus is the Son of man, notice. Though that was the consistent emphasis of Matthew, Mark, and Luke. In John, however, the emphasis changes. John shows that the period of Jesus' ministry to the Jews as Son of man, his life on earth in Israel, was *also* accompanied by divinely given signs of a glory yet to come in a dispensation still to be revealed.

John selects exactly seven prophetic signs, weaving them together with Christ's doctrine to form a continuous narrative, in order to show forth what would be fulfilled by the glorious heavenly ministry of the Son, following on from the descent of the Holy Ghost on the day of Pentecost. This is that ministry which would be—and now is—characterised by the Father's revelation of the Son, a ministry indicated beforehand by the confession of Peter, 'Thou art the Christ, the Son of the living God.'

Nevertheless, twelve times over John does refer to the Son of man, though in a light transcending that of the first three —synoptic—gospels. With John, it is a matter of emphasizing *who* is the Son of man, rather than recording his actual pathway as such. John's emphasis consistently states, *This* is the Son of God.

Observe the references in John. Heaven would open, and men should see the angels of God ascending and descending upon the Son of man. This was said at the threshold of Jesus' ministry to the Jews. Once more: No man had ascended up to heaven, but he that came down from heaven, even the Son of man which was in heaven. This declaration came whilst Jesus stood on earth in the presence of all the Jews.

Again: As Moses lifted up the serpent in the wilderness, even so must the Son of man be lifted up, that whosoever believeth in him should not perish, but have eternal life. Men were not to labour for the meat which perished, but for that meat which endured to everlasting life, which the Son of man should give them, for him had God the Father sealed. Indeed, except men should eat the flesh of the Son of man, and drink his blood, they had no life in them; and did this hard saying offend them? then what and if they should see the Son of man ascend up where he was before?

But when they had lifted up the Son of man, then should they know that Jesus was he, and that he did nothing of himself, but as his Father had taught him, so spake he these things.

Some time later, prophesying of his death, Jesus declared, 'The hour is come that the Son of man should be glorified. Verily, verily, I say unto you, Except a corn of wheat fall into the ground and die, it abideth alone: but if it die, it bringeth forth much fruit.' Shortly after this he affirmed, 'And I, if I be lifted up, will draw all unto me.' This he said, signifying what death he should die.

But what did the Jews know either of the Son of man or of his death? The people answered him, 'We have heard out of the law that Christ abideth for ever: and how sayest thou, The Son of man must be lifted up? Who is this Son of man?' Yet whatever the blindness of the people, the counsel of the LORD was sure. Hence John records, 'Therefore, when Judas was gone out'—that is, to betray Jesus; in consequence of which he should be lifted up upon the cross—Jesus said, 'Now is the Son of man glorified, and God is glorified in him.'

The synoptic gospels each provide many passages on the return of the Son of man at the last day, but with the exception of John 5:27—which states that the Father had given to the Son authority to execute judgment also, 'because he is the Son of man'—there is a striking difference between the fourth gospel and Matthew, Mark and Luke.

There are no passages in John prophetic of the return of the Son of man, no references to the signs and the glory accompanying his return under this title, nor of the great day, the last day, the day of judgment, when the Son of man shall sit on the throne of glory judging all nations.

The difference is marked, a difference finding its cause in the setting forth of the ministry of the Son of man in the first three gospels, as opposed to taking from it the signs of the coming revelation of the Son of God in the case of the last gospel.

v. 'Son of man' from Acts to Revelation

Following the thirty-two places in which the Son of man is mentioned in Matthew; the fourteen in Mark; the twenty-six in Luke; and the twelve in John; there remains only *one* definite reference to the Son of man throughout all the rest of the new testament. These figures in themselves speak volumes.

This one reference appears in Acts 7:56. Here the last and most momentous sight of the Son of man is proclaimed by Stephen to the rulers of Israel. The rejection of this testimony proved to be the final cutting off of the Jewish nation in unbelief. This marked the end of Israel as the sphere of God's operations upon the earth. Thereafter nothing remained of the old legal dispensation, or to earthly Israel as such. Nothing, that is, but the fulfilment of the prophecies in the gospels of the coming again of the Son of man in the clouds of heaven with power and great glory. For now the wrath had come upon them to the uttermost.

After Acts 7:56, however, it is perfectly true that three other passages mention the words Son of man. Nevertheless, the references are not as obvious as they appear.

The first passage—Hebrews 2:6—refers to man's progeny, not the Son of man as a Person. Heb. 2:6 is in fact a quotation from Psalm 8:4, 'What is man, that thou art mindful of him? and the son of man, that thou visitest him?' This is clearly a reference to mankind, and to the children of men, nothing to do with the Son of man sent from heaven in his ministry to Israel. The translators have rightly indicated this fact by the use of the lower case 's' for 'son of man' in both Psalm 8:4 and Hebrews 2:6. Whereas, when referring to Jesus as 'Son of man', invariably they have used the capital 'S'.

The two remaining passages, both from Revelation, appear to give more difficulty. Both have capital 'S' for 'Son of man'.

Observe, however, that in the glorious manifestation of Revelation 1:13, the writer carefully abstains from stating that this vision of Christ was one in which he appeared as Son of man. He states specifically, 'One *like unto* the Son of man'. Evidently this appearance of Christ had a likeness to that ministry in which he came to the Jews, fulfilling the office of Son of man. Yes, but only a likeness, not exactly the same thing. It could not be the same thing.

The allegorical idiom of the book of Revelation draws from many vivid passages of scripture, but the Spirit's wording is always precise and careful. Not 'the Son of man' but 'One *like unto* the Son of man'.

The same observation applies to Revelation 14:14. 'And upon the cloud one sat *like unto* the Son of man.' The truth is that the last vision of the Son of man, as such, appeared in Acts 7:56. Of necessity, that was a vision to all Israel, represented by the chief priests, elders, and rulers of the people sitting in council.

'Son of man' was the title of the office in which God's Son was sent to the Jews—God's ancient people Israel—to turn that people to the kingdom, to bring them to the service of God, and to declare in their ears the long-promised grace sent to them from on high. All this was embodied in the Person and ministry of the Son of man.

Had the Jews received it, the blessing would have gone out from them throughout all nations upon the earth. But they rejected the kingdom, despising the Messiah. They refused the service, spurning the Servant of God. And they trampled underfoot the grace of God, denying that Just One. In a word, they crucified the Son of man, hanging him upon a tree.

Did God straightway blot out that nation? No, he did not. Did he then call out a remnant according to the election of grace, breaking off every natural branch of Israel? Not then.

What then? Then he raised the Son of man from the dead, elevating him to his own right hand. From thence, notwithstanding their dreadful words and deeds against him, he poured out his Spirit from on high even at Jerusalem. What for? To bless them, in turning away every one from his iniquities. But they would not.

At this point appears the significance of the last, the final vision of the Son of man in Acts 7:56.

vi. The vision of the Son of man in Acts 7:56

Stephen, a man full of faith and of the Holy Ghost, was called as a witness before the chief priests, elders, and scribes, sitting in council on behalf of all Israel. Which council, looking steadfastly on him, saw his face as it had been the face of an angel.

Arraigned before the leaders of the people, Stephen gave testimony by the Holy Ghost to the hardness and obduracy of the children of Israel against the successive gracious and merciful dispositions of the God of glory. The more the grace and mercy, the worse the disobedience and obstinacy of the tribes of Israel throughout the centuries of their long history as the people of God.

Finally the Holy Ghost charges by the mouth of Stephen, 'Ye stiffnecked and uncircumcised in heart and ears, ye do always resist the Holy Ghost: as your fathers did, so do ye.' 'Which of the prophets have not your fathers persecuted? and they have slain them which showed before of the coming of the Just One; of whom ye have been now the betrayers and murderers: who have received the law by the disposition of angels, and have not kept it.'

When they heard these things, they were cut to the heart, and they gnashed on him with their teeth.

But Stephen, being full of the Holy Ghost, looked up stedfastly into heaven, and saw the glory of God, and Jesus standing on the right hand of God, and said, 'Behold, I see the heavens opened, and the Son of man standing on the right hand of God.'

In this final vision of the Son of man, witnessed by Stephen, with the testimony of the Holy Ghost, the Jews came to the fulfilment of that which Jesus had spoken whilst on earth: 'What and if ye shall see the Son of man ascend up where he was before?' 'Hereafter ye shall see the Son of man on the right hand of the power of God.'

Standing before the selfsame priests and rulers which slew him, Stephen presently testifies by the Holy Ghost of the fulfilment of the very words which not long ago they had heard from Jesus' own lips. Now, in front of their eyes, all had come to pass. Will they repent?

By this heavenly revelation through Stephen, full of the Spirit, the testimony of the Holy Ghost below bears witness to the glorified Son of man above. Glorified: but standing. Not yet seated. The erect posture of the Son of man indicates readiness to move. As if poised to see whether Israel—even at the very last—would receive this merciful testimony of grace, that of the Holy Ghost himself, by the mouth and witness of his servant Stephen.

And what grace appeared! In glory the Son of man yet lingered, still standing, ready to bless them: 'How shall I give thee up, Ephraim? how shall I deliver thee, Israel?' He who wept over Jerusalem now tarries in glory above it, whilst the last, the ultimate, the full testimony of God is completed, the Holy Ghost descended, bearing witness before the whole council of Israel.

As if eternity stood still whilst the Son waited, poised, watching. Would the vision of the Son of man turn the battle in the gate? Though Israel had slain the prophets; broken the law; refused the promises; denied the Just One; condemned the Son of man; crucified the Lord of glory; gainsaid the resurrection; persecuted the apostles; disobeyed the gospel; and refused the Holy Ghost: yet the Son of man in heaven would turn Israel from destruction.

But as they had been to the Son of man on earth, so they were to the Son of man in glory. And as they had been to the Holy Ghost in glory, so they were to the Holy Ghost on earth. So it was that at the very moment of truth they cried out with a loud voice, stopped their ears, ran upon Stephen with one accord, cast him out of the city, and stoned him. Hitherto they had blasphemed the testimony of the Son of man. Now they blasphemed the witness of the Holy Ghost. This was the final rejection by the Jews of the ultimate testimony to the Son of man, that of the Holy Ghost himself, sent down from that glory to which the Son of man had been raised up in the ascension.

This was the end. The door now shut on the old, earthly, dispensation. No more shall the vision or the prophecy return to Israel. Here the natural branches are broken off.

From Acts 7:56 the silence holds till the end of time. This is the last express reference to the Son of man. No more shall he appear to the Jews in this present life. Never again shall they hear his voice in the world that now exists.

But as the ages run to a close, as the last day draws near, as the sands of time run out to the final grain, all the prophecies and all the signs of the coming of the Son of man shall come to pass. Then shall every last word that he spoke of himself in the gospels concerning the day of judgment most assuredly be fulfilled.

The momentous significance of the rejection of the Son of man by the Jews has neither been fully understood nor appreciated, either by the world or by the professing 'church'. Although it was Israel that rejected him, this was not under the name of Son of Abraham or Son of David—which might be considered peculiar to the Jews—but Son of *man*.

Mankind reacted. The will of man was made manifest. Expressed in Israel, yes, but nonetheless the will of man. Israel expressed the will of the flesh—as such—when confronted with the Son of man.

From the beginning—although a separated people—Israel was never seen in isolation from mankind, but as that chosen race which God had called and would cultivate from among men, and from among all peoples. However this cultivation was in order that, when the Son of man should come, blessing would multiply from Israel to all nations, his saving health from the Jews to all peoples, from the land of promise to the ends of the earth. But they crucified him.

And if *they* crucified him, a people whom God had prepared for ages and generations, who were Israelites, to whom pertained the adoption, and the glory, and the covenants, and the giving of the law, and the service of God, and the promises; whose are the fathers, and of whom, as concerning the flesh, Christ came: I say, if *they* crucified him, what then of the world, sunk in superstition and darkness?

If after all that God had wrought for the Jews, *they* crucified the Lord of glory, what would the Gentile nations have done? Nations sunk in idolatry, without God in the world, without the law, nations given over to a reprobate mind, nations wholly in bondage to the power of the god of this world?

God had long taken up man, as such, in Israel. God gave to Israel the promises in Abraham: but they despised them. God gave them the law: but they did not keep it. God sent them the prophets: but some they beat, some they killed, some they stoned, and all they rejected.

Last of all, God, having yet therefore one Son, his well-beloved, sent him also, saying, Surely they will reverence my Son. But no. They said among themselves, This is the heir; come, let us kill him, and the inheritance shall be ours.

And they took him, and killed him, and cast him out. But God raised him from the dead, and in visions of glory, by the mouth of Stephen, in the presence and power of the testimony of the Holy Ghost, yet once more he stood in heaven to bless them, if so be they might repent.

But they blasphemed the Holy Ghost and his testimony. They stopped their ears. And they stoned Stephen outside the gate. That is the will of man. That is the will of the flesh. That is what mankind decided. Because—not simply the Jewish mind but—the carnal mind is enmity against God.

He was in the world, and the world was made by him, but the world knew him not. He came unto his own, but his own received him not. They all with one consent began to make excuse. Going about to establish their own righteousness, they would not submit to the righteousness of God. They would not. Said he of them, 'Ye will not come to me that ye might have life.' They would not. They hated him without a cause. For his love he had hatred.

There was none, no, not one in Israel, that understood, none that sought after God. Hence the Son of man went as it was written of him. And if this was the glorious revelation of the love of God, it was the more so for being the shameful manifestation of the enmity of man.

Of mankind. Hence he said, 'Now is the judgment of this world.' And again, 'When he the Spirit of truth is come, he shall convince *the world* of sin.' Why? 'Because *they* believe not on me.'

It was expressed by Israel, this damning unbelief, yes, but it was the will of the flesh. It was the will of man, it was the *world*: 'Because they believe not on me.'

'They have both seen and hated both me and my Father.' It was not merely that they had failed to keep the law. That was of old. Now, they had despised and rejected the Son of man. They had both seen and hated both him and his Father.

Hence it is said, 'Once *in the end of the world* he hath appeared.' Not the end of the world in point of time: the end of the world in point of judgment. How is this? Because the will of man had been fully exposed by the presence of the Son of man among the Jews. Man was brought to light in his true and inmost condition. Man slew that Just One. Man was seen always to resist the Holy Ghost.

It was not that Israel alone had been exposed. Israel manifested the will of man, when the will of man had been indulged with every possible divine favour and kindness, in the most gracious light, even that of the very presence of the Son of God in manhood. Man under responsibility was proved to be worthless: more could not have been done than had been done by the love of God. Otherwise, the Son of man, coming to man according to promise, would have taken up man according to the flesh, and blessed the whole earth.

But man in the flesh knew him not, denied him, rejected him, crucified him, and, after all this, finally blasphemed the Holy Ghost. Thus man proved his own total depravity. How? Because of what was manifested when once brought to the light of absolute virtue. In terms of the Son of man, man had brought upon himself a final, an irrevocable condemnation: 'Now is the judgment of this world.'

But God had reserved a hidden mystery. And that hidden mystery was Christ's assembly—the *ecclesia*.

As to how that assembly should be raised up, or built, it was to be by revelation, leading to the confession, 'Thou art the Christ, the Son of the living God.' This was revelation from the Father in heaven. It was not from the religious knowledge, the will, or the building, of man on earth.

Of those to whom the Father, from heaven, revealed the Son, Christ would build his assembly, his *ecclesia*.

Thus the stone which the builders rejected became the head of the corner, disallowed indeed of men, but chosen of God, elect and precious. Here was that living stone, to whom Peter first, then all to whom the Father in heaven would reveal the Son, should come as lively stones, being built up a spiritual house, an holy priesthood, to offer up spiritual sacrifices, acceptable to God by Jesus Christ.

But Israel's outward, earthly house, the temple made with hands, was left unto them desolate. The nation which rejected the Son of man was rejected of him in turn, their priesthood defunct, their sacrifices obsolete, and their service for ever terminated.

5. The Confession of Peter

i. The revelation of the Son of God

The revelation of the Son of God to Peter, Matthew 16:16,17, was not—and could not have been—either objective or outward. Of necessity it was subjective and inward. That is, there was no outward alteration in the appearance of Jesus—objective to Peter—to prompt Peter's confession.

Unlike the transfiguration, Mt. 17:2, Jesus remained exactly the same in appearance before, during and after the revelation to Peter.

Then the change was within Peter, that was where the alteration took place, it was subjective, something happened within Peter, suddenly, that caused him to see Jesus in an entirely new light. But it was not the light of the sun without: it was the revelation of the Father within.

That was how the change took place.

Had Peter so confessed Jesus as the Christ, the Son of the living God, at the transfiguration, when 'Jesus was transfigured before them: and his face did shine as the sun, and his raiment was white as the light', then a confession in such circumstances might well be thought to have been the direct result of Peter's having seen the transformation in Jesus.

Then it would have been the objective and outward change—transfiguration—of Jesus, nothing to do with what was within Peter, that would have caused such a confession. But that was not at all the case at Caesarea Philippi. At Caesarea Philippi Jesus' appearance was precisely the same as it had been throughout the preceding years during which Peter had followed him.

Then the change was within Peter, it was subjective and inward, something vital and transforming happened interior to Peter—for nothing happened exterior to him—causing him to cry out 'Thou art the Christ, the Son of the living God.' And since this is the rock on which Christ builds his assembly, it behoves us to understand exactly what took place in Peter, and to understand it very clearly indeed.

It is essential for us to understand what took place in Peter because when Christ builds his *ecclesia*, even to this present day, he does so by building with those in whom Peter's experience is repeated, not by building on Peter's experience. Nothing other than the continuous repetition of Peter's experience in others could provide the 'living stones' with which Christ would build his future assembly or *ecclesia*. Peter's confession, which caused Christ to say, 'Thou art Peter, and on this rock I will build my assembly', therefore cannot mean that what happened to Peter was unique to him: it was exemplary in him.

Yet people think, when they read of Peter's experience in the bible, that they have finished with the question of revelation. To them it was a biblical revelation to Peter, nothing to do with their own inward condition. Indeed, as to themselves, they are far too balanced to be disturbed by such extravagant notions.

They suppose that what happened to Peter was sufficient for all, given that all read of it, and assent to what they read. In that case, Christ had finished building his assembly for—it is supposed—nothing further was to follow but the reading of and assenting to the biblical record of the apostle's experience. But I will show that what was to follow was the repetition of that experience: 'On this rock I will build my assembly'; that is, *commencing* with Peter.

The divine light of that revelation from the Father in heaven which shone *first* in Peter must *afterwards* be experienced in like manner by everyone that is to be built by Christ into his *ecclesia* even unto the end of the age.

This the apostle Paul confirms, writing to those Gentiles who had never seen Christ outwardly, who did not know Peter, nor had read of his experience at Caesarea Philippi. Yet most certainly they shared Peter's experience, for Paul testifies of Christ having built them together as his own *ecclesia*, Eph. 2:19-22, 'Ye are built upon the foundation of the apostles and prophets, Jesus Christ himself being the chief corner stone; in whom all the building fitly framed together groweth unto an holy temple in the Lord: in whom ye also are builded together for an habitation of God through the Spirit.'

Now, if anyone can come into such an experience as this, or be built spiritually into a temple in the Lord, or become an habitation of God through the Spirit, without a revelation from the Father in heaven, equivalent to that experienced by Peter, I should very much like to know how.

Certainly, if that upon which Christ builds his assembly required nothing more than our assent to an objective, historical record of an experience unique to Peter, then it might be understood how God could dwell in 'churches' of stone, wood, bricks and mortar, there being then no alternative to these temples made by hands.

In such a case, simply to read of Peter's experience, Mt. 16:16-18, confessing it to be the biblical revelation, the scripture, and giving vocal assent to the outward letter and record of the gospel, might be all that were necessary by way of salvation. But this is very far from the apostles' doctrine, just as it is very far from the nature of Peter's confession.

Mere consent to the written narrative of the experience of another, far removed in time and place, completely exterior to one's own person, is not and cannot be that upon which Christ builds his own *ecclesia*. What happened to Peter must happen to us. And what happens to us must have happened to Peter.

It is not enough for us—or for Peter—merely to give assent to the inspired record of scripture. Peter had the scripture—but not the revelation—before Caesarea Philippi. It is not enough for us—or for Peter—simply to confess Christ from outward appearances. Peter confessed Christ from outward appearances before Caesarea Philippi. But it was the inward revelation *at* Caesarea Philippi that made the difference. Because nothing that is external can reveal the heavenly vision of the Son of God. 'But my Father, which is in heaven, he hath revealed it.' On this, and on nothing else, Christ builds his *ecclesia*.

The Father's revelation of the Son *could not* be peculiar to Peter, although it was exemplary in Peter. If the revelation from the Father—which Christ calls 'this rock'—I say, if this rock were peculiar to Peter, then the *ecclesia* would already have been built, for, says Christ, 'On this rock I will build my *ecclesia*'. If none but Peter received the revelation, then none but Peter comprises the *ecclesia*.

Obviously both rock and *ecclesia* must extend beyond Peter to the experience of all the elect to the end of the age. Otherwise, who else has seen and believed upon the Son of God? Peter's confession—before the cross, before Pentecost—was in a sense given beforehand. It was a sign for the time then present of things shortly to be fulfilled. But they have been, they are being, and they will be fulfilled, even to the end of the age, in a great multitude whom no man can number. Of which multitude, Peter is one. But an exemplary one.

The revelation of the Son of God—on which, according to the apostles' doctrine, the assembly should be built up—properly belongs after the cross, beyond the burial, in the light of the resurrection, and from the ascension. 'Declared to be the Son of God with power, according to the spirit of holiness, by the resurrection from the dead.' Mark that, the declaration of the Son of God with power, according to the spirit of holiness, is by the resurrection from the dead.

This declaration is equally clear from the preceding context of Matthew 16:18. Mt. 16:4, 'A wicked and adulterous generation seeketh after a sign; and there shall no sign be given unto it, but the sign of the prophet Jonas.' The interpretation of that sign is clear: Mt. 12:40, 'As Jonas was three days and three nights in the whale's belly; so shall the Son of man be three days and three nights in the heart of the earth.' Thereafter Jonas rose up, as if from the dead, to preach unto the Gentiles.

After Jesus referred to his future building of the *ecclesia*, the following context, Mt. 16:21, asserts with equal force that Peter's confession must be seen in the light of the death and resurrection of Christ. 'From that time forth began Jesus to show unto his disciples, how that he must go unto Jerusalem, and suffer many things of the elders and chief priests and scribes, and be killed, and be raised again the third day.'

From which it follows that the revelation to Peter does not pertain to this present life which perishes, but to that life beyond death which shall never perish.

Observe, moreover, that this revelation was not a disclosure of the Son of man, or of what was temporal, or of Israel, or of man, or of what pertains to this present world, or to the ages of time. It was a revelation of the Son of God, of what was spiritual, what was of heaven, what was of God, what was from the Father. If so, it pertained to everlasting life, to the world to come, to eternity.

It was not a new manifestation of the old law, presaging a building again of earthly temples made with hands. It was not a light to confirm the old and grievous bondage, the ministry of condemnation. This revelation shed no radiance on the sentence of death, or the killing sentence, or the dreadful curse. It was a revelation of the new testament, of the assembly of the living God, of glorious liberty, of the ministry of justification, of the gift of life, of saving grace, of the promised blessing.

This revelation was not an appearance of angels, a giving of tables of stone, of blackness, darkness, or an horrible tempest. It was not a sight of the mount all on a fire, with the people trembling at a veiled, terrible, unknown, and distant Jehovah. It was an interior illumination of the Son of God, the shining of light, the quickening of life, the indwelling of love. It was a rent veil, a way into the holiest by the blood of Jesus, an entrance into the temple not made with hands, a coming into union with God revealed in Father, Son and Holy Ghost.

The revelation of the Son was not from man, it did not stand in man's will, or Peter's will. It was from God, from the will of the Father. It stood in an everlasting election, a gratuitous 'adoption', determined and assured in Christ before the foundation of the world or ever time began.

It was not an education in divinity, or truth taught by men from the pages of scripture, or religious instruction about certain biblical texts. This was outside of man, exterior to this world, a revelation from divine, uncreated, unearthly light beyond death, from eternity. It was a revelation of the deity, the revelation of a Person, a divine Person, of a divine Person in everlasting relationships. It was a revelation to the inward man, causing the receiver of it to become a partaker of the divine nature, so that such an one cannot but cry out, 'Thou art the Christ, the Son of the living God.'

On this rock, and of it, Christ will build his assembly, or *ecclesia*, receiving from the Father every one whom the Father had given to him from eternity and drawn to him in time. Now, although the revelation of the Son is from the Father, and by the Holy Ghost, and is a divine mystery, nevertheless it is a mystery the giving of which is recorded and described in divers places in holy scripture.

Hence any subsequent divine giving, and human receiving, of this revelation must accord and agree with the experience of Peter recorded in the scriptures, for thereunto were they given. It is essential to compare spiritual things with spiritual, to try experience by that rule of holy writ which infallibly declares the work of the Father, the Son, and the Holy Ghost, as it was in the beginning.

To this end, it is most necessary to trace and understand the places in holy scripture in which the revelation of the Son of God—or reference to the Person of the Son of God—is recorded, and to do so carefully, and with disciplined thoroughness.

ii. References to the Son of God in Matthew

The gospel according to Matthew refers to the Son of God sixteen times. But this needs some qualification. Of the sixteen references, one—now being considered, Mt. 16:16—mentions 'the Son of the living God'; one 'My Son'; two 'My beloved Son'; and four, 'the Son'. This leaves a remainder of eight references to 'the Son of God' in Matthew. Of these, two are spoken by the devil; one by devils; one by the high priest of the Jews; one by revilers; one by the chief priests, the scribes, and the elders; and one by a Roman centurion.

One text remains. This refers to the single occasion on which the name 'Son of God'—as such—was confessed by the disciples without subtraction or addition. This happened when Jesus walked on the water, saved Peter from sinking, and stilled the wind. 'Then (the disciples) that were in the ship came and worshipped him, saying, Of a truth thou art the Son of God.'

The nature of these references, together with the character of the speakers, shows clearly that the *revelation* was not of the Son of God during the days of his flesh, but of the *place* that the Son of God took in his ministry to the circumcision: that of Son of man. Observe this statement closely.

This observation is confirmed by the sheer numerical weight —thirty-two references, usually spoken by Jesus himself—of the title 'Son of man' in the gospel according to Matthew, over against half the number—often spoken by evil men or devils—of references to the Son of God.

However, once Jesus was risen from the dead, once he had ascended into heaven, once the Holy Ghost was given, then the *revelation*—not now to Israel but to the whole *ecclesia*—was no longer that of the Son of man, but of the divine Person who had taken the lowly place of Son of man in his earthly ministry to the Jews: the Son of the Father, eternal in divine relationships, God manifest in the flesh.

Being raised from the dead to everlasting glory, henceforward the Son of God should be revealed by the Father from heaven, through the Spirit on earth, to every one whom Christ receives, of whom he builds his assembly, even to the end of the age.

iii. References to the Son of God in Mark

Mark shows exactly the same thing in principle, although on face value there could appear to be a contradiction in the immediate use of the name Son of God, Mk. 1:1.

Because the purpose of this gospel is to make known the Servant and Service of God; because that Servant is not a slave but a Son; and because that service is not on earth in the flesh—although it began there—but from the glory in the Spirit, therefore Mark commences 'The *beginning* of the gospel of Jesus Christ, the Son of God', Mk. 1:1.

The place which the Son took in relation to the Jews, being manifested to them in his ministry as the Son of man, was the *beginning* of the gospel of Jesus Christ. The *continuation* of that gospel became apparent when—having made one sacrifice for sins for ever, and being ascended into heaven, Mk. 16:19,20—that same Son of man was 'declared to be the Son of God with power, according to the spirit of holiness, by the resurrection from the dead.'

Then, just *who* had taken the lowly place and service of Son of man was made manifest. In what way? In that he was no longer veiled under the earthly terms of a ministry and relationship to the Jewish nation, but henceforth revealed in terms of his own intrinsic deity and divine relationships declared in his glorified manhood risen from the dead.

Although Mark 1:1 commences with the statement 'the beginning of the gospel of Jesus Christ the Son of God', only seven other references—taking in all ways of mentioning his Sonship—occur in the book. Whereas there are fourteen passages, all from Jesus' own mouth, referring to the Son of man.

Out of the total of eight references to Jesus' divine Sonship, one is to 'the Son of the Blessed', and was spoken with hostile intent by the high priest. Yet another is to 'the Son of the most high God', and was uttered by an unclean spirit.

Jesus refers to himself as 'The Son' on only one occasion.

Twice however—once at his baptism and once again at his transfiguration—the Father from heaven calls him 'My beloved Son'. Both occasions were of a private nature, involving first the Baptist, then Peter, James and John respectively.

Otherwise there are but three explicit references to 'the Son of God'. One, the opening verse, is narrative. Another is spoken by unclean spirits. The last is the comment of a Gentile centurion.

Clearly the place taken by the Son of God in his service to the circumcision, that of Son of man, is the main thrust of the doctrine in Mark. Notwithstanding, there appear allusions from time to time of the coming service of the risen Son of God from the heavenly glory, God having been glorified on earth by his death on behalf of sinful men.

iv. References to the Son of God in Luke

This observation is confirmed in the gospel according to Luke, not least by the proportion of references to the 'Son of man' and 'Son of God' respectively. Luke refers to the Son of man twenty-six times. References to the Son of God—and similar terms—total twelve in all.

This in itself speaks volumes. Especially when one notes by whom and in what circumstances the respective references were made.

Regarding passages referring to the 'Son of God', but not using that wording precisely, Luke records the use once of 'The Son of the Highest'; twice of 'My beloved Son'; and three times of 'the Son'. The first was spoken by the angel Gabriel, the next two by the Father from heaven, and the last three by Jesus himself.

This leaves the final six passages, all of which expressly state the words 'the Son of God' in full. Of these, one was spoken by the angel Gabriel; two by the devil; one by devils; one by a demoniac; and one by the hostile elders, chief priests, and scribes of the Jews.

Hence, though in no wise discounting the importance of the six oblique references, it remains a fact that there is but one unequivocal use of the title 'the Son of God' of divine origin in the gospel according to Luke. This is in the message spoken to Mary by the angel Gabriel.

Even if the six oblique—and divinely given—references to the Son be added to the only specific passage using the words 'the Son of God', still this number must be set over against the twenty-six references to the Son of man, virtually all positive, and mostly, if not all, from the mouth of Jesus himself. It is noteworthy that these references to the Son of man cover the entire span of Jesus' public ministry on earth.

Without doubt therefore, 'Son of man' is Jesus' own name for himself in his earthly ministry to the Jews, whereunto he was sent. 'I am not sent but unto the lost sheep of the house of Israel.'

v. References to the Son of God in John

The difference between John, and Matthew, Mark, and Luke—the so-called synoptic gospels—must always be kept in mind. It is a fundamental difference. Uniquely, John selects seven signs—*sēmeion*—given during the ministry of the Son of man on earth, in order that by these he might signify what was to be revealed thereafter, following upon the resurrection and ascension, when Christ should enter into his glory.

These signs indicate who it was that had come into the world, appearing to the Jews as the Son of man, and what was that heavenly ministry which should succeed when he entered into glory, ministering the gospel from on high, by the power of the Holy Ghost below, bringing his people into union with the Father. All this, which was to follow thereafter, was wonderfully signified beforehand in the days of his flesh.

These are the signs which constitute the main body of the doctrine in the gospel according to John. 'These (signs) are written'—not that ye might believe that Jesus is the *Son of man* notice, but—'that ye might believe'—as did Peter, Mt. 16:16—'that Jesus is the Christ, the Son of God.' Jn. 20:31.

Therefore it is not surprising to learn that the preponderance of references in the first three gospels to the Son of man, over above those to the Son of God, is reversed in the case of the fourth gospel. Here the numerical weight is overwhelmingly in favour of the name 'the Son of God'.

Whereas John refers to the Son of man twelve times, references—of every form—to the Son of God amount to no less than thirty-two.

Once John records Peter as saying 'the Son of the living God'; there is one narrative reference to 'his Son'; two to 'the only begotten Son'; and one to 'the only begotten Son of God'. Eighteen times—three in the narrative and fifteen times spoken by Jesus himself—John refers to 'the Son'; and nine times there are direct references to the name 'the Son of God'.

Of the nine specific references to the name 'Son of God', once the name is used by Nathanael, once by John the Baptist, four times by Jesus himself, once by Martha, once by the Jews, and once the name 'Son of God' occurs in the narrative.

One cannot overstress the remarkable fact that—in contrast with the synoptic gospels—over against twelve references to the

Son of man in John, there are thirty-two to the Son of God. Furthermore, of the thirty-two references, only one is used with hostility—by the Jews. This leaves thirty-one positive references. This is a complete reversal to the proportional balance found in Matthew, Mark, and Luke.

Evidently the express purpose of the Holy Ghost in John is to reveal the rare disclosures and openings on the Person, name, and nature of the one who was made flesh, and dwelt among us. Disclosures made, that is, whilst as yet his divine Sonship was in a manner still hidden behind the veil of the flesh in which he appeared to the Jews as the Son of man.

vi. References to the Son of God from Acts to Revelation

Now, further to what has been observed from the four gospels, nothing could be more confirmatory than the fact that, apart from the vision of Stephen in Acts 7:56, from the Acts of the Apostles to the Revelation of Jesus Christ there are no references to the Son of man whatsoever. Everywhere and in all places in the epistles it is the revelation of the Son of God.

Since it is in the epistles that the hidden mystery of the *ecclesia* is brought to light, and since this mystery stands in the interior revelation by the Father of the Son of God, the exclusive use of the name 'Son of God' is precisely what should be expected from Acts to Revelation.

For now is Christ risen from the dead, and, having ascended into heaven, sending down the Holy Ghost, it follows that what is heavenly, what is spiritual, what is divine, what pertains to the eternal purpose of God, must be that which is to be made known in the new testament. This is the mystery of his will to all who are brought into the fellowship of the mystery, into the union by one Spirit with the Father and the Son.

But what has this to do with an earthly ministry, the ministry of the Son of man—however glorious—in and of this present world to the Jews?

The revelation of the Son from heaven by the Father, though prefigured in Peter, actually takes place after the rejection and crucifixion of the Son of man by the Jewish nation. It is a revelation following on from the descent of the Holy Ghost, in which the Father, by that same Spirit from heaven, makes manifest the risen and ascended glory of the Son of God.

In the epistles constant reference is made to the Son of God, or to some form of that name, or, equally explicit, to the Lord Jesus Christ, the full title peculiar to the risen, triumphant Son, glorious in his reign in heaven.

The epistles commence with the assurance of victory in Christ, from the other side of death, from the heavenly glory, from the glorified Son of God at the right hand of the Father. Grace and peace have been secured and assured to the assembly, from God the Father, and the Lord Jesus Christ.

The Son of God; his Son; his Son Jesus Christ our Lord; his own Son; My Son; the Son of God Jesus Christ; his dear Son; a Son; the Son; Son; My beloved Son; Jesus Christ his Son; his Son Jesus Christ; his only begotten Son; the Lord Jesus Christ the Son of the Father: all are referred to, ranging from Acts, Romans, One and Two Corinthians, Galatians, Ephesians, Colossians, Thessalonians, Hebrews, Peter, John's epistles—for example, a staggering twenty-two references in the small first epistle of John—and, of course, The Revelation of Jesus Christ.

From all of which it is abundantly clear that whereas God sent his eternal Son to the Jews to go as it was written of him in his ministry and office as Son of man, nevertheless the revelation of the Son in and of himself follows after the ascension. It is a revelation consequent on the descent and administration of the Holy Ghost from heaven.

Properly, on the foundation of Christ's work on earth, the new testament dispensation begins from the glory. That is, after Jesus had suffered many things of the chief priests, the elders, and the rulers of the Jews, was slain, and the third day was raised from the dead, thereafter to ascend into heaven.

If so, the revelation of the Son of God belongs to a new realm. It begins a new order. It pertains to what is beyond death, outside of time. It is neither of the flesh, nor of this present world.

The revelation of the new testament belongs to what is divine, heavenly, spiritual, eternal, glorious, and it views in prospect the heavenly city, the new Jerusalem, the bride, the Lamb's wife, and the eternal ages of everlasting glory. Now, with these things corresponds the assembly, 'my *ecclesia*'.

This is the called-out congregation which Christ builds, and none other: 'My assembly'. It is the assembly which stands in the revelation of the Son of God by the Father, through the Holy Ghost, to the inward man of all whom the Father will draw to the Son. Were it not so, the *ecclesia* would be impossible of realisation.

To all those, especially the professedly religious, to whom it is not so, such a thing is not only impossible, it is absolutely incomprehensible.

Impossible, because being divine, spiritual, heavenly, it is beyond their ability—beyond all the ability of man—to build this assembly. Christ's assembly stands in the revelation by the Father of the Son, and in the Son receiving those to whom that revelation has been given from above, integrating them together with their brethren into his *ecclesia*. And this is a thing utterly beyond the will of man to perform.

Incomprehensible, because the carnal, the worldly, the will-worker in religion cannot comprehend how these things can be: they are wholly beyond his comprehension. They may be beyond his comprehension, but he cannot deny that such things are in the bible, and are the only things in the bible, regarding the only 'church' that God owns, Christ builds, the Spirit fills, the scriptures describe, the apostles taught, the heavens receive, and the everlasting glory beckons.

Peter's confession of the Son of God, Mt. 16:16, was in a sense not for the time then present, rather it was to signify what should follow from the day of Pentecost. A sign given in the days of Christ's earthly ministry, so that from his own lips—and therefore recorded in the gospel—might sound forth the truth of that upon which the *ecclesia* should be raised up when once the Holy Ghost was given.

Hence this confession of the Son of God was in view of a revelation properly belonging to the ascension of the Son, and the consequent descent of the Holy Ghost. It was the result of a revelation from the Father, a revelation which brought forth the cry 'Thou art the Christ, the Son of the living God'. After the ascension, the manifestation of this work of the Father from heaven would provide the spiritual material from which Christ would build his *ecclesia* throughout all generations even to the end of the age.

The truth that Peter's confession of the Son was to set forth that on which Christ builds his assembly, and therefore that it was illustrative of what should follow from the giving of the Holy Ghost, is evident from the unfolding of the name 'Son of God'.

This is the name proper to Christ in deity from eternity, the name of him whom the Father sent into the world, but it is not the name by which—save for few exceptions—this same Son of God declared himself publicly in Israel in his ministry to the Jews.

When the Jews rejected and crucified the Son of man, God raised him from the dead to his own right hand. From thence the Holy Ghost was given. Then the heavenly gospel declaration began to be preached in all the world: 'declared to be the Son of God with power, according to the Spirit of holiness, by the resurrection from the dead.'

The references to the Son of God in the new testament confirm this. The passages in the gospels show it. Particularly is this true when comparing Matthew, Mark and Luke—all of whom primarily detail Christ's ministry as Son of man to the Jews on earth—comparing these, I say, with the fourth gospel.

For John's purpose is quite different: it is to signify the heavenly ministry of the Son of God from the glory, selecting for this purpose suited figures, signs, and discourses from the thirty-three years of Jesus' life on earth in this present evil world.

Having first considered the number of occasions on which the name of the Son of God occurs in Matthew, Mark, Luke and John respectively, now it is needful—so essential is this to the understanding of the *ecclesia*—to observe the passages themselves.

Such passages graphically illustrate the truth that he who by the incarnation had come to the Jews in his office as Son of man awaited the resurrection, the ascension, and the giving of the Holy Ghost fully to be revealed in his divine nature as Son of God.

In a word, the true, the interior, the spiritual knowledge of the Son of God, anticipated by that given to Peter in Mt. 16:16, properly belongs to the ascension, and the giving of the Spirit. This revelation of the Son by the Father from heaven, through the Holy Ghost, gives an unmistakable character to all those whom Christ builds into his *ecclesia*. They become as pure gold, like unto clear glass.

6. The Ministry of the Son of God

i. The Son of God perceived in Matthew

First, observe the passages in the gospel according to Matthew.

The first instance is the quotation from the prophet 'out of Egypt have I called my Son'. The Authorised version uses a lower case 's' for Son. But since the text—which asserts the fulfilment of the prophecy—states specifically 'My' Son, there is no warrant for using the lower case so as to give the reading 'son'. Only the Geneva bible, 1652—out of all the versions in the King James tradition—renders the correct, capital, 'S'. There can be no doubt from the context however, that the allusion is to the Son of God, and that the interpretation soars spiritually into the realm of the heavenlies.

Next, at the threshold of his earthly ministry, Jesus is baptized of John in Jordan. Going up straightway out of the water, 'the heavens were opened unto him, and he saw the Spirit of God descending like a dove, and lighting upon him, and, lo, a voice from heaven, saying, This is my beloved Son, in whom I am well pleased.'

According to Matthew, this was a vision which appeared to Jesus himself. Observe, 'the heavens were opened unto *him*, and *he* saw the Spirit of God descending'. This vision was in fact significant of the ministry which should follow after his resurrection and ascension, when he had delivered his people from the law and its curse, having been submerged on their behalf beneath the waters of death at the hands of retributive justice.*

Thereafter, in the inward parts of all those for whom Christ had died, there would sound the witness of the Holy Ghost

*Read 'The Messiah', pp. 52-65, The Publishing Trust. See advertising pages.

below, echoing the voice of the Father above, in the revelation of the Son. 'This is my beloved Son, in whom'—not *with* whom, notice, *in* whom—'I am well pleased.' As to being 'in' the Son, this refers to the indwelling of the Spirit, through whom Christ comes to abide in his own: 'I will not leave you comfortless, I will come to you.' Hence, 'At that day ye shall know that I am in my Father, and ye in me, and I in you.'

After Jesus' baptism follows his ministry to the circumcision, in which the Son took the lowly place of ministry in manhood to the Jews in the things of God as their Messiah, bringing to them the kingdom of heaven. Here the Son of man goeth as it is written of him.

Hence it is the manifestation of the Son of man: not the revelation of the Son of God.

But *who* was this Son of man? This could not entirely be hidden. The devil himself knew: 'If thou be the Son of God, command that these stones be made bread'. 'If thou be the Son of God, cast thyself down.' The demons knew: 'What have we to do with thee, Jesus, thou Son of God?' It was only the Jews—the professing people of God—who knew nothing. And the reason was, they were blinded by the very religion in which they trusted.

'No man knoweth the Son but the Father; neither knoweth any man the Father, save the Son, and he to whomsoever the Son will reveal him.' Then, any work of God cannot proceed on the basis of exterior religion, or of the law, or of the knowledge of the letter of scripture. It must proceed on the basis of the revelation of the Father and the Son.

This the disciples saw, and none other, 'Of a truth thou art the Son of God.' As to the Jews, they knew not so much as whether there should be a Son of man.

But Peter cried 'Thou art the Christ, the Son of the living God', a revelation proper to a finished atonement, a glorious resurrection, and the Spirit given to bring in the *ecclesia*. Hence it is said, 'On this rock I *will* build my assembly.'

All others are superseded: 'This is my beloved Son: hear him'. Not Moses; not Elias: not anyone else. Who else can once compare with the Son? But the Jews, full of hatred, that they might have wherewith to condemn him out of his own mouth, taunted him: 'Tell us whether thou be the Christ, the Son of God.'

However, this knowledge was by the inward revelation of the Father. The self-sufficient Jews despised such knowledge. Yet, for all their presumption in the scriptures, they knew not so much as the Son of man before their very eyes. Hence they crucified him, mocking, 'If thou be the Son of God, come down from the cross'. But the Gentile shamed them, confessing, 'Truly this was the Son of God'.

But God raised him from the dead. Risen, he commanded the eleven to teach these things—*these* things—among all nations, baptizing them in the name of the Father, and of the Son, and of the Holy Ghost.

This completes the sixteen references—of all kinds—to the Son of God, as opposed to the thirty-two specific texts concerning the Son of man, found in the gospel according to Matthew.

ii. The Son of God perceived in Mark

Straightway Mark opens the gospel with his first reference to the Son of God. 'The beginning of the gospel of Jesus Christ the Son of God.' Immediately Mark follows this by pointing to the place—in a figure—from which the service was to begin, that is, from Jesus' baptism: 'Thou art my beloved Son, in whom I am well pleased.'

And is this he, who, being in the form of God, thought it not robbery to be equal with God? Did *he* make himself of no reputation? Was it *he* who took on him the form of a servant? *He* who was made in the likeness of men? Yes, it was. He was the servant, found in fashion as a man, who humbled himself, and became obedient unto death, even the death of the cross. For he came not to be ministered unto, but to minister, and to give his life a ransom for many. It was he who came to serve the Jewish people, appearing to them in his service as the lowly Son of man.

Then what of the Jews? Did they not know? Had they not heard? The devils knew, and trembled. They trembled at the very truth they themselves prevented the blinded Jews from perceiving. Unclean spirits, when they saw him, fell down before him, and cried, saying, 'Thou art the Son of God'. And again, 'What have I to do with thee, Jesus, thou Son of the most high God?'

Yet secretly to Peter, James, and John, alone in a high mountain apart, the Father testified, saying, 'This is my beloved Son: hear him.' Nevertheless, Jesus forewarned them that they should tell no man that he was the beloved Son of the Father, till the Son of man—mark that, *the Son of man*—was risen from the dead.

Then, then, should this gospel be preached abroad among all nations. And that till the very last day. But of that day knows no man, no, not the angels in heaven, neither the Son, but the Father.

Next, the high priest, not from any believing, nor even calm enquiry, but from bitter malice, attempted to trap the Son of man into 'blasphemy', enquired, 'Art thou the Christ, the Son of the Blessed?' But neither the high priest, nor the elders, nor the rulers, nor the people, so much as believed him to be the Son of man, of whose coming and ministry their own scriptures—which they professed—testified.

Yet the Gentile said at his death, 'Truly this man was the Son of God.'

Thus Mark concludes the eight references of all kinds to God's Son. That is, in contrast with some fourteen references to the Son of man.

iii. The Son of God perceived in Luke

In the gospel according to Luke the angel Gabriel was sent from heaven to announce the incarnation of the Son to the virgin Mary: 'He shall be great, and shall be called the Son of the Highest.' He declares, 'The Holy Ghost shall come upon thee, and the power of the Highest shall overshadow thee: therefore also that holy thing which shall be born of thee shall be called the Son of God.'

Luke next records the name of the Son at his baptism: 'Thou art my beloved Son; in thee I am well pleased.' But the devil said unto him, 'If thou be the Son of God, command this stone that it be made bread.' And once more, 'If thou be the Son of God, cast thyself down from hence.'

Thereafter follows the ministry of the Son of man to the Jews, during which references to his Sonship are both sparse and hostile: 'And devils came out of many, crying out, and saying, Thou art Christ the Son of God'.

Another man, which had devils a long time, fell down, crying, 'What have I to do with thee, Jesus, thou Son of God most high?'

Nevertheless, privately to Jesus' disciples there came a voice from heaven out of the cloud saying, 'This is my beloved Son; hear him.'

And, said he, 'All things are delivered to me of my Father: and no man knoweth who the Son is, but the Father; and who the Father is, but the Son, and he to whom the Son will reveal him.' This spake Jesus alone to his disciples, as he rejoiced in spirit, observing that these things were hid from the wise and prudent, but revealed unto babes.

Then the new testament—and therefore the *ecclesia*—cannot proceed on the basis of man's knowledge of the scriptures, or of his conformity to the externally revealed will of God, or of an exterior sight and hearing of Christ, for all these things the Jews had, yet they were blind both to the Father and to the Son. More: the only true knowledge of the Father and the Son, that is, that which comes by divine, interior revelation from heaven, God himself had hidden from them in a secret place inaccessible to all the wisdom, intelligence and will of man in religion.

After this passage, Luke 10:22, Luke is silent concerning the divine name of the Son of God for some twelve chapters, a silence broken only by the malign clamour of the elders of the people, the chief priests and the scribes, seeking to trap Jesus that they might crucify him. 'Then said they all, Art thou then the Son of God?' Luke 22:70.

Luke 22:70 is the final quotation mentioning Jesus' divine Sonship of the twelve—in all forms—recorded by Luke. As opposed to twenty-six references to the Son of man.

iv. The Son of God revealed in John

It is abundantly clear that the relative use of the terms 'Son of man' and 'Son of God' in John is in inverse proportion to that recorded in Matthew, Mark, and Luke. John does not write to declare the ministry of the Son of man—as is the case with the first three evangelists—but takes from that ministry the unique signs which reveal the divine Person and work of the Son of God.

Far from recording an earthly, chronological, or historical sequence, John selects from the testimony of Jesus the signs which reveal the Father and the Son. Strictly this revelation is prophetic: it foreshadows that heavenly, ascended ministry which should follow after the giving of the Holy Ghost on the day of Pentecost.

Then, redemption having been accomplished, all righteousness fulfilled, God having been glorified on earth and the Son in heaven, that should be brought to pass which had been so marvellously set forth in the seven signs constituting the gospel according to John.

It was not possible that such glory, proper to the Person of the Son, should be altogether hidden in the days of his flesh. Nor that it should be altogether obscured behind the veil of his humanity during the period of his ministry to the Jews as the Son of man. Not possible. And it falls to John to bring out from the earthly life of Christ just how glorious and prophetic was the outshining of the Son of God throughout that earthly ministry.

Now, this is what Peter, John's constant companion, meant by his confession of 'the Son of the living God'. The gospel according to John, more than any other, expressed the meaning of Peter's confession, on behalf of all the believing disciples.

Whereas the term 'Son of man' occurs but twelve times in John, Matthew refers to this title thirty-two times, Mark fourteen, and Luke twenty-six times.

The name 'Son of God'—or its equivalent—however, occurs in the gospel according to John thirty-two times, in contrast with Matthew's sixteen times, Mark's eight, and Luke's twelve references.

This contrast alone shows the difference in purpose between the three synoptic gospels and John.

Nothing confirms this more surely than Jn. 20:30,31. 'And many other signs truly did Jesus in the presence of his disciples, which are not written in this book: but these are written, that ye might believe that Jesus is the Christ, the Son of God; and that believing ye might have life through his name.'

With these words John writes long after Christ's resurrection, ascension, and departure from sight, to those who had never seen him, that they might believe on him in view of the revelation given in the gospel, and that they might share his divine life in consequence. This John does by taking seven signs from Jesus' earthly life and ministry, showing by them what would be the glorious administration from the ascension, revealing the Father and the Son.

Peter, at the time of his confession, may not have conceived all that concerned the hidden mysteries of the glorious gospel of Christ. But whatever he did not know, he knew enough by heavenly revelation from the Father to say 'Thou art the Christ, the Son of the living God.' Furthermore, Peter had been taught by the voice of the Son of God to believe and know, together with John, by experimental hearing—'blessed are your ears, for they hear'—all that is written in the fourth gospel, from the first sign to the last.

In the gospel according to John the first occurrence of the name Son of God—or of a similar form of that name—occurs in the narrative: 'No man hath seen God at any time; the only begotten Son, which is in the bosom of the Father, he hath declared him.'

But not the bare writing on the page of this gospel, nor the recitation of some contrived creed to that effect, enables one to receive this declaration of the Father by the Son. For, 'No man knoweth the Father but the Son, and he to whom the Son will reveal him.'

Then, to receive what the Son has declared of his God and Father, is a question of revelation. It is to receive the inward revelation of the Father by the Holy Ghost. Just as receiving what the Father has declared of the Son is a question of revelation. It is to receive the inward revelation of the Son by the Holy Ghost.

'And of his fulness'—that is, what is within him—'have all we received'—and, if so, within ourselves—'and grace for grace.' So that, if, by the Spirit, the Father in heaven reveals the Son, then by that same Spirit the Son in glory reveals the Father. This is the wonderful declaration of which John speaks. On this the *ecclesia* is built, and on nothing less. The reception of such divine revelation alone constitutes the assembly. Without this, there is no assembly. Only pretence. However large and accepted that pretence might be.

But did Peter receive revelation of the Son by the Father, and of the Father by the Son, at Caesarea Philippi, Mt. 16:16? Not then in the utmost fulness of it, perhaps. But in the breaking forth of the light of it, a sign of what eye had not seen, nor ear heard, neither had entered into the heart of man to conceive, the foretaste of all that God had prepared for them that love him, then, yes, Peter did receive it. Otherwise how could Jesus have responded to Peter, 'flesh and blood hath not revealed this unto thee, but my Father which is in heaven', and, 'on this rock I will build my assembly'?

He who sent John to baptize said unto him, 'Upon whom thou shalt see the Spirit descending, and remaining on him, the same is he which baptizeth with the Holy Ghost.' And he who heard the voice of God, and saw the descent of the Spirit, testified, saying, 'And I saw, and bare record, that this is the Son of God.'

Who else? Who else could 'baptize with the Holy Ghost'? Who but the only begotten Son, which is in the bosom of the

Father? How else could men be filled with all the fulness of God? How otherwise could men receive that spiritual and interior baptism, imparting the light, life, and love of God? None but he, and nothing but this, can bring in the knowledge of Father, Son, and Holy Ghost. Now, that is the new testament, and that is the *ecclesia*. Nothing else, and nothing less.

Amazed at the prescience of Jesus, Nathanael confesses him to be the Son of God, joining to this name, the King of Israel. However, Jesus first points him to the knowledge of the Son of man, who, going as it was written of him, should open the heavens, bring heaven and earth together, and unite God and man in his own Person, by nothing other than the death of the cross.

And if all the heavens be opened, shall the whole earth be limited to the land of Israel? In no wise, for God loved the world, *so* loved the world, that for it he gave his only begotten Son. But is he not the God of the Jews only? Nay, but of the Gentiles also, that whosoever believeth in him should not perish, but have everlasting life.

For God sent not his Son into the world to condemn the world; but that the world through him might be saved. Here is a new testament, here a disclosure of the love of God, and here a revelation of God through the Son of his love, with a witness. After the long ages of the old covenant, the love of God expands from Israel to the whole world. And after centuries under the old law, the grace of God sends forth the new testament to the ends of the earth.

Now appears an unprecedented, an absolute criterion. He that believeth on him is not condemned. But he that believeth not is condemned already. Why? Because he hath not believed in the name of the only begotten Son of God.

All is new, and all declares the pre-eminence of Christ: For he whom God hath sent speaketh the words of God: for God giveth not the Spirit by measure unto him. All declares his pre-eminence, and all is absolute. He that believeth on the Son hath everlasting life: and he that believeth not the Son shall not see life; but the wrath of God abideth on him.

The Jews sought to kill Jesus, because he not only had broken the sabbath, but said also that God was his Father, making himself equal with God. Then answered Jesus and said unto them, Verily, verily, I say unto you, The Son can do nothing of himself, but what he seeth the Father do: for what things soever he doeth, these also doeth the Son likewise. The Jews had said, he made himself equal with God. This was false. He did not make himself equal with God. However, being in the form of God, he thought it not robbery to be equal with God.

As to what he made himself, 'He made himself of no reputation, and took upon him the form of a servant, and was made in the likeness of men: and, being found in fashion as a man, he humbled himself, and became obedient unto death, even the death of the cross.' So far from the Jewish slander that Jesus exalted himself to a place not his, namely, equality with God, the truth was that from a place rightfully his, he had humbled himself with a sevenfold abasement, that blessing might be theirs. He did not exalt himself, as they did. He abased himself, which is what they would never do.

Abased, his language to them in answer to what he 'made himself' was this: He did—he could do—nothing of himself: but what he saw the Father do. The Jews, however, did everything of themselves, they could not see anything that the Father did. But when they saw the Son doing the works of the Father, they sought to slay him.

Indeed, the work of God, the true knowledge of the Father and of the Son, was the very opposite to all their notions, creeds, conceptions, traditions, and works of religion. And so it is to this day in all those that are of the dead letter and outward form.

But how was it that the Father showed Jesus that to which the Jews were blind? Because the Father loved the Son, and showed him all things that himself doeth. But the Father did not love the Jews, for, said Jesus, I know you, that ye have not the love of God in you.

Why not? Because they loved themselves, honouring one another: 'How can ye believe, which receive honour one of another, and seek not the honour that cometh from God only?'

They went about to establish their own righteousness, though the fountain of their life issued in sin and death, which they would not confess, polluting all their works, which they would not admit. For nothing would induce these hypocrites to submit to the righteousness of God.

They esteemed their scripture learning, and their honourable degrees as the acme of attainment. But, 'That which is highly esteemed among men is abomination in the sight of God.' Jesus, however, humbled himself, spake nothing of himself, did nothing of himself, knew nothing of himself, judged nothing by himself, and sought nothing for himself. He sought only the words, works, judgments, glory and honour that pertained to the Father.

And the Father loved him, as he testified. For, though Jesus had all things beyond human measure or conception, he became as nothing, for nothing but his Father's glory. This—it is true—is what he 'made himself'. And him the Father honoured in consequence.

The Father showed him all things that he himself did. Nor was that all. He would show him greater works. Greater, for example, even than the raising up of the impotent man at the pool of Bethesda, that the Jews might marvel. But what greater works can there be than the raising of the impotent man? Why, the raising of the dead. The work of resurrection itself, the greatest work of all. For as the Father raiseth up the dead, and quickeneth them, even so the Son quickeneth whom he will.

The Father judgeth no man, but hath committed all judgment to the Son. What judgment is this that is committed to the Son? That which is committed to the Son is his judgment as to whom he shall quicken, and whom he shall not quicken.

And whom shall he quicken? All that the Father hath given to him, all these shall he quicken. For the Father shall draw them to him, and reveal him to them, as he revealed him to Peter, Mt. 16:16. Therefore Peter, with all his brethren from the beginning of the world to the end of it, will the Son quicken. With what effect? That all—that is, all of them—should honour the Son, even as they honour the Father.

He that honoured not the Son, honoured not the Father which had sent him. But who dishonoured the Son, and how was he dishonoured? The Jews honoured not the Son, professing instead to honour the scriptures, claiming to honour the law as their rule of righteousness and life. But they broke the law, and they dishonoured the scriptures. For the scriptures, which they dishonoured, testified of Christ, witnessing that righteousness and life came by him, and by him alone.

As to that righteousness, it was by the death of Christ. As to that life, it was life from the dead. For all that is in the world, and all that is born of the flesh, appears as nothing but sin and death in the sight of God. Nevertheless, 'The hour is coming, and now is, when the dead shall hear the voice of the Son of God: and they that hear shall live.'

Which dead are these? Those dead, without righteousness and without life, that then heard his voice, together with all who should hear it thereafter, to the end of the age.

This voice does not refer to his outward, audible, voice. For many then, and since, should hear his voice in the gospel, but it would not penetrate the sepulchre of their hearts to the dead soul within. Then again, many others then, and since, should hear his inward voice in the gospel, and it would penetrate the sepulchre of their hearts to quicken into life the dead soul within. 'And they that hear, shall live.' This is called, The first resurrection.

For as the Father hath life in himself, so hath he given to the Son to have life in himself. That is, given to him for the fulfilment of the 'greater works' of the resurrection of the dead. Moreover he hath given him authority to execute judgment—that is, *the* judgment—also, because he is the Son of man. Mark that, judgment also, because he is the Son of man.

Before, it was said that the Father would show him 'greater works'—it is plural—greater, that is, than the raising up of the impotent man at the pool of Bethesda.

The first of these greater works has been observed: that by his voice then on earth, and throughout the age by the gospel, he should quicken into life the interior souls of those dead in sin. This is the 'greater work' of spiritual resurrection, in which the inwardly and spiritually dead pass from death unto life, whilst still in this present evil world.

But what other work can there be, added to such a work—to make the plural, greater *works*—that is of commensurate greatness? Why, the resurrection from the dead at the great and notable day of the Lord, the last day, the coming day, the day of judgment, when the Son of man shall appear in the clouds with great glory. That last, final, 'greater work'.

Then, all that are in the graves—not just the spiritually dead in the sepulchre of the flesh—the literally dead, from the beginning of the world to the end of it, mouldering into dust throughout the earth, then, then they shall hear his voice.

'And the sea gave up the dead which were in it; and death and hell delivered up the dead which were in them: and they were judged every man according to their works.' 'And I saw a great white throne, and him that sat on it, from whose face the earth and the heaven fled away, and there was found no place for them.' 'And I saw the dead, small and great, stand before God; and the books were opened: and another book was opened, which is the book of life. And the dead were judged out of those things which were written in the books, according to their works.'

'For', declares John, 'the hour is coming, in the which all that are in the graves shall hear his voice, and shall come forth. They that have done good, unto the resurrection of life; and they that have done evil, unto the resurrection of damnation.' This is the last resurrection. And it is the final judgment.

Who then can be saved? 'And this is the will of him that sent me, that every one which seeth the Son'—by revelation, as did Peter, Mt. 16:16,17—'and believeth on him'—in consequence of that revelation—'may have everlasting life: and I will raise him up at the last day.' That is, to the resurrection of life. All these shall assuredly be saved. No wonder therefore that Simon Peter answered him, saying, 'Lord, to whom else shall we go? Thou hast the words of eternal life. And we believe and are sure that thou art that Christ, the Son of the living God.'

The Jews, in bondage to sin, that is, inbred sin under which all are sold in the Fall, yet professed liberty as Abraham's seed. But Jesus informed them that the servants were not free, neither abode they in the house for ever. A servant comes in but to serve, afterwards to be dismissed to his quarters.

But the Son abideth ever, for the house is his. If therefore, and only if, the Son should make men free, then their liberty in the house should be assured for ever. And who other than he could afford to purchase such a freedom for Abraham's seed? And at what price?

But what was that to self-justifiers, who claimed that they were not in bondage, but alive before God, when the yoke was heavy upon them, and the chains bound fast their dead souls from birth? They were bound by the legal yoke, and none but Christ could deliver from that. And his deliverance, they despised, claiming to be free already.

How different was the case of the man born blind, who knew what darkness was, who felt his blindness, and could tell the slavery of the Fall—from birth—by bitter experience. But with clay made from Jesus' spittle, by the anointing of his eyes, having washed in the pool of Siloam, he had been made to see. Therefore, seeing, the Saviour had been revealed; and by whom but the Father?

Hence, when asked 'Dost thou believe on the Son of God?' like Peter he replied, 'Lord, I believe'. This is perfect freedom: it results in worship; it comes by faith; it separates from the synagogue; and it eschews all dead works.

To the self-righteous, who sought to approve themselves to God by their religious lives, what the blind man, now seeing, believed, was blasphemy. Indeed, to them, Jesus himself had blasphemed. Hence Jesus asked them, 'Say ye of him, whom the Father hath sanctified, and sent into the world, Thou blasphemist; because I said, I am the Son of God?'

But if he were not the Son of God, how could he have opened the eyes of the blind?

If seeing the Son were not the result of the inward revelation of the Father, why was it that the man born blind, who came seeing, could perceive clearly what was utterly obscure to the blind Jews, though they claimed sight? The man whose eyes had been opened could see that the Father was in the Son, and that the Son was in the Father. Could not the Jews? It was evident. Why then did they not believe, even if only for the work's sake?

But, like all the religious in the dead letter, without the interior revelation from the Father in heaven, they say, 'We see', whilst as yet they are blind. And because they say, 'We see', therefore their sin remaineth.

Lazarus, by birth dead in sin, even as others, died of his sickness. Yet this was not that he should abide in death, but for the glory of God, that the Son of God might be glorified thereby. How else glorified, other than by the resurrection of the dead? The resurrection of all was signified—and assured—by the raising of one, even Lazarus. For the Son shall raise the dead, and this is his glory.

Indeed, he is himself the resurrection and the life. He that believeth in him, though he were dead—as Lazarus was dead, who had believed in him—yet shall he live—as Lazarus lived, and was raised to life again to testify to the resurrection of the dead. Yea, whosoever liveth and believeth in him—further to the first, the interior, resurrection—shall never die—that is, never die the second, endless death. Believest thou this? Martha believed it, saying, Yea, Lord: I believe that thou art the Christ, the Son of God, which should come into the world. Which is what Peter believed, Mt. 16:16.

All is in Christ. As to the law and its rule, he that believeth in him is dead to the law by the body of Christ, that he should be married to another, even to him who is raised from the dead. Then shall he bring forth fruit unto God. All is in Christ, and he that is joined unto the Lord is one spirit.

As to bringing forth fruit, Jesus said, He that believeth on me, the works that I do shall he do also; and greater works than these shall he do; because I go unto my Father. And whatsoever ye—the disciples—shall ask in my name, that will I do, that the Father may be glorified in the Son. If ye ask any thing in my name, I will do it.

At that time Jesus prayed, lifting up his eyes to heaven, saying, Father, the hour is come; glorify thy Son, that thy Son also may glorify thee: as thou hast given him power over all flesh, that he should give eternal life to as many as thou hast given him. This prayer, that the Father should glorify him, anticipates his rising from the dead.

In an earlier passage, but in the same context, he had prayed concerning his death: Now is the Son of man—mark that, the Son of man—glorified, and God is glorified in him. This refers to the atonement, when the Son of man should be made sin, bear sins, receive the curse of the law, and answer to the righteousness of God on behalf of sinners in the place of judgment.

When he had taken away the sin of the world, made an end of sins, borne the last sentence of the broken law, and glorified God in righteousness: when no vengeance remained, and all justice was satisfied: then came in the prayer, and the answer, that remained: Father glorify thy Son, that thy Son also may glorify thee. How else would the Father glorify him but by raising him from the dead? For he was raised from the dead by the glory of the Father.

'Father glorify thy Son, that thy Son also may glorify thee.' How would he also glorify the Father? By giving eternal life to as many as the Father had given him. First by bringing in the righteousness of God on their behalf, that it should be imputed to them. Thereafter to give to them eternal life from the throne of glory in the heavens. This he should do for all whom the Father had given him, throughout this present age, even by the effectual working of his own power. This is to glorify the Father. And it does glorify the Father. As it was in the beginning, is now, and ever shall be, Amen.

This is the ministry of the Son of God; this is what it is to believe on the Son of God; this is what is revealed from the Father in heaven. This is the quickening of the first resurrection on earth; this is that glorious, triumphant, life-giving, abiding work of the Son of God; this is what Peter meant by 'The Son of the living God', Mt. 16:16. And this is that upon which Christ builds his *ecclesia.*

For all that God sent his Son into the world to be clothed upon with flesh; to take upon him the seed of Abraham; to veil his ineffable deity behind that perfect humanity; to come as Son of man in meek lowliness to the Jews, that they might receive the promises; that deity—as John shows so graphically—could never be hid. Behind the veil of flesh, beyond the nature of that humanity, shining through the ministry of the Son of man, a glory, a mystery, true deity was revealed. It was this that brought the Jews to a murderous fury: 'We have a law, and by our law he ought to die, because he made himself the Son of God.'

No. He did *not* make himself the Son of God. He *was* the Son of God. He made himself of no reputation.

'And these signs'—of what should break forth in full glory after the resurrection—'are written, that ye might believe that Jesus is the Christ, the Son of God; and that believing ye might have life through his name.' This last passage—John 20:31—completes the references to the Son of God in the gospel according to John, unique among the four evangelists.

Of all the apostles, John was the closest to Peter, and hence the most apt to show the meaning of that apostle when he exclaimed, Matthew 16:16, 'Thou art the Christ, the Son of the living God'.

v. The Son of God revealed from Acts to Revelation

The understanding of what Peter meant, Mt. 16:16, is no question of academic interest to the student. It is a matter of salvation to the lost. It is not an option for the learned. It is of the essence to the perishing.

The apostles were to go and teach all nations. But teach them what? Teach them *all things* whatsoever Jesus had commanded them. That teaching, and those commands, are in the four gospels. But whatever else was in that teaching, nothing is more important than the truth of the Son of man, or the revelation of the Son of God. 'On *this* rock I will build my *ecclesia.*'

If that Builder is not made known, or if that building should be obscured, then Christ's assembly cannot be built. And if Christ's assembly cannot be built, so as visibly to be perceived, then we are no better off than would have been the family of Noah without the ark.

All this about the Son of man and Son of God? Most religious people—including their priests, pastors, ministers and teachers—would say, 'What has all that kind of thing got to do with the 'church'?' The answer is, literally and absolutely *everything*. But they have detached the *ecclesia*, or assembly, from the knowledge of the Son of man, and they have despised the revelation of the Son of God. But take that knowledge and that revelation away, and nothing exists with which Christ is to build his *ecclesia*. And with little or no exception that is precisely the position today.

Nothing is more clear than that the revelation of the Son by the Father from heaven alone provides that from which Christ will build his *ecclesia*. It is not what one does, or persons do for one, or what any body or organisation claims to do for others in Christianity. All that counts is what the Father does from heaven to the inward and spiritual man, so as to reveal his Son. Nothing else provides that from which Christ builds his assembly.

No matter what the claims on earth, if a man lacks this, he is neither of the *ecclesia* nor suited to it. But if a man has got this, he is of the *ecclesia*, and should be united with it. And with nothing else. All this appears so idealistic and unreal to professing Christendom—Roman, Protestant, Evangelical, Reformed, it makes no difference—that it is dismissed as mystical and visionary extremism. It is neither. It is Christ's assembly. Which is not theirs. Otherwise they would have no such objection.

It is because those who refuse this doctrine reject that Stone, and set themselves up as builders, that they are against it. Because they are builders they are against it. Hence they refuse to consider—will not even contemplate—with whom, why, and what Christ builds, even to this latest day.

Whereas mention of the Son of man disappears, references to the Son of God abound in the epistles, together with the coming in of Jesus' full ascended title: The Lord Jesus Christ. This speaks of the glorified Son seated on the throne of his Father in the heaven of heavens. This becomes the light and life of the assembly, and the glory that shines in the gospel: Grace unto you, and peace, from God our Father, and the Lord Jesus Christ.

From the ascended Son, the apostles, having received grace and apostleship from on high, for obedience to the faith among all nations, were charged to preach the gospel with the

Holy Ghost sent down from heaven. The faith which they preached, and to which they were obedient, was called 'The faith of the Son of God.'

The saints, to whom revelation from the Father in heaven had been given, were called into the fellowship of God's Son. To them, into their hearts, was sent forth the Spirit of his Son, crying, Abba, Father. They were predestinated to be conformed to the image of his Son. For the Son of God, Christ Jesus, was preached unto them, not as yea and nay, but yea and Amen, for all the promises of God in him were yea, and in him Amen, unto the glory of God by the apostles.

For when Christ ascended up on high, he gave the apostles to the assembly—and others, too, prophets, evangelists, pastors and teachers, in this same heavenly and glorious ministry of the Son of God—for the perfecting of the saints, for the work of the ministry, for the edifying of the body of Christ. For what purpose, and until when? Till we all come in the unity of the faith, and of the knowledge of the Son of God, unto a perfect man, unto the measure of the stature of the fulness of Christ. Then, till the very end of time.

Indeed, by the Holy Ghost, the assembly was in God the Father, and in the Lord Jesus Christ, one *ecclesia*, variously manifested. One body, and one Spirit, called in one hope of this calling; one Lord, one faith, one baptism; one God and Father of all, above all, and through all, and in all. How then could it have been other than one assembly, and one *visible* assembly at that?

That assembly visibly answered to the revelation of the Son of God from heaven by the Father, through the Holy Ghost, given to indwell all saints gathered into one unity below.

The saints and faithful brethren had been translated into the kingdom of God's dear Son—a separate, lowly, heavenly and glorious company—and they waited for the return of God's Son from heaven. One body, and nothing but that one body manifested in each assembly, united in Father, Son, and Holy Ghost. Here was a people, a people of God, holy and harmless, separate from the world, always persecuted and despised, a people called 'the sect that is everywhere spoken against'.

It should be remarked that more than any other epistle—though it is one of the shortest—the first epistle of John abounds with references to the Son of God. The same feature distinguished the gospel according to John when compared with the three synoptic gospels. The five short chapters of the first epistle of John contain no less than twenty-two references to the Son. These range from three occurrences of 'his Son Jesus Christ'; one of 'Jesus Christ his Son'; one of 'his only begotten Son'; four of 'his Son'; five of 'the Son'; and eight occurrences of 'the Son of God'.

The first epistle of John declares the humanity of Jesus Christ, the Son of God, come in the flesh. It affirms what is recorded in the four gospels, that which the apostles heard, saw with their eyes, looked upon, and which their hands had handled, of the Word of life.

The Spirit, the water, and the blood bear witness. That is, witness to Jesus Christ, come in the flesh, raised from the dead, ascended to glory, revealed by the Father, and manifested by the Holy Ghost. For he that believeth on the Son of God hath the witness in himself. And this is the witness: that God hath given to us eternal life, and this life is in his Son.

He that hath the Son hath life, and he that hath not the Son of God hath not life. And we know that the Son of God is come, and hath given us an understanding, that we may know him that is true, and we are in him that is true, even in his Son Jesus Christ. This is the true God, and eternal life.

And this is what Peter meant, when he said, 'Thou art the Christ, the Son of the living God', Mt. 16:16

From the foregoing it is abundantly clear that the *ecclesia* is that which Christ builds up by uniting together those to whom the Father has revealed the Son, and none other.

Neither is there any different, or alternative, *ecclesia.*

The one, the only *ecclesia,* is of divine initiative, spiritual character, heavenly origin, holy life, mysterious nature, glorious destiny, and visible unity. Though inward in its life, it is outward in its assembly. This is the assembly of those to whom the Father reveals the Son. Who, in consequence, are built together and united in one body by the filling of the Holy Ghost sent down from Christ above.

There is nothing here of the will of man; no quarter for the will of the flesh; no place for anything of the world; no room for the intrusion of any human organisation. Not in Christ's *ecclesia.* All is of God, in Father, Son, and Holy Ghost; and all is of God from the ascension; all is of God out of heaven; and all is of God in an entirely new creation in Christ Jesus. It is *his* assembly.

Whosoever esteems the 'church' anything less, or settles for anything short of it in practice, is not only blind to the truth, knowing nothing yet as he ought to know, but he is downright disobedient to the heavenly vision, the holy scriptures, the words of the Lord Jesus, and the doctrine of the apostles. Such a man will find at the last day that what was at this time a matter of indifference to him, was very far from a matter of indifference to Christ, who presents to his people neither alternative nor variation for what he calls 'My *ecclesia*'.

When the Son of God laid aside that glory which he had with the Father before the world was, making himself of no reputation, and taking upon him the form of a servant, being made in the likeness of men, and come among men, it was, therefore, in the fashion of a man that he was judged of mankind. The Jews saw that manhood. Yet they would not even once concede that he was the promised Son of man. Much less would they ever admit *who* it was that had been made flesh, to dwell among them as Son of man. In this, they were typical of all mankind.

Albeit veiled by the flesh of his humanity, that eternal life which was with the Father, was manifested to the Jews in the Person of the Son. Far from perceiving that eternal life, or that divine Sonship, a life and relationship which subsisted between the Father and the Son from eternity; far from being aware that he was in the world who had made the world; the Jews despised even the purpose of his manhood.

Israel neither knew him, nor received him, even as Son of man, though he was manifested so wonderfully to them. And if they refused the Son of man, their own Messiah, as man, before their own eyes fulfilling all scripture, every prophecy, each type, everything that was written of him, how should they believe on him who had come to them out of eternity, out of deity, out of glory, out of heaven, to fulfil his lowly, humiliating office in manhood?

But the Son was refused, despised and rejected by the Jews.

This refusal manifested the blindness of mankind—born blind—to all that was divine, all that was heavenly, all that was spiritual. Though set before the eyes of all humanity, confirmed by a thousand signs, still, 'He was in the world, and the world was made by him, and the world knew him not.'

Then nothing, no incarnation, no miracle, no sign, no scripture, no Messiah, no Son of man, no Son of God, no gospel —though manifested and made known objectively before the very face of mankind—could possibly penetrate the darkness of the mind of man, or the blindness of the human heart.

Then shall all fail because of the hardness of the heart of the Jews, and the blindness of the mind of fallen mankind? Not at all. Despite the unbelief of the Jews, for all the darkness of the world, there has appeared light from heaven, revelation from the Father, and illumination from the glory. 'Arise, shine; for thy light is come, and the glory of the LORD is risen upon thee. For, behold, the darkness shall cover the earth, and gross darkness the people: but the LORD shall arise upon thee, and his glory shall be seen upon thee. And the Gentiles shall come to thy light, and kings to the brightness of thy rising', Isa. 60:1-3. Now, this light is Christ. But it is Christ revealed by the Father from heaven.

Supernatural vision, answering to the revelation by the Father from on high, enabled Peter to perceive that glorious light from heaven manifesting the Son of God, the very deity veiled in manhood. This experience caused him to cry, 'Thou art the Christ, the Son of the living God'. That is the mystery. And upon the revelation of it, Christ builds his *ecclesia*.

Here is a penetration, a seeing beyond what is visible, a passing into the supernatural. It is a revelation, not of what Christ does for man, but of what he is in himself. Here the Son is illuminated by the Father in his own nature and in his divine relationships. This is to see, and to see indeed, that 'the life was manifested'.

This heavenly light came from above; and it came within. It was not visible to the eye, it was manifest in the spirit. It was of divine prerogative, from the Father in heaven. This was not man choosing Christ, or man 'deciding for Christ'. This was not what Christ can do for one, or for another, or for all mankind. This, from above, happened to Peter. He did not initiate it. He saw the Son by revelation, and he saw the Son in his own nature. If so, he saw the Father. 'For he that hath seen me, hath seen the Father.'

Of those who receive such a revelation—a revelation coming not from Christ, but coming from the Father in heaven revealing Christ—and of those alone, Christ builds his *ecclesia.*

7. The Son of the living God

i. The living God

Finally, concerning the confession of Peter, notice the qualification: 'Thou art the Christ, the Son of the living God.' Why the *living* God? Here is an emphasis evidently vital to the experimental vision given to those from whom Christ builds his assembly.

So obvious is the expression 'living' in relation to God, that one might have thought that such a qualification was not necessary. But it is necessary.

'Life' or 'living' may be considered either in terms of the length of days, the lifetime, as in 'he is still alive', or 'still living'; or else it may be viewed in terms of existence, the fact of being lively, the vitality, the 'quickness', the quality of the life. When predicated of God, in the first case this points to his eternal duration: that he is everlasting; in the second to his Being, to the nature of the life of God, that his is divine life, uncreated life.

In both applications, one addresses concepts past all human comprehension: these things lie beyond the ability of men even to imagine. And yet they lie at the heart of the revelation to Peter, and, if so, at the heart of the revelation to all the people of God, to every one whom Christ builds into, and of whom he composes, his own *ecclesia.*

Both concepts are implied in the words 'the *living* God'. Firstly, everlasting life is implied. It is everlasting in terms of duration. Not only has what is everlasting no end: by definition, it has no beginning. It *is*. It is the life of 'I AM THAT I AM'. From eternity past no commencement existed to the everlasting life of God, it is life without conception, it is life that will never end, it is immeasurable.

Time is totally irrelevant to eternal life; death is meaningless; neither beginning of lifetime, nor ending of days can be projected into these realms, such notions are but limited ideas that have no bearing on the deity. In the things of God these temporal concepts are irrelevant.

Secondly, considered in terms of the quality of the life, the vitality of the life of the deity—the *living* God—this is not only eternal life, or everlasting life—life without beginning or end—it is that unique life of God himself, within himself.

This transcends all, soaring absolutely above all created life, whether in heaven, or on earth, or under the earth; whether of angels, or men, or of living creatures. If for no other reason than that it is the uncreated life of him who gives transient breath to every creature that has ever lived, is living, or will ever live. But, 'thou takest away their breath, they die, and return to their dust. Thou sendest forth thy spirit, they are created: and thou renewest the face of the earth. The glory of the LORD shall endure for ever.' All these are nothing but a passing wind, beginning from nothing save his word, and ending in the dust at his command.

It is impossible for man, the possessor of human being, or human life, even to imagine the likeness of divine life. Indeed, there is no likeness to divine life. It is not merely superhuman: it is beyond all human conception, outside of all conscious existence, it is life transcending all created ability to comprehend.

It is expressed in terms that are absolutely immeasurable, unfathomable, incomprehensible to man. It is *other*, beyond the grasp of cherubim, seraphim, archangels, angels, the heavenly host, the principalities, powers, the unseen beings in the heavens: all these fall down in wonder. Then how much more mankind, how much more human nature? No creature can comprehend the life of God. Yet this is revealed in the gospel. It is what Peter experienced. It is what he meant by 'the living God'.

ii. The life of the ecclesia

O, staggering truth! this is that life which fills the *ecclesia*. And shall men experience such things? Yes, they shall.

But how can this be? 'For what man knoweth the things of a man, save the spirit of man which is in him?' Then how can man conceive of the life of God, the living God?

'Even so the things of God knoweth no man, but the Spirit of God. Now we have received, not the spirit of the world, but the spirit which is of God; that we might know the things that are freely given to us of God.'

Such as everlasting life, the life of God, the living God, the life of the Father and the Son. 'That eternal life, which was with the Father, and was manifested unto us', I Jn. 1:2. Man can never comprehend, no; but the Spirit of God can and does communicate to the *ecclesia* of Christ 'the things freely given to us of God'. And what more than everlasting life in the Son?

As to man, 'Cease ye from man, whose breath is in his nostrils: for wherein is he to be accounted of?' As to man, it is not in Adam that all live, for, 'In Adam all die'. From Adam came nothing but sin and death.

As to Christ, he was not born of man, but of woman; and the living seed that is in Christ, quickened by the Holy Ghost, answers to that spoken of Eve—not Adam—'She shall be called the mother of all living.' 'This is a great mystery, but I speak concerning Christ and the *ecclesia*', Eph. 5:32.

iii. Life in the Son

The phrase 'the living God', used by Peter, and inspired by the Holy Ghost, has reference to Christ's Sonship. 'The *Son* of the living God.'

This is not only a revelation of Sonship absolutely, in deity, from eternity, but of Sonship *then*, in manhood, it is the Son *as sent*.

'As the living Father hath sent me', Jn. 6:57. If so, sent in manhood, and sent into the world. But Peter saw beyond the manhood to the one whose manhood it was; he saw past all that was visible in the world, to what was invisible from heaven. He saw outside of everything that was of man, of the flesh, to all that was of God, of the Spirit.

To this he had been begotten, and the revelation from the Father marked that begetting. 'As the living Father hath sent me, and I live by the Father: so he that eateth me, even he shall live by me.'

This 'eating' indicates a spiritual assimilation of the Son, the 'Prince of life', the 'quickening spirit'. In consequence, the Spirit of sonship is conveyed to and manifested in all who receive that revelation from the Father which was first distinguished in—and set forth by—Peter at Caesarea Philippi.

'The living God' or 'the living Father' are themselves terms revealing how God would quicken into being those whom he had before chosen to the 'adoption of children' by Christ Jesus. 'Having predestinated us unto the 'adoption of children' by Jesus Christ to himself, according to the good pleasure of his will.' That is, God calls into being an elect people, whom he had chosen to sonship by Jesus Christ unto himself before all worlds. 'According as he hath chosen us in him before the foundation of the world', Eph. 1:4.

These elect children—'Behold I and the children which God hath given me', Heb. 2:13—having been redeemed by the blood of Christ, are now quickened by the Holy Ghost: 'Therefore if any man be in Christ, he is a new creature.'

These new creatures are distinguished in that they look for a new creation—being now crucified to the old—because the earnest expectation of the creation waiteth for the manifestation of the sons of God. Because the creation itself shall be delivered from the bondage of corruption into the glorious liberty of the children of God.

And not only so, but ourselves also, which have the firstfruits of the Spirit, even we ourselves groan within ourselves, waiting. Waiting, that is, for the resurrection of the body in the last day. Waiting for a new heavens and a new earth. For a new creation, wherein dwelleth righteousness.

The 'living God' is a term of quickening life, life given to the 'adoption', to the children of God. It is a question of how God does this: it is a matter of generation, of life.

Not, as with human generation, by corruptible seed, objective to and distinct from the progenitor, causing conception. But, unique to divine life, by an everlasting, a living, a spiritual fountain of life. This generation is a wellspring flowing out of eternity from the Father, through the Son, by the Spirit, springing up as a fountain of living water in the elect seed, life from the 'living Father'.

Before the foundation of the world the elect were chosen to sonship in Christ, and to redemption through his blood.

Hence, 'because ye are sons'—that is, sons from eternity, effectually redeemed in time—'God hath sent forth the Spirit of his Son'—now, at present, by revelation—'into your hearts, crying, Abba, Father', Gal. 4:6.

This inward Spirit is the sure mark, exemplified in Peter, of sons chosen in Christ before the foundation of the world: 'For as many as are led by the Spirit of God, they are the sons of God.' All these, like Peter, chosen and elect of the Father, having been redeemed by the blood of Christ, receive in time the revelation of the Son from above at the Father's initiative.

'For ye have not received the spirit of bondage again to fear; but ye have received the Spirit of 'adoption' whereby we cry, Abba, Father. The Spirit itself beareth witness with our spirit, that we are the children of God: and if children, then heirs; heirs of God, and joint-heirs with Christ; if so be that we suffer with him, that we may be also glorified together', Rom. 8:15-17.

Some fourteen or fifteen times the word 'living' is applied in one way or another to the deity, and, usually, it is applied in relation to the quickening of the children of God.

In relation to the election, therefore, in time, out of a dead and dying world, he is revealed as the 'life-giving God'. This is not a relationship borne to man in Adam, the man of sin and death. It is a relationship borne to the election in Christ, the Man of righteousness and life. Hence he is called 'the quickening spirit', I Cor. 15:45.

The life bestowed by the living God is not human but divine; not mortal but immortal; not corruptible but incorruptible; not temporal but eternal; not carnal but spiritual; not earthly but heavenly; not transient but everlasting; not created but uncreated. Evidently: for what is bestowed is the life of God.

This was what the forerunner and exemplar of all the *ecclesia*, Peter, experienced, by which he was illuminated, for, 'the life was the light of men.' This was that through which he was quickened at Caesarea Philippi. Hence it is said—whether spiritually or physically dead, it makes no difference—'As the Father raiseth up the dead, and quickeneth them; even so the Son quickeneth whom he will.' Then such life is interior to the body, but in the resurrection raises the body.

'For the hour is coming, and now is, when the dead shall hear the voice of the Son of God: and they that hear shall live'. And, 'If the Spirit of him that raised up Jesus from the dead dwell in you, he that raised up Christ from the dead shall also quicken your mortal bodies by his Spirit that dwelleth in you.'

All is in Christ. The election, the 'adoption', is in Christ, and so is the quickening: 'The world seeth me no more; but ye see me: because I live, ye shall live also.' So affirmed Paul: 'I live; yet not I, but Christ liveth in me.' Jesus said, 'I am the resurrection, and the life: he that believeth in me, though he were dead, yet shall he live: and whosoever liveth and believeth in me shall never die.'

Several times the term 'the living God' is applied to the 'adoption'. That is, to the eternally chosen, effectually redeemed, and presently quickened children of God. Hence they say, 'Thou art the Christ, the Son of the living God'.

The elect are called 'the children of the living God', Rom. 9:26, on account of this life bestowed upon them. This is because they have been born from above. It is because 'the living God' has begotten them, by the life peculiar to himself, to be his own sons in Christ. This is of the Spirit, not the letter. For 'the letter killeth, but the Spirit giveth life.' Because the new testament is written on the hearts of these children by 'the Spirit of the living God'. In their minds also, because in their foreheads, each one, they bear 'the seal of the living God', Rev. 7:2,3.

Therefore they are full of life. Uncreated, heavenly, spiritual, divine, everlasting, supernatural, mysterious life from the Father, the Son, and the Holy Ghost. Full of life, these children of the living God are called 'the temple of the living God', II Cor. 6:16; 'the city of the living God', Heb. 12:22; and 'the assembly of the living God', I Tim. 3:15.

Hence the term 'the living God' is not a term made known in Adam. It is a reality made known in Christ. It is not known in or by the world. Nor known, indeed, in or by the professing 'church', filled with the vast multitude led by the hirelings and false shepherds to talk of the things which they have never experienced, and which they do not possess. But these things are experienced by and possessed of the elect, that is, all those quickened into life in Christ.

Such spiritual things are the real possession of all who are predestinated unto the 'adoption of children' by Jesus Christ unto the Father, according to the good pleasure of his will. All these are illuminated, called, and quickened: this being that interior regeneration made known to all the elect by the 'life-giving God', that is, by 'the living Father', in his generation of sons by Jesus Christ unto himself.

For, 'the living, the living, he shall praise thee, as I do this day.'

These, and none other, Christ takes and builds up into his assembly, for the glory, praise, and worship of God and the Father, world without end, Amen.

IV

Fatherhood and the Ecclesia

'AND Jesus answered and said unto Peter, Blessed art thou, Simon Bar-jona: for flesh and blood hath not revealed it unto thee, but my Father which is in heaven.'

Here, Jesus first pronounces the blessing upon Peter.

Now, the blessing is not the haphazard and general thing that most suppose it to be. On the contrary, it is specific and particular.

1. The Blessing

i. The blessing and the blessed

'Blessed art thou, Simon Bar-jona.' The blessing is pronounced upon the chosen seed, and upon the chosen seed alone.

'For when God made promise to Abraham, because he could swear by no greater, he sware by himself, saying, Surely blessing I will bless thee, and multiplying I will multiply thee.' Now, this is the blessing, and all other blessings are briefly comprehended therein. It is a blessing exclusive to the seed of promise, and outside of it there is nothing but a curse.

The blessing is not arbitrary: it stands in relation to the character of the blessed. Mark that, the character. Jesus taught, Mt. 5:3-11, 'Blessed are the poor in spirit; blessed are they that mourn; blessed are the meek; blessed are they which do hunger and thirst after righteousness; blessed are the merciful; blessed are the pure in heart; blessed are the peacemakers; blessed are they which are persecuted for righteousness' sake; blessed are ye when men shall revile you, and persecute you, and shall say all manner of evil against you falsely, for my sake.' This is the character of the blessed.

Now, all these traits were manifest in Peter. From poverty of spirit: 'Depart from me; for I am a sinful man, O Lord', Lk. 5:8; through peacemaking: 'Seek peace, and ensue it', I Pet. 3:11; to being persecuted for his name's sake: 'And when they had brought them, they set them before the council: and the high priest asked them, saying, Did not we straitly command you that ye should not teach in this name? Then Peter and the apostles answered, and said, We ought to obey God rather than men', Acts 5:27-29. Every trait was manifest in Peter: 'Blessed art thou, Simon Bar-jona.'

Moreover the blessing stands in relation to the circumstances of the blessed: 'Blessed be ye poor; blessed are ye that hunger now; blessed are ye that weep now; blessed are ye when men shall hate you, and when they shall separate you from their company, and shall reproach you, and cast out your name as evil, for the Son of man's sake.' Now, these were Peter's circumstances precisely: 'Peter therefore was kept in prison', Acts 12:5; he was a 'partaker of Christ's sufferings', I Pet. 4:13.

Peter endured divers fiery trials and sufferings, being kept through them all, though oft 'weeping bitterly'. Thus he was enabled by his own temptations and experiences to comfort others of the elect in like afflictions. Now, this is the man upon whom Jesus pronounced the blessing.

Correspondingly the curse—which rests on all those not under the blessing—is not arbitrary, but is thoroughly warranted by the character of those upon whom it is pronounced. Therefore there is a woe unto them: 'Woe unto you that are rich; woe unto you that are full; woe unto you that laugh now; woe unto you, when all men shall speak well of you.'

But none of these circumstances was true of Peter, to whom Jesus said, 'Blessed art thou, Simon Bar-jona.' Nor are such circumstances ever true of any of the chosen seed whatsoever.

Rather, the very persons who were the cause of this blessing being pronounced upon Peter—that is, his persecutors, who reviled him, spoke evil of him, and separated him from their company—why, these very persons by the same actions brought a woe upon themselves! 'Woe unto the world because of offences; woe to that man by whom the offence cometh. It were better for him that a millstone were hanged about his neck, and that he were drowned in the depth of the sea.'

'Woe unto you, Pharisees! for ye tithe mint and rue and all manner of herbs, and pass over judgment and the love of God; woe unto you, Pharisees! for ye love the uppermost seats in the synagogues; woe unto you, scribes and Pharisees, hypocrites! for ye are as graves which appear not, and the men that walk over them are not aware of them.'

Now we all know that it was not the blessing, but the curse, that sounded against these dead hirelings. For upon them, and upon their dead congregations, a dreadful woe was pronounced by Jesus himself.

But not upon Peter, for he was not dead, but living, as it is said, 'The living, the living, he shall praise thee, as I do this day'; which is precisely what he did when he said, 'Thou art the Christ, the Son of the living God.'

ii. The blessing and justification

But life comes through righteousness, not without it, just as death comes by sin, not apart from it. On the one the blessing is pronounced; and on the other falls the curse.

Here is the line that divides mankind; and there is not another.

Then whence comes that righteousness that brought the blessing upon Abraham and his seed for ever? It came by the blood of Jesus Christ, God's own dear Son, and it is called, 'The righteousness of faith'. And so it is written, 'Abraham believed God, and it was counted to him for righteousness.' 'Even as David also describeth the blessedness of the man, unto whom God imputeth righteousness without works, saying, Blessed are they whose iniquities are forgiven, and whose sins are covered. Blessed is the man to whom the Lord will not impute sin.'

Here the forgiveness of iniquities, the covering of sins, and the not imputing of sin, are together equated with the imputing of righteousness without works, the experience of both David and Abraham. And if so, since the blessing is pronounced upon the man—'Blessed is the man'—to whom these things occur, it must be the blessing of Abraham, to whom it was sworn by the Almighty, 'Surely blessing I will bless thee'.

But is this blessing of righteousness, imputed without works, distinct from Christ? God forbid! By no means, for Christ brought in that selfsame righteousness for all the chosen seed when he died and shed his blood as their substitute. This imputed righteousness, brought in by the blood of his cross, is called 'The righteousness of God by faith of Jesus Christ', and it is 'unto all and upon all them that believe.' And so is the blessing.

As to the curse, it is clean removed from such a people, for, having been justified by grace, the Spirit being given, they are enabled to say 'Thou art the Christ, the Son of the living God'. Here is sure evidence of that blessed people whom God has chosen, and to whom he freely imputes righteousness without works. These are the blessed. 'Blessed art thou, Simon Bar-jona.'

Where then is the curse, which, naturally, they brought upon themselves under the law?

It is paid in full by the redeeming death of Christ. 'Christ hath redeemed us from the curse of the law, being made a curse for us: for it is written, Cursed is every one that hangeth on a tree: that the blessing of Abraham might come on the Gentiles through Jesus Christ; that we might receive the promise of the Spirit through faith', Gal. 3:13,14.

iii. The blessing and the curse

Galatians chapter three sets before the assemblies of Galatia the blessing and the curse. The blessing is by the gospel of Christ; the curse is by the law of Moses.

The blessing, even that sure blessing unto Abraham and to his seed for ever—'Surely blessing I will bless thee'—rests upon those freely justified by grace, and stands in the righteousness of faith without the works of the law. Hence it is written, 'The scripture, foreseeing that God would justify the heathen through faith, preached before the gospel unto Abraham, saying, In thee shall all nations be blessed.' So we see that they which be of faith are blessed with faithful Abraham.

As to the curse, this lies heavy upon all who would justify themselves by their own deeds, on all the self-righteous, that is, all the world. These, religious or not, have hope towards God that he will be lenient to what they consider to be the good that is in all men, and the comparatively decent life which they consider themselves to have led.

But that is their rule, it is neither the rule of law, nor that of God. By their own invented and subjective rule, measured so as to justify themselves, they may, or may not, make a fair show of self-righteousness. But they are not wise. God's rule is the law, which is an objective rule, and the true rule, measured according to that righteousness which is owed to God and men by every accountable being.

As to that rule, the only just rule, the rule by which the world will be judged—and from which the religious will not escape—in the last day: 'As many as are of the works of the law are under the curse: for it is written, Cursed is every one that continueth not in all things which are written in the book of the law to do them.'

For that no man is justified in the sight of God by the law is evident, for by the law is the knowledge of sin. And against sin sounds the curse. Hence a woe lies heavy upon all those under the deeds of the law, who justify themselves by works, upon all the self-righteous, world without end.

iv. The blessing and sonship

All those predestined to the 'adoption', chosen to sonship before the world was, are the blessed in Christ. Such are the true seed of Abraham, justified freely by grace, to whom righteousness is imputed, not of works, lest any man should boast. These are not under the law, but under grace. Neither do they walk by the law as a rule of life, for they walk by faith, even as did their father Abraham some four hundred and thirty years before the law was heard of in the world.

For when the fulness of time was come, God sent forth his Son, made of a woman, made under the law, to redeem those that were under the law, that every heir of promise might receive the 'adoption' of sons. Thus faith is the rule, and the Spirit of sonship the power, by which the heirs of promise walk in the steps of Abraham, the father of the faithful.

And, saith Paul to the blessed Galatians, 'because ye are sons'—mark that, because ye *are*: that is, by eternal election in Christ—'God hath sent forth the Spirit of his Son into your hearts, crying, Abba, Father.' Sonship was precedent.

God chose them in Christ from eternity; the Son redeemed them in time at the cross; the Father illuminated them from heaven in their experience; thereupon the Spirit of sonship was sent forth into their hearts. And this same Spirit witnessed with their spirit that they were the children of God, crying, Abba, Father.

To this elect seed in Christ pertains the promise made to Abraham, for all the promises of God are in him Yea, and in him Amen. They are justified by faith without the works of the law; the promise of the resurrection is theirs; the world to come is their inheritance. These heirs of promise, having been given to Christ from eternity, and having been brought to him in their experience by the revelation of the Father, cry out, 'Thou art the Christ, the Son of the living God.' They are sons. Of these Christ builds his *ecclesia*. But not of the world. He prays not for the world, Jn. 17:9.

Neither prays he for the self-justifying, nor the self-righteous. For they, being under the law of works, are under the curse, and to them pertains the sentence, 'Depart, ye cursed, into everlasting fire, prepared for the devil and his angels.' 'And these shall go into everlasting punishment.'

But those upon whom the Lord pronounces the blessing, who share Peter's character, circumstances, and experience—'Blessed art thou, Simon Bar-jona'—assuredly shall hear this word, 'Come, ye blessed of my Father, inherit the kingdom prepared for you from the foundation of the world.'

And these shall come into life eternal, for the blessing attendant upon justification by faith is everlasting life. This life is freely bestowed by grace upon all the chosen seed, on all the 'adoption', as it is said, 'Behold I and the children which God hath given me.'

2. The Revelation

'Blessed art thou, Simon Bar-jona: for flesh and blood hath not revealed it unto thee, but my Father which is in heaven', Mt. 16:17. Here a revelation is given, in consequence of which Christ builds his *ecclesia*.

By definition, at any time, in any age, and with any generation, none but Christ can build this *ecclesia*. It is his *ecclesia*.

By definition, Christ's *ecclesia* is built up by him of none save those who receive precisely the same divine revelation from the Father in heaven as did Peter.

And, by definition, such as these, and these alone, though receiving what is inward and spiritual, are outwardly and visibly united in consequence of Christ's building them together.

From whence it follows absolutely throughout the age that prior to the being built into the *ecclesia* or assembly of Christ —the one divinely authorized and acknowledged assembly, or *ecclesia*, that exists—the Son must be revealed to the inward sight by divine and spiritual illumination from the Father in heaven.

This is the present subject, the basic subject, the basis of the very existence of the *ecclesia* of Christ, without which it cannot exist at all.

It is impossible to stress too strongly that *the revelation of the Son from the Father in heaven* is the ground, the whole ground, and the only ground, upon which Christ builds his assembly. In fact, as has already been shown, and as will yet appear even more clearly, this *is* the rock. Therefore, given the vital importance of this revelation to the existence of the *ecclesia*, the closest attention must be paid to the doctrine of Christ and his apostles from every place in which this matter is disclosed in holy scripture.

i. The word 'revelation'

The Greek noun *ἀποκάλυψις*, *apokalupsis*, occurs some eighteen times in the new testament, and is the word which has been roughly transliterated into English in the title of the book of the Revelation: the Apocalypse.

The translators have not uniformly rendered *apokalupsis* by the English word 'revelation', although they have done so in the majority—two thirds—of the cases.

Their use—for example—on one occasion of the word 'coming', on another of 'appearing', once again of 'manifestation', smacks more of interpretation than translation, the English 'revelation' being adequate for every occurrence of the Greek *apokalupsis*.

The reader is quite safe to read 'revelation' in all instances, although the concept of that revelation being in consequence of an unveiling should be borne in mind.

Also there appears in the Greek new testament a verb form of this word, and that of course is the form used in Matthew 16:17. Here the word is *ἀποκαλύπτω*, *apokaluptō*, uniformly translated by the English 'reveal' in every one of its twenty-six occurrences.

Both the noun—*apokalupsis*—and the verb—*apokaluptō*—are compound words, each commencing with the preposition *apo*, the basic meaning of which conveys the idea of 'forth from'; or 'away from'.

Apo, therefore, according to circumstance, may indicate departure; distance of time or place; riddance; or derivation from some given source. This is the preposition which qualifies the basic meaning of *kaluptō*—or *kalupsis*—so providing the compounds *apo-kaluptō* and *apo-kalupsis* respectively.

The fundamental meaning, however, is in the word *kaluptō*, a verb used as such eight times in the new testament, being rendered 'cover' five times, and 'hide' three times.

This Greek word has a variety of applications in the original, all possessing the basic idea of hiding or covering from sight, as, for example, by a veil.

In fact the noun formed from the same root has been translated 'veil' on each of its four appearances in the new testament, being devoted to the concept of a covering over the face, or the head, that is, a head-covering.

From this it is clear that the root meaning, To cover, to conceal, to hide, has a particular application of To cover, conceal, or hide *the face* or *the head*: that is, to *veil*. However, the range of meaning often extends beyond this: for example, to a ship being 'covered' with waves, Mt. 8:24; to persons being 'covered' by earth and rocks, Lk. 23:30; or to the 'hiding' of the gospel from those that are lost, II Cor. 4:3.

As has been indicated, to this verb *kaluptō*, 'to cover', or, 'to hide', has been added the prefix *apo*, and it is the addition of this preposition that forms the compound *apokaluptō*.

But the addition does not merely form a compound: it radically alters the meaning of the verb.

It nullifies the verb.

The meaning of 'away from', in this instance conveying the idea of 'riddance'—inherent in one use of the prefix *apo*—means that *the covering* is qualified by this expression, one is rid of it; in a word, the covering has gone, the veil is 'taken away'. Then, all is 'revealed'.

That is the word *apokaluptō*: all is revealed. Not as if it were not there, it was there, but it was covered. Now the cover is drawn off, it is away, one is rid of the veil. Hence what was behind the covering is opened up and manifest to sight.

ii. The revelation not of flesh and blood

This lifting of the veil to Simon Bar-jona, effectually hiding the Son of God from his sight, was not a work of flesh and blood. 'Blessed art thou, Simon Bar-jona: for flesh and blood hath *not* revealed it unto thee.' It was not only that flesh and blood had not revealed it: flesh and blood could not reveal it. For, 'No man knoweth the Son but the Father'.

The reason is this: a veil lies upon the heart of man and a covering hides the face of all flesh from the spiritual sight and experimental knowledge of the living Person of the Son. Here is a veil, and here is a covering, which no flesh and blood can ever penetrate, much less remove.

Others, senior or superior to Simon Bar-jona in Israel, whether the ancient fathers, or the scribes and priests, or else the Jewish Rabbis, did not and could not teach Peter on this matter. No, not though they laboured at the scriptures from dawn to dusk, year in and year out. Because it is not a question of education, but of revelation. But here is a thing beyond the competence of elders to teach their youngers, of tutors to instruct their pupils, or of professors to impart to their students.

Such a conclusion is implied in the words 'Simon Bar'—*son of*—'Jona'. Here, the flesh and blood which begat Simon, that is, his father Jona, is excluded. The revelation came not from human antecedents.

It cannot be conveyed by the instruction of another, however biblical or scriptural, because it is not a matter of religious knowledge or of doctrinal teaching from the bible. It is a matter of divine illumination, of light radiating from the Father in heaven.

And no man, however erudite in the scriptures, however exalted in religion, I say, no man can convey this to another. It is a divine prerogative and a heavenly operation exclusive to the Person of the Father.

Neither can a man come to this revelation in and of himself. For if his father be but 'flesh and blood', he himself also must be the same. Nothing but 'flesh and blood'. And 'flesh and blood hath not revealed it unto thee.'

No matter how devout, how earnest, how intent, all was but 'flesh and blood'. No matter what had been learned from the law or the prophets, no matter how sincerely John the Baptist's ministry had been received, all was but 'flesh and blood'. No matter that Jesus had been followed outwardly, wholeheartedly, the mind having been given to his ministry, the heart to his Person, the attention to his words, all was but 'flesh and blood'. And 'flesh and blood hath not revealed it'.

For it all, 'No man knoweth the Son, but the Father.'

It was not of man, either of Simon, or from others. It cannot be from man, because it is a supernatural, a divine, a heavenly revelation, radiating from that uncreated light which 'no man hath seen, nor can see'. It is, and can only be, revealed by 'My Father which is in heaven'.

'Flesh and blood hath not revealed it.' Nor could flesh and blood ever perceive it, in view of the state of flesh and blood. And—hypothetically—were flesh and blood not in the state that it is, were it as innocent as it was in Adam at the first, still there could be no reaching to this light.

For this is uncreated light, altogether above and beyond the senses of created man. This heavenly light cannot be reached by flesh and blood; it must be radiated down from the Father above, in the Spirit, shining within. Even then the natural eye is incapable of receiving it. 'Flesh and blood hath not revealed it, but my Father, which is in heaven.'

And if created flesh and blood—albeit in innocence in the garden of Eden—cannot attain to what lies outside its proper sphere and element, how much less can such things be, in view of the actual state of flesh and blood since the Fall? For 'flesh and blood cannot inherit the kingdom of God.'

Why not? Because flesh and blood is a state at once corrupt and corruptible, in which, even though under the most profound exterior religious influences, and gifted with the most abundant scriptures, and scribes to interpret them, as with the Jews, still, 'the veil is upon their heart'.

It is true that, when Moses received the law by the disposition of angels, his face shone with the light of the glory. Thereafter Moses' countenance was alight with such an unearthly brightness that the children of Israel could not stand it, and at their request Moses must needs put a veil over his face. What! Could not Israel, which had voluntarily embraced the law, stand the light? No, Israel could not, hence it was that not only Moses' face was veiled, but says the scripture, a veil was upon their heart. And worse. Their minds were blinded. Why?

Because by the energy and deeds of flesh and blood—for these are the works which the law requires—they presumed to attain to the knowledge of God. Which is to be blind indeed.

'But their minds were blinded: for until this day remaineth the same veil untaken away in the reading of the old testament; which veil is done away in Christ. But even unto this day, when Moses is read, the veil is upon their heart', II Cor. 3:14,15.

That may be true of the law, but what of the gospel?

To this also they are blinded, 'According as it is written, God hath given them the spirit of slumber, eyes that they should not see, and ears that they should not hear; unto this day.' For, 'if our gospel be hid, it is hid to them that are lost: in whom the god of this world hath blinded the minds of them which believe not, lest the light of the glorious gospel of Christ, who is the image of God, should shine unto them.'

Where then is this shining light of the glorious gospel? is it not in the grasp of flesh and blood? No it is not. It is in nothing save the prerogative of God's commandment. 'For God, who commanded the light to shine out of darkness, hath shined in our hearts, to give the light of the knowledge of the glory of God in the face of Jesus Christ', II Cor. 4:6.

The prophet Isaiah also describes this glorious shining of revelation, saying 'I will bring the blind by a way that they knew not; I will lead them in paths that they have not known: I will make darkness light before them, and crooked things straight.' Mark that threefold 'I will'. This work of God refers to the removing of the old veil, the shining of divine light, and the giving of sight to the blind, with a witness.

So that a great deal more is needed than the taking away of the spiritual veil hiding the true nature of the Son. The covering must be taken off the heart also. Moreover the light must shine from heaven. And, besides all this, sight must be given to the blind.

This is what happened to Peter, and of necessity the same must happen to all whom Christ receives from his Father to be built into his *ecclesia*. The Father vouchsafes to destroy in this mountain the face of the covering cast over all people, and the veil that is spread over all nations, when he causes the heart to 'turn to the Lord'. Then shall the eyes of the blind be opened, the veil shall be taken away, and a voice shall come from heaven to the heart, saying 'Arise, shine, for thy light is come, and the glory of the LORD is risen upon thee.'

Now this is revelation. In this light the Son is seen. But it is certainly not from flesh and blood. It is a revelation that cannot be but from 'my Father which is in heaven'. On this rock Christ builds his *ecclesia*.

iii. The revelation from the Father in heaven

In consequence of such a revelation from the Father in heaven, Peter had seen the Son in a light that could never come from nor be received by human nature.

This revelation was the inshining of divine, heavenly, spiritual, supernatural and uncreated light, radiating from another realm, a realm inconceivable to human nature, lighting up dimensions otherwise beyond the ability of man to comprehend. It was this, I say, together with the opening of Peter's eyes, that caused him to cry out 'Thou art the Christ, the Son of the living God'.

Now, this was not something unique to Peter, above the experience of the Christian. It *is* the experience of the Christian. It is not something peculiar to the *ecclesia* in the Acts of the apostles, unique to that age. It is common to Christ's assembly in all ages. Of course it is. This is to see Christ. And to see him by revelation is to believe upon him.

But the revelation preceded and caused the seeing, and the seeing resulted in the believing, as it is written, 'The world seeth me no more; but ye see me.' And again, 'And this is the will of him that sent me, that every one which seeth the Son'—that is first—'and believeth upon him'—that follows in consequence—'hath everlasting life.' The cause of this 'seeing' —the result of which is believing—is revelation.

Any other 'believing', any other 'faith' than that resulting from the spiritual sight of Christ, in consequence of the revelation from the Father in heaven, is nothing but presumption.

This truth is what will-working Arminians cannot stand. Even, if not especially, when that Arminianism is cloaked under the outward appearance and form of 'Fundamentalist', 'Reformed', or 'Calvinist'.

And the reason that these chameleon-like species of Arminians cannot stand the revelation of the Son from the Father in heaven is this: it takes everything out of the hand and ability of man. It places everything entirely in the prerogative and power of Almighty God. That is, not in 'Reformed' or 'Calvinistic' theory, but in actual practice. These chameleons cannot stand this. Not in practice. For the whole of the religion of these lizard-like creatures consists in their taking on the colour of their chosen surroundings, without the least change in their intrinsic nature.

Nevertheless there is a people in the earth who bless God for this truth, and of all such, and none other, Christ says 'Blessed art thou, for flesh and blood hath not revealed it, but my Father which is in heaven.' Now, this is that revelation, the result of which causes opened eyes to behold the interior and spiritual sight of the Son. Those who receive it believe indeed, and of them, Christ builds his *ecclesia*.

The revelation given to Peter—from the English wording—would appear to be the direct and immediate result of the inshining of divine light from heaven. But we have seen that the words *apokaluptō*, 'reveal', and *apokalupsis*, 'revelation', imply more: there must be an interior divine operation prior to that inshining, in order that it should be unhindered in its radiance within the heart.

Indeed the words 'light' or 'shining' are not inherent in the word *apokaluptō*. The concepts inherent in the word *apokaluptō* are 'cover', 'hide', or 'veil', on the one hand, and 'away', 'away from', or even, in context, 'be rid of', on the other. Now, when the veil is taken away, when one is rid of what prevents the entrance of the light, when the cover is taken away from the face, *then*, given the divine command, the light will shine in at God's direction.

But it is the operation of taking away the veil, of achieving riddance of what obscures the light, and of removing the covering from the inward eyes, that the word *apokaluptō* properly describes.

Then, the eyes having been opened, the veil now taken away from within and without the heart, divine radiance from the Father in heaven floods the interior spirit to give the light of the knowledge of the glory of God in the face of Jesus Christ. Then one cannot but believe, even as one cannot but confess, 'Thou art the Christ, the Son of the living God'.

Ten times the two words *apokaluptō*, 'reveal', and *apokalupsis*, 'revelation', occur in the gospels, five times in Luke, four in Matthew, and once in John.

The first occurrence, Mt. 10:26—the parallel passage is in Luke 12:2—informs us that there is nothing covered that shall not be revealed. This was spoken by Jesus of the deceitfulness of the religious leaders, who had called Jesus 'Beelzebub', and would call his servants the same thing. This was the leaven of the Pharisees, which is hypocrisy.

Those leavened with this leaven, to this day, are so agreeable in their outward appearances; so fair in their sheep's clothing; so sound in their voluble profession of the scriptures. But Jesus admonishes, Beware of them. It is all the leaven of deceitfulness, all form and show, and, as to the scriptures, they neither believe in them in heart nor practice them in life. But the servants of Christ are not to be daunted by this swarm of hypocrites. 'For there is nothing covered'—like their lying hearts—'that shall not be revealed.'

Here it is a clear example of the removal of the cover so that the hidden guile beneath the outward show of religion might be exposed for the hypocrisy that it is in fact.

Observe however this use of the word 'revealed'. Strictly it is the removal of a cover to expose what is there: in this case hypocrisy. The inshining of light from heaven, together with the opening of the interior eyes, is not remotely implied by the word 'revealed' in Mt. 10:26 and Lk. 12:2. Although in other instances the removal of the old veil on the heart, the dismissal of the cover, joined together with the opening of the eyes of the blind, allows the radiance of the glory of the Father, illuminating the Son, to shine into the inward man.

Notwithstanding, in the strictest sense—whatever may be implied in certain instances—the concept of the word is limited to the veil or cover being taken 'away from' what is otherwise hidden, that is, the interior heart.

The next two passages, Matthew 11:25 and 27, correspond with those in Luke 10:21 and 22. Here, Mt. 11:25, Jesus gives thanks that the Father, the Lord of heaven and earth, has kept spiritual things hidden from the wise and prudent.

But such thanksgiving as this is something into which no natural man can possibly enter. On the contrary, natural men would consider it to be the antithesis of true religion, a denial of the love of God, that God should *hide* what was essential to salvation from *anybody*. Not so Jesus; he gives thanks to the Father for hiding these things from the 'wise and prudent', and he does so without the least hesitation.

Now, first, who are the wise and prudent, and, second, how are the things concerning Christ hidden from these persons?

First, who are the wise and prudent? All Israel after the flesh; for these, in their wisdom, rejected Christ, saying, We will not have this man to reign over us. They believed, however, that all was well. They were of Israel, they were Abraham's seed; God would never leave them nor forsake them. It would be folly to think otherwise.

But, 'they are not all Israel which are of Israel.' Indeed, 'Though the number of the children of Israel be as the sand of the sea', yet only 'a remnant shall be saved.' Again, 'Neither, because they are the seed of Abraham, are they all children.' 'That is, they which are the children of the flesh'—Abraham's flesh—'these are not the children of God.' They had boasted, 'We have Abraham to our father'. But Jesus had replied, 'Ye are of your father the devil.'

Yet so sure were the Jews, the children of Israel, that, because their line went back to Abraham, and because they were called the people of God, and held to the traditions of their fathers, the temple of God and his service being theirs, they were safe. Indeed this was all their wisdom, and the sum of their prudence.

They had the scriptures, which the wise among them had prudently considered, in order to prove their election of God to their own satisfaction. Yet their wisdom and prudence, according to which they laboured to establish their own righteousness, by which they would justify themselves, and through which they rested in their own traditions, actually proved to be to their destruction. Professing themselves to be wise, they became fools.

However, the term 'wise and prudent' cannot be limited to Israel, neither can it be confined to the Jews. These words extend to the Gentiles, and must be enlarged to take in the whole professing 'church'. On what grounds? Because Jesus thanked the Father as 'Lord of heaven and earth'. If of the earth, then not the land of Israel merely. If not, then neither as God of the Jews only, but of the Gentiles also.

Evidently, 'wise and prudent' was not meant in natural terms, or in terms of the arts and sciences, but in terms of religion. But religion is not limited to Israel. Then, the professing 'church' and 'churches' throughout the age.

The words extend to Christendom, if so be the 'churches' consider themselves to be 'wise and prudent'. But which of them considers themselves to be foolish and ignorant? They all think that they know everything, they all lay claim to be the people, all come under the stricture, 'No doubt but ye are the people, and wisdom shall die with you.' Indeed, were men to look in the earth for those habitually opinionated, bigoted, complacent, know-all's every one, the whole world knows where to find the greatest concentration.

And the more 'fundamental', the more 'scriptural', the more 'reformed', the more 'Calvinistic', the more 'evangelistic', then the more they think that they know everything, and the more they are past being taught anything. They are the wise and prudent, you see. Paul addresses these, saying, 'Thou art confident thou art a guide of the blind, a light of them which are in darkness, an instructor of the foolish, a teacher of babes, which hast the form of knowledge and truth in the law.'

Yes, the form of it, for in their own opinion, they are the wise and prudent. They are the ones who instruct babes, not the babes who are to be instructed.

But Jesus thanks God for hiding these things from the wise and prudent, and revealing them unto babes, saying in another place, 'But now ye say, We see; therefore your sin remaineth'. For all their wisdom, all their prudence, the religion of such is of the flesh, from the world, in the letter and form of scripture. But everything that the babes possess comes by revelation from God out of heaven.

Now, secondly, how are the things of Christ hid from the wise and prudent?

Why, by leaving them to themselves. This is what they wish. They, and their followers, are confident of their ability, of their learning, or at least of their libraries from which to parrot, copy, or otherwise steal the words every man of his neighbour.

They are confident of the scriptures, that is, of their own ability to search them. Or, at least, to rob the spiritual of their words, plundering them out of their books and mouths, and putting them into their own books and mouths. And this they do when their hearts are far from such matters, and their souls void of the experience which brought forth such reality from the inward parts of the spiritual.

These are the sort who are able to exercise mental judgment, who have acquired an ability to assess which men—past or present—are spiritual and which are not, and whose words will impress their hearers and whose will not—stealing them in order to get a name for themselves with the people. But their own hearts remain as dark as night, and their own souls continue as barren as the desert.

It must be so. God has hid these things from them, they are left to their own devices in religion. They must strive perpetually to draw up water from their own dry well, turning the wheel to no effect under the sentence of hard labour from the old law. And, since they are so wise and prudent in biblical religion, of what can they complain?

They have the traditions of their fathers to enable them to find their own way; the wisdom to be educated by others like themselves; the prudence to lift up themselves upon their high places. They boast in such things. Then why should it be any wonder to find them contemptuous of revelation?

Nor need we be surprised to find that they stumble upon the dark mountains, groping for the wall like the blind, muttering without authority as the scribes. All this, whilst they act a part not theirs, in the tradition of the hypocritical Pharisees, blind as bats to their own condition.

What else would you expect to find from those whose cultivated wisdom in 'the church', whose prudent moderation in evangelicalism, whose polite conversation in the gospel, earns for them from God a blinding sentence, a perpetual darkness, an everlasting confusion, and an impenetrable veil?

As to that veil, it is upon their hearts, just as the covering is upon their face. From whence? From God. And should one rejoice at that? 'In that hour Jesus rejoiced in spirit, and said, I thank thee, O Father, Lord of heaven and earth, that thou hast hid these things from the wise and prudent.'

Now, beholding the 'wise and prudent' in religion in our day, where are those who will echo Jesus' thanksgiving at the Father's hiding of these things from such people in his day? Those only who abide in the unchangeable Spirit of Christ, viewing such persons in religion even until this present time, I say, those only will react in this contemporary age, as did he when confronted by the 'wise and prudent' in his own generation.

And so it was from the beginning, as David speaking by the Spirit of Christ testified, saying, 'Let their eyes be darkened, that they see not'. Which prayer God answered. Otherwise no cause had been found for Jesus to lift up the voice and give thanks that the Father, the Lord of heaven and earth, had 'hid these things' from the wise and prudent.

Again Jesus saith 'Therefore speak I unto them'—'them' being such as the blind leaders of the blind—'in parables: because they seeing see not, and hearing they hear not, neither do they understand.'

'And in them is fulfilled'—continued Jesus in his saying—'the prophecy of Esaias, which saith, By hearing ye shall hear, and not understand; and seeing ye shall see, and not perceive: For this people'—that is, the foolish blind people who in their benighted wisdom follow the worldly prudent—'this people's heart is waxed gross, and their ears are dull of hearing, and their eyes they have closed; lest at any time they should see with their eyes, and hear with their ears, and should understand with their heart, and should be converted, and I should heal them.'

Here it is plain: leaders and followers alike, they were wise and prudent, they were confident that they were guides to the blind, they cried indignantly, 'Are we blind also?' They knew that they had no veil on their heart, and as to the very idea of their minds being blinded, it was they who compassed heaven and earth to gain one proselyte, being a light to those who sat in darkness. What need had they of revelation?

To them revelation was—and is—dangerous. Their own minds, their own traditions, their own ability in scripture, their own service, the 'church': here lay safety. Here was their wisdom and prudence.

Yes, but these are those whom God has blinded, the veil is upon their hearts, and the Father has hidden from them the revelation of Jesus Christ, so that they can never find it. Jesus goes on in his rejoicing, and exults further in his thanksgiving: 'And hast revealed them unto babes', Mt. 11:25. Of such he says 'To you it is given to know the mysteries of the kingdom of heaven, but to them it is not given', Mt. 13:11.

In another place also Jesus pronounces the blessing, saying, 'Blessed are your eyes, for they see: and your ears, for they hear', Mt. 13:16.

The heart of the blessed has been turned to the Lord, II Cor. 3:16, and, withal, the veil has been taken away. The gospel has been preached by the voice of the Son of God from heaven to these poor babes: 'And the eyes of the blind shall be opened.' Though born blind to the light from heaven, now, at the sound of this jubilee, far from their minds being blinded, they receive their sight in a moment, the veil is taken away, and all becomes light in the Lord.

Suddenly they are no longer conformed to this world, or its religion, but they are transformed by the renewing of their minds, Rom. 12:2. They are no more carnally minded, which is death, but spiritually minded, which is life and peace, Rom. 8:6. At the command of the Father in heaven the light of the glory shines in upon them, their light is come, and the brightness of his rising illuminates all within, even as a light from heaven above the brightness of the sun.

Every obscuring veil, each thick covering, all blindness, the deepest shade of the night, the blackness and darkness under the law, in an instant, at the twinkling of an eye, in a moment, all dissolve. Everything is taken away, and the light of the glorious gospel of Christ shines in upon their hearts: 'And hast revealed them unto babes.'

That these things are so, and so immediately, in no way implies that there is no interior work of God prior to the revelation of the Son by the Father.

As in the case of Peter, Matthew 16:17, and of the 'babes', Matthew 11:25, it is obvious that there was such a preparatory work.

It is clear that Peter had attended John the Baptist's ministry, together with his brother, and others, all John's disciples, John 1:35-42. And if they were John's disciples, as surely they were, then they would have been subject to his preparatory ministry. The word of God by John the Baptist must have wrought effectually in them, even to the full range of his doctrine, that is, 'prepare ye the way of the Lord'.

The Baptist's voice would have cried out to them in the wilderness of their own souls, John 1:23, and in them every valley would have been exalted, every mountain and hill brought low, all the crooked places would have been made straight, and every rough way smooth, Lk. 3:5.

This was the preparing of good ground for the sowing of the heavenly seed, Mt. 13:23, which preparation preceded the work of divine sowing, just as it did the shining forth of the heavenly revelation.

Is this same preparatory work also predicated of all those called 'babes', not only then, but now also? It should be noted that the term 'babes' was applied by Jesus to all those who receive the revelation of the Son by the Father from heaven.

The things of Christ are said to be revealed unto 'babes'. Clearly indicating that this term was descriptive of their state at the time of the revelation, not as a consequence of it. 'Thou hast revealed them unto babes'. Then they were babes beforehand. And since none are 'babes' by nature, we may safely conclude that their becoming so was due to a work of God preparing them for what was about to be revealed.

And we know that except we become as little children we shall in no case enter into the kingdom of heaven. Where the becoming little children precedes the entrance into that kingdom. Showing, of course, a work of God preparatory to the receiving of the glorious revelation of the Son by the Father from heaven, in which that kingdom is made manifest which is neither meat nor drink, but righteousness, peace, and joy in the Holy Ghost.

But how many 'churchmen', how many 'reformed-men', how many 'Protestants', how many 'evangelicals', how many 'Charismatics', how many other 'Christians', so confident of their standing, can see eye to eye with this preparatory work in their experience?

How many, I say, can lay their hand upon their heart, whilst declaring sincerely with their mouth their testimony of God's mighty inworking? How many can give us an account of the experience by which they became babes through the effectual inworking of a preparatory ministry? How many can then go on to enlighten us as to their interior sensations which they felt when they received the revelation of the Son from the Father in heaven?

How many? Why, every one whom the Father has called, every one to whom he has revealed his Son from heaven.

In a word, all those called babes, for whom, each one, Jesus gives thanks, saying, 'I thank thee O Father, Lord of heaven and earth, that thou hast hid these things from the wise and prudent, and hast revealed them unto babes. Even so, Father: for so it seemed good in thy sight.'

This illuminating work of the Father must be inwardly experienced, felt in the interior spirit as a revelation, an unveiling of things beyond all human sensations, beyond the senses, supernatural, outside of anything created.

It is the shining of divine light. Not created light. Created light is transient, coexistent with heat or burning: it is not self-existent. Given the reduction of burning matter to ashes, whether artificial light, or that of the sun and stars, radiance no longer exists. All is darkness. Outer darkness.

The sight of the eyes corresponds with created light. But not with uncreated light: no sense, no sight, can correspond with this.

Uncreated light is not visible to the eye. Sublimely independent of matter, divine light shines in a realm and from a dimension outside of and beyond all human comprehension. 'God is light.' That is what the 'babes' have experienced. And will yet experience. 'And the city had no need of the sun, neither of the moon, to shine in it: for the glory of God did lighten it, and the Lamb is the light thereof.'

Just as 'no man knoweth the things of a man save the spirit of man which is in him'—humanity, the comprehension of the human spirit, being utterly beyond the fowl of the air, the beast of the field, and the fish of the sea, incomprehensible to them—'even so the things of God knoweth no man, but the Spirit of God.'

To see this light, is to see God. This will never come by the law. By the law is a covering veil, blackness, obscurity, a concealing behind the dark and lowering clouds of judgment. But the light of God—for God is light—shines from the countenance and Person of Jesus Christ.

God is a Spirit, and is light, and that light and spirituality is revealed in his Son and none other: 'Who only hath immortality, dwelling in the light which no man can approach unto; whom no man hath seen, nor can see.'

That is, whom no man can see after the flesh. He cannot be seen by the outward eye: it is not possible.

But Paul in spirit saw Christ revealed from heaven. He spoke of the vision as 'A light above the brightness of the sun.'

This is the exceeding radiance of Christ glorified, in whom the glory of God shines with that light 'which no man can approach unto', so illustrious is the glorious manhood of the Son of God, so resplendent, so radiant beyond conception.

In the ascended and glorified humanity of the Son of God, truly flesh and bones, risen from the dead, the ineffable deity in which he dwelt with the Father from eternity shines out from his divine Person in heaven with a radiance unbearable, unendurable, unimaginable. Yet a radiance resplendent in manhood.

'And now, O Father'—said he, in view of his coming death, resurrection, and ascension—'And now, O Father, glorify thou me with thine own self with the glory which I had with thee before the world was.' This prayer was answered. But the glory which he had with the Father, as Son, in one Spirit, before the world was, was a glory wholly spiritual, for God is a Spirit.

Now, the humanity of the Son of God, his glorified manhood, radiates with that same ineffable, uncreated, eternal, and divine light: the light that *is* God, but God made known in grace through the Son of his love. Now, the beams of that same light are those which inwardly are revealed to babes in the revelation of the Son by the Father from heaven.

The absurd and impudent claims of those—typically, papists; Pentecostals; and Charismatics—who assert that they have seen visions of Jesus standing before them, that they have 'seen the Lord' as a physical figure, are entirely repudiated by this truth: they *could not* so see him. Paul in spirit saw the uttermost beams of that unbearable light which streams from his Person in heaven, a light 'which no man can approach unto' —that is, after the flesh, by the senses, or by natural sight—a light 'above the brightness of the sun'. That light blinded him for three days. And are *they* apostles?

Paul the apostle cried out to the heavenly Being so glorious that he could not be seen for the very brightness of his radiance,

'Who art thou, Lord?' Out of that unapproachable light came the reply, 'I am Jesus'. Is that *their* Jesus? No it is not. Theirs is *another* Jesus, II Cor. 11:4.

And yet the beams radiating from his wonderfully glorified Person—the Father taking away the veil; opening the eyes; commanding the light to shine out of darkness—the beams, I say, radiating from the Son of God, are those which shine into the heart to give the light of the knowledge of the glory of God in the face of Jesus Christ. At this Jesus gives thanks and declares of all who receive it 'Blessed art thou, for flesh and blood hath not revealed it, but my Father which is in heaven.' Of such he builds his *ecclesia*; none other.

It is this light, and this light alone, that reveals doctrine: 'In thy light we shall see light.'

Theologians, professors, doctors, masters, reverends—as they name themselves and each other contrary to the word of Christ—blunder about with the scriptures in the dark. But like the scribes and doctors of old, they are far, far, below the heavenly light, with nothing but traditions and dead men's writings to help them to receive their various honours and rewards the one from the other.

But they are confounded. They blunder. They just cannot get it right, try as they will.

And wherefore? Because they are full of darkness and unbelief about the very things from which they have chosen to make a living, deceiving the people. 'How can ye believe, which receive honour one of another, and seek not the honour that cometh from God only?'

'For that which is highly esteemed among men is abomination in the sight of God.'

The honour that comes from God only, and that which is highly esteemed in his sight, is the revelation of his own dear Son from heaven. In this radiant light, the scriptures fall open, the doctrine glows with divine rays, and all truth unites to the glory of his Person from whom all light proceeds.

'Now when they saw the boldness of Peter and John, and perceived that they were unlearned and ignorant men, they marvelled; and they took knowledge of them, that they had been with Jesus.' Mark that, these 'unlearned and ignorant men' had been 'with Jesus'. Is this example nothing to those who the rather, lusting to be thought learned and wise, have been with their professors and doctors in the classrooms of their divinity academies and universities? Do they prefer these inventions to the revelation from the Father in heaven?

As to Jesus himself, have they never read what men said of him? 'And the Jews marvelled, saying, How knoweth this man letters, having never learned?' Jesus answered, 'My doctrine is not mine, but his that sent me.' Then, in the light of him that sent him, he saw light. And in his light, we see light, who are but babes and sucklings.

Every divine ray of light pulsates and radiates from Christ. In the light of the heavenly glory streaming from the Son of God, invisible in the heavens, the apostles saw and wrote the doctrine of the gospel, the doctrine of Christ.

And in nothing but the light of that same radiance shining within can the gospel be apprehended and understood.

Otherwise it is all the dead letter, all dark, disconnected, all confusion to the carnal mind: 'Lest the light of the glorious gospel of Christ, who is the image of God, should shine unto them.' But it shined unto the apostles. It shined unto Paul.

It pleased God to reveal his Son in Paul, Gal. 1:16. Paul the apostle received his gospel in the light of that same heavenly revelation by which the Father had revealed the Son. Illuminated by the beams which shone from heaven, above the brightness of the sun, he says, 'I certify you, brethren, that the gospel which was preached of me is not after man. For I neither received it of man, neither was I taught it, but by the revelation of Jesus Christ.'

Only by such ministers can light and life be communicated through the gospel; only by ministers sent and taught of God by revelation. Only these will labour mightily in prayer that the God of our Lord Jesus Christ, the Father of glory, might give unto us the—same—spirit of wisdom and revelation in the knowledge of him, the eyes of our understanding being enlightened, even by his divine radiance, Eph. 1:17,18.

Literally, and physically, of course, the apostles had seen the Lord. But this did not, and could not, bring the revelation.

Nothing but the light from the glory, by the revelation of the Father, in the ministration of the Holy Ghost, caused them to say 'Wherefore henceforth know we no man after the flesh: yea, though we have known Christ after the flesh, yet now henceforth know we him no more.'

Now, this was after the Spirit, not the flesh. For the Spirit took of the things of Christ and revealed his heavenly glory unto them, according to the will of God and the Father.

It is true that the apostle Paul could 'come to visions and revelations of the Lord', II Cor. 12:1, and that John received a vision of 'the revelation of Jesus Christ'.

But both John and Paul were holy apostles, the distinguishing feature of whom was the appearance and calling of the Lord himself in a singular way visibly made manifest to them. In this, they were unique. And in the case of Paul, if any one claims similar 'visions and revelations'—outwardly—as those of which Paul wrote, well. Then let us see in them also his sufferings, his persecutions, his thorn in the flesh, his scars, his dreadful afflictions, and his being counted the offscouring of the earth. But this is what such absurd pretenders will never produce, for they are all mouth and no reality.

In the case of the other apostolic vision cited, that of John in the Revelation, the effect was to cause him to 'fall on his face as dead', struck to the heart with fear at the glorious majesty revealed in the vision. These attendant circumstances and humiliating reactions never appear in the puerile affectations of the Pentecostal and Charismatic sort. Such solemn frames are beneath their contempt who lay claim to such impious and presumptuous 'visions' of divine things.

These pretensions are very far from that light of revelation which shines from the Father in heaven upon the Son of his love. And far from that soul-abasing effect, of which we speak, upon those who are subject to the apostles and their doctrine.

The light of the glory of Christ was that which communicated to the apostles their gospel and its doctrine, and in the same light it is both received and illuminated. 'For our gospel came not unto you in word only, but also in power, and in the Holy Ghost, and in much assurance', I Thess. 1:5.

The gospel was revealed to the apostles, and in the new testament we read of its being preached, received, and applied. But that gospel at this time must be the subject of the same power in present day ministers, if it is to be equally effectual to contemporary hearers.

Then such ministers must be prepared and sent on the same apostolic principles: 'How shall they hear without a preacher? And how shall they preach, except they be sent?'

The same light and power must be communicated now through the chosen vessels sent from Christ in heaven to preach to today's hearers, as that poured out upon those sent from him in the apostolic ministry at the beginning.

'We have this treasure in earthen vessels', says the apostle. And, in another place, glorying in infirmities and sufferings, he affirms that this is so that 'the power of Christ may rest upon me.'

Likewise Peter endured great persecutions and afflictions. The treasure was in an earthen vessel. Nevertheless, 'While Peter was yet speaking, the Holy Ghost fell upon them.'

These are chosen vessels, and, without such chosen vessels, and the attendant work of God accompanying them, all is but dark confusion, actors playing a part from their dead scripts. 'Having the form of godliness, but denying the power thereof.' Adds the apostle, 'From such turn away.'

Nevertheless under the spiritual ministry of those sent by the commandment of the everlasting God, and the Lord Jesus Christ, by the Holy Ghost from heaven, in the mighty power of God, abundant light and revelation from the Father is attendant, and the word of God is preached according to his own will. But not attendant to all. Such ministry separates and divides, as did Christ's in the days of his flesh. It has, and must have, exactly the same effect as then, if, by his sent servants, Christ himself ministers from heaven in our own day to this generation.

Sharply divided asunder as in an instant, straightway the hearers fall into two parts.

Like David's line, the one part is unto death on this side, the other part for life on that side: 'To the one we are the savour of death unto death; and to the other the savour of life unto life', II Cor. 2:16.

Now the one part blesses God for the ministry sent to them from heaven, hearts full of light and life and love at the revelation of the gospel of Christ. The other part, however, is filled with darkness, desperation and hatred. Such gnash their teeth against the faithful ministers whom they would fain stone with stones and heap with lying slander. As it was in the beginning, is now, and ever shall be. Amen.

The gospel is a revelation, and it is received by revelation. That is, in all those in whom it is effectual.

This revelation follows each unfolding of the doctrine.

'For the wrath of God is revealed from heaven', Rom. 1:18. As men sent of God, full of the Holy Ghost, thunder out the truth of God, so heaven itself, and Christ in heaven, accord an answer with a spiritual echo that reverberates within the soul. With interior flashes of wrath from the heaven of heavens, arrows of conviction strike into the inward parts of all those alarmed and awakened under such divinely sent preaching.

The wrath of God is not only revealed in the gospel preached, it is likewise revealed by the Holy Ghost in the inmost soul of all who hear it effectually. That is, wrath is revealed—and felt—from heaven *against them personally.* Now, this is evangelical work; this is the old work; this is that work of revelation with which all effectual calling and hearing commences in the gospel.

'The LORD also thundered in the heavens, and the Highest gave his voice; hailstones and coals of fire. Yea, he sent out his arrows, and scattered them; and he shot out lightnings, and discomfited them.' Here is the wrath of God revealed from heaven to the inward parts, by the gospel, with a witness.

In like manner to the wrath from heaven, so with the day of judgment.

One may read about the judgment, pray over it, be aware of the scriptures, memorise them, even—if it were possible today—hear preaching upon the very subject; one may earnestly seek to imbibe that truth, and plead to feel deeply about such a great and notable day of the LORD. Yes, but when the revelation of the day of vengeance actually breaks in upon the heart and conscience, all the efforts of others, and those of oneself, pale into insignificance beside the felt reality.

For the 'day of wrath and revelation of the righteous judgment of God', once revealed by the Holy Ghost to the convicted sinner, make the soul to cry out in terror. 'Fearfulness and trembling are come upon me, and horror hath overwhelmed me'.

Immediately, such an alarm, such an awakening, such a conviction is felt. Straightway the company of man is shunned. God is sought in earnest. The petition is put up with strong crying and tears, 'O LORD, rebuke me not in thy wrath: neither chasten me in thy hot displeasure.' 'For thine arrows stick fast in me, and thy hand presseth me sore.'

Nor is this transient, or passing, as legal convictions, or those evangelical impressions which come from without.

These deep spiritual convictions, leading a soul to Christ, are from within, from the Holy Ghost, they do not pass away, they get stronger and stronger. This is revelation, not yet of the Son of God, but of the day of wrath and revelation of the righteous judgment of God.

This revelation makes one cry continually, 'My sore runs in the night, and ceases not: I refuse to be comforted.' No, not by men. Nor by 'claims' out of the dead letter of scripture. Only by the Comforter, the Spirit of truth.

He is the only authority, the only relief, the sole consolation sent from heaven by the Father, through Jesus Christ, to the wounded conscience and terrified soul. 'And in that day thou shalt say, O Lord, I will praise thee: though thou wast angry with me, thine anger is turned away, and thou comfortedst me.'

How is this? By the revelation of Jesus Christ, the Son of God, to the inner man. For by this revelation the heavenly beams of divine glory shine into the heart, and, traced to their source, the glory of God is seen to shine in mercy in the face of Jesus Christ, the Son of God.

The judgment of God is perceived not simply as abated, but quenched, in the five glorified scars in his body. The righteousness of God appears not merely as suspended, but satisfied and appeased in the sprinkled blood upon the propitiatory. Whilst the law, and its righteous sentence, met in a crucified Saviour, is seen not just as vindicated, but actually magnified and made wholly honourable.

The soul stands in awe, aglow with heavenly light, trembling with divine life, as, both from without by the inspired preaching, and within by the interior illumination, the glorious revelation of the gospel radiates grace, mercy, and peace from God our Father, and the Lord Jesus Christ. The evangel appears as unspeakably precious, beyond price, transcendent. 'For therein is the righteousness of God revealed from faith to faith: as it is written, The just shall live by faith.'

Here is revelation, not by flesh and blood, but from the Father in heaven, revealing the Son, shining out of and from within the evangel, in which the righteousness of God by faith of Jesus Christ is pronounced unto all and upon all them that believe. The joyful soul, now brought to faith by the sight of Jesus Christ, and him crucified, declared in the gospel, lies prostrate in worship, lost in wonder, love and praise. Now, this is revelation.

And it is salvation. And, more or less, this is the way in which God and the Father brings every one whom he draws to the Son, that all such may be built by him into 'My *ecclesia*'. As it is written, 'They shall be all taught of God.'

'Every man therefore that hath heard, and hath learned of the Father', saith the Son, 'cometh unto me.' And none other. All others come to a delusion of their own heart, deceived of men, and blinded by the god of this world. All such blunder on through false versions of scripture, attending and attendant under bondage to those teachers which a fallen 'church' has heaped to itself, having itching ears. These are those possessed of a veil upon their heart; error in their mind; flattery in their mouth; and a lie in their right hand.

But the word of the Lord endures for ever: 'No man can come to me, except the Father, which hath sent me, draw him.' This drawing is by that revelation of the Father from heaven exemplified in Peter, Matthew 16:17. Brought to faith in the Lord Jesus, the love of God is shed abroad in the heart. Christ is revealed within his people as their glorious hope: 'Christ in you, the hope of glory.' The way in which this work of God began in the soul, is that by which it continues, as the God of our Lord Jesus Christ, the Father of glory, bestows 'a spirit of wisdom and revelation in the knowledge of him' upon those now gathered in the unity of one body.

This keeps the soul meek, lowly, and self-distrusting, it makes the heart melted and broken, it preserves an interior separation between the flesh and the spirit. This begets a yearning to be rid of this vile body and the present evil world, setting one to look for the appearing of the great God and our Saviour Jesus Christ.

'Let that therefore abide in you, which ye have heard from the beginning. If that which ye have heard from the beginning shall remain in you, ye also shall continue in the Son, and in the Father', I Jn. 2:24. This is to have oil in the vessel with the lamp.

Baptized by one Spirit into one body, built into Christ's assembly with every living stone, in such a people spiritual Jerusalem appears as a city compactly built together. Self-judgment marks them, the esteeming each better than himself. They abide in the faith, in the living seed, experimentally. They keep out of presumption, out of the working of the flesh. The entire assembly of such a people looks for and longs after the world to come, whereof we speak. All look for a city—that is, an heavenly—of which the builder and maker is God.

Revelation is longed after, not only inwardly, but outwardly, the glorious revelation of the Lord Jesus Christ from heaven, coming again for his own at the resurrection of the dead. In that day there shall appear the creation of the new heavens and new earth, the revelation of the holy city, new Jerusalem, adorned as a bride for her husband. Then what a blessed hope shines within and before the *ecclesia* of Christ! Nor are these glorious things looked for only, they are *lived* for.

Separation to Christ from the world, as an entire system, therefore marks the company of God's people. They are separate socially, religiously, politically. Whilst denying ungodliness and worldly lusts, living soberly, righteously and godly in this present world, they look for that blessed hope and the glorious appearing of the great God and our Saviour Jesus Christ.

They stand out in the darkness as strangers, sojourners, pilgrims, as lights in the world. They are the citizens of a better country, that is, an heavenly. Wherefore God is not ashamed to be called their God: for he hath prepared for them a city, Heb. 11:16.

Thus the saints in unity in Christ's *ecclesia* are made 'partakers of the glory that shall be revealed', looking for the revelation to be brought unto them at the appearing of Jesus

Christ. The whole assembly is seen to be walking in the light of 'The revelation of Jesus Christ, which God gave unto him, to show unto his servants things which must shortly come to pass.'

Faith, love and hope are kept alive in the light, life, and love of God, by the ministry of Jesus Christ from heaven.

In the assembly that same revelation is the rule, by which, from the first, the evangel was manifested, the scriptures opened, and the ministry of the Spirit declared. The word is, 'I shall speak unto you'—that is, from the word of the truth of the gospel—'by revelation'. This, being in the unction of the Holy One, always agrees with and opens up the apostolic doctrine of Christ with divine enlightenment.

The same rule holds good among the brethren in the midst of the assembly. Here is no congregation of the dead, presided over by some hireling 'pastor' paid to 'conduct worship', as they think of it, whilst they sit in dumb silence. Rather, the rule in the *ecclesia* is, 'Every one of you hath a revelation'. Only that this glorious liberty accords with holy writ, answering to the witness of the Holy Ghost dwelling in the midst of the *ecclesia*.

Indeed, even as one speaks forth from the word of God, opening up the gospel of God concerning his Son, so the Spirit spontaneously moves another to glorify Christ in response. Throughout the company the Spirit of truth will use one and another, in harmony taking the things of Christ and revealing them unto the saints one after the other.

Then the first will gladly hold his peace with all meekness, if anything 'be revealed to another that sitteth by'. Thus all are edified, all are comforted, and if any come in from without, he will fall down and confess, 'God is among you of a truth'.

This is Christ's *ecclesia*, and this is the revelation of the Son by the Father, constantly made known in the midst of the assembly by the Holy Ghost sent down from heaven. Thus, Father, Son, and Holy Ghost dwell in the company of the saints, builded together for an habitation of God through the Spirit.

Waiting until the coming again of Christ from heaven, and the gathering together of his own by the resurrection from the dead, the cry rises from the wilderness of this world, from the midst of the assembly: 'Come quickly, Lord Jesus.'

Whilst this mystery was ordained before the world unto our glory, brought in by Jesus Christ through his coming, death, resurrection and ascension, everything for us—who are the called—springs from the revelation of the mystery in the light from heaven within our hearts.

This revelation is not of flesh and blood, neither of man, nor by man, but by God the Father, revealing his Son from on high. 'Blessed art thou, Simon Bar-jona: for flesh and blood hath not revealed it unto thee, but my Father which is in heaven', Mt. 16:17. On this divine and heavenly revelation the *ecclesia* is built.

But scornfully dispensing with such a revelation—indeed with the very idea of revelation—considering it to be utterly impracticable, men everywhere and sects on all hands think to have taken over the building. But they have not. 'This is the stone which was set at nought of you builders, which is become the head of the corner: this is the Lord's doing, and it is marvellous in our eyes.' In ours, yes, but not in theirs!

In their eyes it is an irritating theory, anyway incapable of being realised, in which they do not believe, and which they consider interferes with their plans. To this very moment, as they build up their Baptist, Presbyterian, Methodist, Brethren, Anglican, Independent, Papist, 'New Testament', Reformed, Fundamentalist, Orthodox, and indeed any other of their 'churches', as they call them, they continue to reject the chief corner stone, which is Christ. They refuse to be built up by him as living stones given by the Father from heaven. Meanwhile, they grudge, scorn, and despise Christ's building, as 'a sect', impertinently calling it 'yet another denomination'!

Why do they do this? Because they are confederate with one consent to repudiate the very idea of Christ building his own a spiritual house. No *they* will do it, or they will stand in bitter opposition. However, they are all in favour of building people—preferably the saints—into their own particular party governed by their own personal authority and self-interest. And where is the Father's revelation from heaven, or Christ building *his* assembly upon it, in that?

Because we dare to say such things, they rage at us, accusing us of doing exactly the same things as they do themselves. By these words they bear testimony against their own deeds, blaming us for what they excuse in themselves. Otherwise, of what are they accusing us? For what do they blame us, but what they admit doing themselves?

Yet in truth we are not doing what they do. They are doing the building. We deeply repent of man's building, loathing ourselves in our own sight for this our evil presumption in times past. Now, however, by his grace and inworking we can do nothing but submit to Christ's building, overwhelmed with gratitude that he should not give us up, but take up such poor and worthless material, making of marred clay a new vessel.

Far from doing the same thing as them, we are saying that *notwithstanding* all that man does, Christ still builds his own *ecclesia*, but that this is on no other basis than that of the revelation of the Son by the Father in heaven.

As to us, with weeping and penitence ceasing from our own works, with overwhelming brokenness of heart, we find ourselves to be the work of his own hands. Then why do they not do likewise, seeing that they condemn their own activities?

We who have seen the Son, and believed upon him, can conceive of no other pathway for faith than to turn in submission to the Son of God. Would that all saints might come out in brokenness, to be built up together by him, and in him, for the glory of God and the Father.

But that is what present-day Christendom—evangelical, reformed, Brethren or otherwise: it makes no difference—neither looks for, nor owns as practicable, nor cares about, nor believes in, either for themselves or for anyone else. No more can they stand it when it is held forth, Christ's work being manifest in faithful ministers and brethren before their very eyes in our own day.

They affect to laugh us to scorn with disdain and contempt. Or else they peddle the pathetic slanders of those abject liars whom God has already judged and excluded. But, in truth, they would, if they could, like their fathers before them, wipe us off the face of the earth. On our part, we are careless of their rage, and indifferent to all that they can do to us, for our eyes have seen the King in his beauty, and we have observed the scars incurred by the persecutions he himself endured in his pilgrimage through this world, on his way to glory. And who are we to expect any different treatment?

These would-be builders therefore obscure Christ's building, and, whilst they would never admit it, they hate his building. Just as their 'unity' of denominations and 'churches'—pretending that such a fabrication of sects is 'one church'—obscures the reality of the unity of Christ's *ecclesia*.

They obscure everything that is from heaven, and darken all that is wrought by the Father, the Son, and the Holy Ghost.

Dispensing with revelation, they would gain over whomsoever they could—including Christ's sheep with their goats—to fill their pews, their 'church' rolls, and their collection plates, so that their 'livings'—if you can call it living—might be sustained, and their systems supported.

Bringing everyone under a thick fog, mixing everything together, they claim a relationship to Christ and an application of scriptural words and texts, to which they have no right whatsoever. They deceive the simple by their amalgamation of 'churches', sects, and denominations, calling it 'one church'—though invisible!—when, patently, it is nothing but a collection of human organisations.

But they have no intention whatsoever of dismantling their systems, no, not even to gain so much as the appearance of justifying their spurious claims to 'unity'.

Yet for all that this is so obvious, nevertheless by it they still manage to obscure the eyes of the world to the truth—and the reality—of one body, built up by Christ himself. This is his own *ecclesia*, filled by one Spirit, owning one Lord, confessing one faith, and indwelt by one God and Father, above all, through all, and in all the assembly of his own people.

iv. The revelation of the mystery

This revelation—on which Christ builds his *ecclesia*—is called elsewhere 'The revelation of the mystery'. This is never disconnected from the gospel, or from the preaching of Jesus Christ.

On the contrary, if it *is* that gospel which is preached, and if it *is* that doctrine of Christ which is made known, then Christ's assembly will follow, and must follow, and cannot but follow, in the nature of the revelation of the mystery.

'Now to him that is of power to stablish you according to my gospel, and the preaching of Jesus Christ, according to the revelation of the mystery, which was kept secret since the world began, but now is made manifest, and by the scriptures of the prophets, according to the commandment of the everlasting God, made known to all nations for the obedience of faith: to God only wise, be glory through Jesus Christ for ever. Amen', Romans 16:25-27.

The word 'mystery'—so intimately connected with 'revelation'—is of great significance in the new testament. On each occasion of its use the Greek *μυστήριον*, *mustērion*, has been rendered 'mystery' in the English.

The word *mustērion* is derived from the Greek *μυέω*, *mueō*, used once only in the new testament, and translated 'instruct'. Phil. 4:12, 'I know both how to be abased, and I know how to abound: everywhere and in all things I am instructed'—I have learned the secret—'both to be full and to be hungry, both to abound and to suffer need.'

Here the wording generally suggests something being opened up by experience, that is, the experience of life, from circumstances both of hunger and of satiation, of a smiling providence and of a frowning heavens. A lesson has been taught to one by life itself. But beyond this lies the secret of Paul's having learned how to answer spiritually to each such extreme of experience: Phil. 4:13, 'I can do all things through Christ which strengtheneth me.'

Then, this is not the stoical fortitude of a soul 'instructed' under distresses and excesses. No, it is the spiritual response to exterior conditions which Paul had learned inwardly, a response conditional upon the ministry of Christ to the inward man, 'Strengthened with might by his Spirit in the inner man.' Hence Paul could say 'I can do all things through Christ which strengtheneth me.'

This shows that the 'instruction' of Phil. 4:12 is spiritual and interior, standing in the power of Christ supplied continuously and invisibly from above. Thus he was in the secret. The matter was naturally 'closed up', but it had been 'opened' to him.

In turn the word *mueō*, 'instruct', is derived from the root word *μύω*, *muō*. This word does not occur in the Greek new testament. The basic meaning conveyed is that of 'close', or, 'be shut'. This has been applied to the eyes, the mouth, or, indeed, any opening, such as that of flowers, and so on. It is a question of what is closed up, or of what becomes closed up. From this unused root—unused, that is, in the new testament —springs the word *mueō*, occurring but once, as observed, in Phil. 4:12.

From *mueō* arises in turn the Greek word *mustērion*, 'mystery', a word of singular importance, occurring twenty-seven times in the new testament.

The use of the word *mustērion* in ancient Greek literature—that is, outside of the scriptures—possesses connotations of secret rites, initiation ceremonies, pagan temple worship, mysticism, and such like things. Notice of this can do nothing but muddy the pure waters of the new testament meaning, and must be strictly separated from the use of the word by the Holy Ghost.

The mere mention of the word 'mystery' in connection with the gospel conjures up a two-headed spectre of extremism. One head of this spectre arises from superstition, the other from fanaticism. The first extreme, superstition, feeds upon sacramentalism. The second extreme, fanaticism, thrives on mysticism. For fear of these extremes, the mystery of the gospel, and the revelation of the mystery, have been shunned by the 'orthodox'. But where is the orthodoxy in shunning the heart of the doctrine of Christ and his apostles?

Ah, but—say the wise and prudent doctors and masters of divinity—this is a matter fraught with danger.

So is religion. Then why do they live off it? So is eating. Then why do they risk their food? So is living. Then why do they abide this mortal coil? Think of the dangers! Yet they eat, they drink; they marry, they give in marriage; they buy, they sell; and they live. What, despite the dangers?

Yet in the matter of the mystery of the gospel—and the revelation of the mystery—taught by Christ and his apostles, mark, they enter not. Why not? Because of the dangers! Did these dangers deter Christ and his apostles? Did Christ not command us, despite the dangers? Then why do these disobey 'because of the dangers'? Here are 'blind leaders of the blind', with a witness. Go not after them. Go after those who admit the dangers, and, avoiding them, notwithstanding enter into the mystery of Christ according to his commandment.

The first extreme is sacramentalism. This consists of dissociating the word 'mysteries'—the Latin equivalent of which is *sacramentum*, 'sacrament'—from that with which Christ and the apostles invariably associate it: the mysteries of the gospel. This is to put asunder what God hath joined together. It is to make void the word of God by their traditions. But this is not the worst. The worst is the unholy alliance which follows. Sacramentalists next associate the word 'mysteries' with their 'sacraments', as they—but never Christ, the apostles, or the scriptures—call them.

These so-called 'sacraments' are all outward forms, some invented, others perverted from the apostolic ordinances, but all invested by them with a 'mystery' clean foreign to holy writ. This sleight-of-hand is done in order to prey upon the superstitions of a deluded world. Upon this system, the right of a 'priesthood' to administer it, and the authority of a 'holy father' to ordain that priesthood, upon this system, I say, popery hangs. And, to a lesser extent—but a very real one—so does the Church of England.

Baptism, in this system, is no sign: it is a mystery. It must be, if, in sprinkling an unknowing infant, the 'priest' can say 'sanctify this'—tap—'water to the mystical washing away of sin.' This is nothing but rank, idolatrous, heathen superstition.

The same applies to the Lord's supper, called by the Lord and his apostles, a 'remembrance', something done 'in memory'.

Sacramentalists, dark with superstition, call it 'the Mass', or 'Holy Communion', or 'Holy Eucharist', words never used of the ordinance of the Lord's supper by the Lord Jesus, or by the holy apostles, or by holy writ. Never once is it called a 'mystery'—or 'sacrament'—for the simple reason that it is not a mystery, it is a clearly explicable ordinance.

Priestcraft, however, confounds the Lord's supper with the words of Jesus in John—John, who nowhere, gospel or epistle, even mentions the Lord's supper!—'Except ye eat the flesh of the Son of man, and drink his blood, ye have no life in you.'

Sacramentalists transfer this spiritual utterance to the bread and wine, making the preposterous claim that in a 'mystery' or 'sacrament', at the words of their 'priest', the bread and wine 'turn into' the flesh and blood of Jesus. They appeal to John 6:53. But this is nothing to do with the supper. Only Matthew, Mark and Luke mention the supper. Never John. Only Paul in the epistles. Never John. Apart from this, Jn. 6:53 speaks of the flesh and blood of the *Son of man*. And what will they make of that?

The fact is that nothing whatsoever in any place anywhere warrants the papist priests' farcical confusion of scriptures, from such diverse contexts, with altogether different conceptions. Quite apart from their dreadful blasphemy. To what kind of grotesque proportions must such 'flesh' and 'blood' mount, swollen generation by generation, century after century?

What kind of a denial is this of the bodily resurrection and ascension of the Lord Jesus? And, however 'mysterious' or 'sacramentalised' they make cannibalism, no other word suits this idolatry, if their scheme but once reach the light of day, let alone the light of the judgment of God.

As to the words of Jesus, after he had addressed his hearers concerning 'whoso eateth my flesh, and drinketh my blood', he enquired 'Doth this offend you?' The Jews were outraged because—like the sacramentalists—they supposed Jesus to mean some form of cannibalism! But he explained, 'The words that I speak unto you, they are spirit, and they are life.'

And so is the eating of the flesh of the Son of man, and the drinking of his blood.

These are spiritual things, inwardly assimilated in the light and life of the Son. But they are nothing, but nothing, to do with the ordinance of the Lord's supper, which is not mystery, neither sacrament, nor any such thing. The supper is no more nor less than what it is called by the Lord Jesus and his apostles: 'a memorial'. Something done 'in memory of me'.

The other extreme by which men have distorted the mystery of the gospel of Christ is that of 'mysticism'. Essentially this fanatical extremism—in one form or another—separates the Spirit from the word; the soul from the body; or, just as erroneous, the individual from the *ecclesia.*

Thus the form may vary, but the essence is the same. It is a putting asunder, under the claims of higher light, or mysterious 'revelation', what God has joined together.

This is most obvious in the case of those who dispense with scripture, save when raving out of it from their own self-conceited 'revelations'. They use the bible as little more than a depository of disconnected sentences randomly selected by them to support their vainglorious hallucinations.

Hence, dismissing the doctrine of Christ, the teaching of the gospel, and the clear exposition of the word of God—the very means by which the true child of God receives powerful divine impressions upon the soul—these claim ecstasies, revelations, prophesies, tongues, spiritual baptisms—or so they say—and second, and other, excited 'experiences'.

Meanwhile they gush forth extravagantly about the 'Spirit' —and themselves—whilst quite ignoring the objective doctrine of both law and gospel, altogether to the detriment of the glory of Christ, and the majesty of Almighty God.

Now this is fanaticism with a witness. And, in reality, it is no more than a branch of that mysticism which separates the Spirit, and so-called experiences and gifts of the Spirit, from the doctrine of the holy word of God.

Whilst it is true that revelation marks the commencement and the continuation of the work in both the child of God and the assembly of Christ, nevertheless that revelation is always by, and in accordance with, the truth. Likewise it conforms with the recorded experience of the people of God set forth in the scriptures.

That such revelation is divine, spiritual, interior, mysterious, heavenly, and powerful, is certain. But it is equally certain that the word of God is that which is used by the Holy Ghost to effect every part of this work. Finally, nothing is without precedent. Everything must agree with the description of the varied sensations of the saints under such operations written from the beginning in the word of God.

For example, at one time David's soul was almost consumed from off the earth. He pleaded with God not to chasten him in his hot displeasure, nor to rebuke him in the fierceness of his anger. If God's hand pressed him sore; if his belly clave to the earth; if his convictions, chastenings, alarms, awakenings, terrors, tremblings, scourgings, caused him to cry, groan, sigh, pray, yearn, weep, entreat; if the enlightenment, revelation, quickening, regeneration, light, life, and love he received seemed to transport him to the heights of glory, to the gates of heaven: what? What then shall we say to these things?

Why, that such deep and divine experiences were all caused —every one of them; the whole range of them—by God's law, word, commandments, testimonies, judgments, statutes, and precepts. The cause of both affliction and revelation was in the word of righteousness, the word of faith, the word of life: in a word, by the first principles of the doctrine of Christ.

No matter how mystical, how spiritual, the cause was in the types, shadows, prophecies, promises, the figures of the true, the gospel before preached unto Israel. I say, it was by the word of God that the Spirit of truth wrought these mighty inward works of God. It was neither without the word, nor by anything other than the word.

Anything else belonged to the false prophets and the carnal, that outward seed of Abraham, which, dispensing with the doctrine of God's holy word, gave itself over to extravagance. Such as these—no better than the priests and prophets of Baal—forfeited that interior work of the Spirit into whose hands the custody of the truth had been placed from the beginning. They left themselves with nothing but an empty pretence to a mysticism which bore no resemblance whatsoever to the experiences of the prophets whom God had sent, or to the true interior sensations of that people called 'the sheep of his pasture'.

The same principle holds good in the new testament. The Spirit of God appears in the word of God. Never without.

If men were pricked in their hearts, it was under the preaching of the gospel. If fear came upon every soul, it was through the apostles' doctrine. If men trembled under the wrath of God, it was the word of truth that made known the terror of the Lord. If men were alarmed and made to cry out at the revelation of the righteous judgment of God, the cause was the word declared in the epistle to the Romans.

Did sinners tremble at the revelation from heaven of the wrath of God? The wrath of God was revealed from heaven in Paul's gospel. Men were born again? It was by that word of God which by the gospel was preached unto them. Men were regenerate? It was through being born again, not of corruptible seed, but of incorruptible, by the word of God. Men were made spiritual, holy, heavenly? Such sanctification of the Spirit was in perfect harmony with the belief of the truth.

Should men have the witness of justification in their hearts? Then it would be through the righteousness of God revealed in the gospel. Should men have the Son of God revealed to them by the Father in heaven? Then straightway they would confess, Thou art the Christ, the Son of the living God. Should men cry out at the light and voice from heaven, Who art thou, Lord? Immediately they would hear in answer to their cry the word of the Lord from heaven, saying, I am Jesus, whom thou persecutest.

Is it so that Christ should speak by the Spirit inwardly to his sheep, calling them by name, sanctifying them? It would be accompanied by 'I have given them the words which thou gavest me', and, 'Sanctify them through the truth: thy word is truth.'

Is it true that the Son of God should be so illuminated, so imparted to the heart of his people, that they would do the will of God even as did he? 'If any man will do his will he shall know of the doctrine, whether it be of God.'

Did Christ love the assembly, did he give himself for it, does he appear to it, all of one with it, sanctifying and cleansing his *ecclesia*? It is by the word of God that he does so, calling this the washing of water by the word, that he might present it to himself a glorious *ecclesia*, not having spot, or wrinkle, or any such thing, but that it should be holy and without blemish.

Shall Christ by his mighty power come from heaven for his assembly, change the living, raise the dead, and glorify the assembly? It will be with a voice, not without one; at the trump—which gives no uncertain sound—not without it; at a shout—the last word—not without utterance. 'I am Alpha and Omega, the first and the last, the beginning and the end.'

And is this mysticism? Not in the sense of the fanatics who separate the Spirit from the word, but in the sense of that revelation by which the Spirit of truth in a mystery uses the word of truth. Then, yes, it is the revelation of the mystery.

Another form of 'mysticism', so-called, is seen in those who would separate the soul from the body, as if the body, and, indeed, any and all matter—matter in and of itself—were innately evil.

But the truth is that the body, together with any and all matter—although permeated with evil from the Fall—was innately good before the Fall. 'And God saw that it was good.' These, however, in their wisdom, differ from the Almighty, and presume that it was bad. There is bad, yes, not in his creation, but since it. And will they see nothing but evil? Is their eye evil because he is good?

Then what do they? If their bodies are nothing other than innately evil matter, what can they produce but—since they intend to appear religious—'A show of wisdom in will worship, and humility, and neglecting of the body; not in any honour to the satisfying of the flesh.' Of this sort are the Trappists, hermits, monks, nuns, recluses, papist clergy, and the like. All with their voluntary will worship vowing themselves either to poverty, or chastity, or silence, or obedience. And all these things with oft fasting, abstinence, and such like things as they do.

But this is what Paul roundly condemns, calling the whole 'the commandments and doctrines of men'. He utterly dismisses such notions of the body, or its functions, or matter, as being intrinsically evil, with the scathing denunciation 'Vain philosophy and deceit'.

Yet another form of mysticism appears in that propensity of self-conceited individuals to detach themselves from the *ecclesia*, behaving as if nothing mattered but their own existence. Never is this more true than in those who think that they have some special ministry: mystical indeed, for no one else can see it. Neither is there the least evidence for such extraordinary presumption.

With these self-seekers, all rights of Christ to his own assembly are contemptuously dismissed. On the other hand, any or—if possible—all the various denominations, missions, movements, become the stage for the singular exercise of this supposedly marvellous ministry, in reality nothing but a theatrical exhibition of staged entertainment. Modern evangelism and the modern evangelist exemplify this specious form of mysticism. Yet none of them think so.

Specious, because, often accompanied by showmanship, extravagance, worldliness and gloss, nevertheless, it is the separation of the individual from the *ecclesia*, so as to be detached from its common discipline.

Actually, therefore, it is a claim to be exonerated from assembly responsibility on the basis of a 'special' work. This in fact places the 'evangelist' in a position superior to anything warranted by the word of God or exemplified by the apostolic ministry. This sort think that nothing like their transatlantic entertainment—which they call 'evangelism'—ever existed before. The deprived generations of many previous ages had to do without them, till they arose, till they arose prophets in Israel—or America—the light of their own wondering eyes.

This is far more of a spiritual evil than is generally recognised.

Like all forms of mysticism in principle, it is a claim, by way of assumed 'divine guidance', to a mode of occupation which cannot be supported by the word of God. The modern 'evangelist' goes to and gets his support from all quarters without a shred of principle. Ostensibly, 'prayer' support is required. But we all know that this is only the sugar coating round the pill. It is *money* that is being solicited. And solicited from all quarters—wherever available!—and from all denominations, irrespective of any articles of belief or communion, a method well understood by these ubiquitous heirs of the vicar of Bray.

Thus the modern 'evangelist', for purely selfish reasons, thrusts himself upon Christendom. He has not a single principle, save to ingratiate himself with every denomination in existence, endorsing all whilst belonging to none, so as to deny the one true assembly of Christ in perpetuity. And what 'mystical' dreams are these?

There is one body. The Spirit and word of God acknowledge and tolerate nothing but one *ecclesia*. That is, the assembly of the living God, the house of God, the pillar and ground of the truth.

No matter what has become fashionable parlance, universal acceptance, or unquestioned tolerance, the truth—mark that, the *truth*—of the gospel leads to and forms Christ's assembly and Christ's assembly alone. That evangelist who evangelizes by the evangel with the one true *ecclesia* in view sets forth the only evangelism sent of God. Everything else is sheer charlatanism. It must be. There is one God and Father, one Lord, one Spirit: there can be but one body, one *ecclesia*, one assembly, answering to that divine unity.

To divide and denominate that unity into parts is to proclaim as many gods as there are divisions. To tolerate anything less than one body in effect is to tolerate a witness to polytheism —many gods—in the name of the Lord Jesus.

False love, universal charity, sentimental affection, may call the hirelings who perpetuate this disobedience 'ministers', or name the opportunists who capitalise upon it 'evangelists', but we will show that they are not, and cannot be, according to the word of God.

Modern American-style 'evangelists' are a kind of latter-day 'mystic', *sans* gospel, *sans* assembly, *sans* self-denial. They are nothing better than itinerant conjurors, wandering from gipsy site to squalid squat, accompanied by a motley crew of minstrel troubadours, quack healers, not to mention other kinds of parasitical entertainers.

How different was the ministry, the evangel, the evangelist, the evangelism, in the beginning! But it ought not to be different, we should suffer no deviation, we should tolerate no departure from the ministry of the new testament. To do so is to be indifferent to Christ, careless of the Holy Ghost, and contemptuous of the most high God.

Consider. When Christ sent forth his apostles, he charged them, since all power was given unto him in heaven and in earth, 'Go ye therefore, and teach all nations, baptizing them in the name of the Father, and of the Son, and of the Holy Ghost: teaching them to observe all things whatsoever I have commanded you: and, lo, I am with you alway, even unto the end of the world. Amen.'

Now here is the evangel, the evangelist, and evangelism, from the very mouth of Christ. Set forth as in no other place. But the place is in Matthew. And Matthew is the only place in which the word *ecclesia* occurs in the gospels. Three times over. And the only place where the word is used by the Lord himself. And used with such effect that time would fail to examine the length, the breadth, the depth, and the height of no more than the half of what Jesus taught when he himself spoke of his own *ecclesia*.

Yet that teaching, together with all the teaching, all that Jesus taught, sums up the matter which the evangelist is to evangelize. 'Teaching them to observe all things whatsoever I have commanded you.' Commanded teaching, observe, that embraces Christ's *ecclesia*, Matthew chapters 16 and 18.

Teaching the hearers to *observe*, mark, not *ignore*. They were to observe this teaching, or doctrine, of Christ. Not talk about it, whilst practically denying it. Much less distorting and accommodating the teaching to persons, situations, denominations and divisions which clean contradicted both doctrine and observation.

This wresting of what was in the beginning to suit what has come to pass in the end precisely summarises the method and the practice of modern 'evangelicalism'. It is what modern 'evangelism' does, and what modern 'evangelists' do. But it is not what the apostles did. It is what they would never do.

What would the apostles never do? They would never separate the evangel, evangelism, or the evangelist from the one *ecclesia* of Christ. Because that *ecclesia* was precisely what the gospel was intended—and they were sent—to bring in for Christ, and for his own glory, by raising up the one habitation of God through the Spirit.

This is seen in the apostolic teaching concerning the ministry in the epistle to the Ephesians. Christ, having ascended up on high, 'gave some, apostles; and some, prophets; and some, evangelists; and some, pastors and teachers.' Here is the unique apostolic ministry; here the prophetic ministry; here are evangelists—the only evangelists authorized by the word of God—and here we find pastors and teachers. This is the entire and manifold heavenly ministry sent from Christ above throughout the age, according to his own will.

But to do what? For what are these persons sent? 'For the perfecting of the saints, for the work of the ministry, for the edifying of the body of Christ.' This, it is clear, is the purpose of the ministry. It is the purpose of evangelism. To perfect the saints. That is, *as united in one body.*

The epistle is addressed to 'the saints which are at Ephesus'. But the saints at Ephesus were *assembled.* They were Christ's *ecclesia* seen at Ephesus. Perhaps not yet perfected, but not left unperfect, for Christ sent the apostles, prophets, evangelists, pastors and teachers that they might be perfected in Christ Jesus. As one assembly. One body in Christ.

Again, the end of evangelism is the work of the ministry. Not *the evangelists'* ministry. The ministry *of the body.*

The one body is that which is to be built up. No apostle, no prophet, no evangelist, no pastor, no teacher, could have any other end than that of the 'edifying of the body of Christ.' Which is one in all the earth, as it is one in every place. Visibly one, with no other unity than the unity of one body, the very idea of division from it being beyond the remotest possibility.

To separate so-called 'evangelism' from that, to ignore the divisions and denominations of Christendom—as if they were 'normal'—nay, rather, to use them to further one's own 'ministry', is not only defiance of God's word, not simply contempt of Christ's things. It is abusing the very evangel, the gospel—or smatterings of it—to assist in the settling and establishment of the Adversary's own work.

That the gospel cannot be separated from the one body, that evangelism cannot be separated from Christ's *ecclesia*, that the evangel is sent to bring in and build up the unity of God's assembly, is made plain throughout the new testament. This is incontrovertible and invariable truth.

There is absolutely no warrant for a 'ministry' tolerant of division or denominationalism. Much less is there warrant to flatter this intolerable sectarianism in order to foster some 'ministry' in particular. As if *that* were the end in view—with denominationalism the means to it—and not Christ's *ecclesia.*

Even given the case of true gift sent from Christ, there is no authority whatsoever for any minister of whatever gift to debase that ministry by the craven servility of trading it for the pulpit favours of fallen denominationalism. Humiliate Christ for the self-interest of a place on the stage? Humiliate the Holy Ghost by hiring out the gift of heaven to a mixed multitude, to silence all others, to require payment, to set oneself in a class apart from one's brethren, and to distinguish this bizarre procedure by absurdities of dress and peculiarities of title?

The apostle Paul speaks for every minister sent from Christ when, declaring his sufferings for the body of Christ, he says, 'for his body's sake, which is the *ecclesia*: whereof I am made a minister.' His ministry, his evangel, his evangelism, were all 'for his body's sake, which is the *ecclesia*'.

That is, Paul viewed this heavenly calling as a heavenly ministry sent to all the assembly, the whole *ecclesia*. 'For the perfecting of the saints, for the work of the ministry, for the edifying of the body of Christ.'

This is what cannot be achieved by confining a ministry to one assembly. Much less to one of the divisions of Christendom at the expense of every other. Neither can it be achieved by ministering to all the denominations so as to tolerate their continued existence. Nor can it be achieved by negotiating 'areas of agreement' between those denominations, largely composed of worldly memberships, and ruled over by unbelieving and unregenerate old men. And women.

It can only be achieved by preaching the gospel with the purpose of gathering Christ's heavenly assembly outside of all the earthly sects, divisions, denominations, organisations, schisms, and assemblies of man's devising.

For in all of these unlawful divisions of men, each claims authority, each claims the scripture, and each claims one and the same gospel to give its particular division some vestige of biblical validity. But such spurious spirituality proclaims one thing with utmost clarity: that all this is nothing other than a dressed up form of mysticism which separates itself from the *ecclesia* of Christ and the apostolic ministry sent from above.

Nevertheless there is a mystery which is divine, and we are not—God forbid!—to neglect it for fear of the fashionable trend toward sacramentalism on the one hand, or to specious forms of modern mysticism on the other.

We are to return to 'that which was from the beginning', unmoved by the fear or the flattery of man, and untouched by the ridicule of the world or the scorn of the worldly 'churches'. We should remain unaltered by the affliction of the path of the stranger, and unchanged by the loneliness of the sojourner passing through this present evil world. For this is the way marked out for the saints from the very beginning.

In this pathway, whatever the covenant, or dispensation, we share the work of God and the operation of his hands with the unbroken line of the people of God ever since Abel by faith offered a more excellent sacrifice than that of Cain. Yet, with the bringing in of the new testament, our endowment and privilege is vastly greater than theirs.

For these are the last days, in which we come into the hidden mystery, the unveiling of the purpose of God in the Son of his love, kept secret since the world began. Ages and generations of the godly saints in times past have looked for and yearned after these things, yet have lived as pilgrims and strangers in a way of suffering affliction which puts us to shame. Nevertheless we have received all that for which they longed. With unabated zeal, the old testament saints searched from the time of the prophets even until John the Baptist. Yet it is to us that Christ's *ecclesia* has been made known, and made known by the revelation of the mystery. Then what manner of men ought we to be, compared with them?

The word *mustērion*, 'mystery', occurs twenty-seven times in the new testament. It is used three times in the gospels, once in Matthew, once in Mark, and once in Luke.

There are two occurrences in Romans, five in the first epistle to the Corinthians, six in Ephesians, four in Colossians, one in the second epistle to the Thessalonians, two in the first epistle to Timothy, and, lastly, four in the book of the Revelation of Jesus Christ.

In order to understand clearly and to establish precisely the meaning and use of the word *mustērion*, each of these passages must be examined in order, and the whole weighed and evaluated to summarize the teaching.

First the three passages in the gospels, the only occasions recorded in which Jesus himself, in the days of his flesh, used the word 'mystery'.

The reference in Matthew provides the introduction of the word *mustērion* to the new testament. 'To you it is given to understand the mysteries of the kingdom of heaven, but to them it is not given', Mt. 13:11. Evidently the kingdom of heaven is shrouded in 'mysteries'. That is, by definition, 'A hidden or secret thing; something beyond human knowledge or comprehension; a secret; hidden or inexplicable matter.'

But to whom are these 'mysteries' of the kingdom of heaven hidden?

To all mankind, seeing that a mystery is 'something beyond human knowledge or comprehension.' Then do any among mankind know the secret? Yes. How? Because 'to them it is given.' Then what of the generality? 'To them it is not given.'

From which it follows that penetration into the mysteries of the kingdom of heaven depends upon this 'being given'. From whom? From God. From whence? From heaven. It is 'the kingdom of heaven.' Then, the things that pertain to it must be revealed—if they are to be perceived at all—by 'my Father which is in heaven'.

What of those not counted as Christ's disciples? Of them all Jesus says, 'Seeing they see not; hearing they hear not, neither do they understand', Mt. 13:13.

But men think that they see, and are convinced of the adequacy of their sight in religion. They are sure that they can hear: they are persuaded of their ability, and are quite sure that their ears are sufficient for the occasion. Of course they understand. Are not with them the wise and prudent?

Understand? Certainly. Rather, it is a question of this fellow, Jesus. Of whether he is right. It is all very well, but many have not *their* eyesight or hearing, much less their sound traditions. Hence they conclude 'He deceiveth the people'. This is a man of whom one must be very careful. Indeed, they can say of such as him,'He seemeth to be some setter forth of strange doctrines.'

For 'we'—who are privileged to be familiar with traditional theology, and reformed orthodoxy—'have not heard it on this wise before'. Hence 'we' warn that 'this people which knoweth not the law are cursed.' But, naturally, 'we' know it, see it, understand it, and people ought to heed 'us', turning away from all these strange mysteries. This is the voice of wisdom and prudence from of old.

'And in them is fulfilled the prophecy of Esaias, which saith, By hearing ye shall hear, and shall not understand; and seeing ye shall see, and shall not perceive: for this people's heart is waxed gross, and their ears are dull of hearing, and their eyes they have closed; lest at any time they should see with their eyes, and hear with their ears, and should understand with their heart, and should be converted, and I should heal them', Mt. 13:14,15.

Contrariwise, of the babes to whom it is given to understand the mysteries of the kingdom Jesus says, Mt. 13:16, 'But blessed are your eyes, for they see: and your ears, for they hear.' Not see and hear his exterior word and doctrine: for all did that. But see and hear the interior revelation and opening: that was peculiar to the inward eyes, and unique to the interior ears, of those to whom it was given. As it is said, 'Blessed art thou, Simon Bar-jona: for flesh and blood hath not revealed it unto thee, but my Father, which is in heaven.'

If the revelation of this mystery be 'given' according to the will of God, then the initiative lies not in the will of man.

If it is given 'unto you', but not 'unto them', then it is not a general or universal giving according to the will of man, but a particular and limited giving according to the will of God. If it is given to the 'disciples' of Christ, then the issue will not be academic talking, but disciplined following. If it be given unto them to 'know' the mysteries, then with them it will not be 'Yea, yea; Nay, nay'; 'maybe' or 'perhaps'; 'Lo, here'; 'Lo, there'; but their knowledge will be at once clear and precise, doctrinal and experimental.

If it is 'mysteries' that they know, then spiritual they are, whose knowledge stands not in the wisdom of men, but the power of God. Whose understanding rests not in education from the dead letter, but in light from the living Father.

Again, if the mysteries be of the 'kingdom', then dominion is predicated. Submission must follow, meekness be in attendance, and subjection be much in evidence. This will appear through self-abasement in the worshippers, and humility in the *ecclesia*. For, 'The LORD is King for ever and ever.'

Once more, if the mysteries be of the kingdom 'of heaven', then such mysteries must be heavenly. If so, those to whom it is given to see them will be heavenly in conversation, and heavenly in knowledge, their vocation will be heavenly, and heavenliness will characterise their assembly.

Moreover, if to all others such things are 'not given', then this is the gift of God not the study of man; it pertains to the world to come, not the world that now is; and it stands in the honour that comes from God only, not that which men confer the one upon the other.

By these marks those in the secret, and those out of the secret, may readily be determined, irrespective of all the claims, postures, or pretensions of the professing 'church', in any or all of its withered branches.

The second reference to the 'mysteries' of the kingdom appears in Mark 4:11. However, since the third and last mention of the same word—in Luke 8:10—is a parallel passage, it will be well to take these together.

These texts in Mark and Luke are similar to that in Matthew, except that both use kingdom 'of God' as opposed to Matthew's kingdom 'of heaven'. All three references come from the lips of the Lord Jesus, and together constitute the full record of his use of the word *mustērion*.

Mark 4:11 reads 'And he said unto them, Unto you it is given to know the mystery of the kingdom of God: but unto them that are without, all these things are done in parables.'

Luke 8:10 states 'And he said, Unto you it is given to know the mysteries of the kingdom of God: but to others in parables; that seeing they might not see, and hearing they might not understand.'

Little need be added to what has been said from Mt. 13:11, the same conclusions being applicable, save that in the last two references Jesus emphasizes not the heavenliness of the kingdom, but its divinity.

In Mark 4:11 and Luke 8:10, Jesus stresses that the kingdom is of God not man; its nature is divine, not human. Until that time there had been a kingdom on earth: it was Israel. There had been a city on earth: it was Jerusalem below. There had been a throne on earth: it was the throne of David on mount Zion.

But now everything would be elevated above all that ear had heard, eye had seen, or the heart of man had conceived. God would set his divine King upon his holy hill in heavenly Zion, in Jerusalem above, declaring the decree, 'Thou art my Son: this day have I begotten thee.'

All that went before now appeared but a shadowy figure of the true. Now the kingdom of God was preached, and all that which had gone before was to wax old, for it was ready to pass away.

The knowledge of the mystery in the new testament was to be given to those with ears to hear. If so, to the spiritual. Those without ears to hear were those uncircumcised in heart and ears, who always resisted the Holy Ghost.

But by the Holy Ghost the ears of the spiritual were circumcised, so that they heard the voice of the Son of God from heaven in the heavenly kingdom. They were his sheep who heard his voice, and his voice declared to them by the Holy Ghost the mysteries of the kingdom of God.

This knowledge of the kingdom was divine; it was of God: 'That their hearts might be comforted, being knit together in love, unto all riches of the full assurance of understanding, to the acknowledgement of the mystery of God, and of the Father, and of Christ; in whom are hid all the treasures of wisdom and knowledge.' Here are the hidden mysteries of the kingdom of God with a witness. Mysteries, that is, though divine, yet disclosed to those to whom it was given, namely, to Christ's disciples, the circumcised in heart and ears, the elect of God, the *ecclesia.*

There are two passages in the epistle to the Romans in which the word *mustērion*, 'mystery', occurs. The first appears in Rom. 11:25, 'For I would not, brethren, that ye should be ignorant of this mystery, lest ye should be wise in your own conceits; that blindness in part is happened to Israel, until the fulness of the Gentiles be come in.' The apostle continues, verse 26, 'And so all Israel shall be saved'.

All Israel? Does this literally mean every single Israelite? By no means, for here is a mystery, and I would not that brethren should be ignorant of it—though, because of premillennialism, brethren are ignorant of it—lest they be wise in their own conceits.

'For they are not all Israel, which are of Israel', Rom. 9:6. If not, then the apostle cannot mean 'every Israelite' by the expression 'all Israel', Rom. 11:26. Because *not every Israelite is of Israel.* As he says, 'They are not all Israel, which are of Israel.'

According to the apostle in this place, they only from among all the Israelites are 'of Israel' who are the children of God according to the election of grace. A much smaller number than the total number of Israelites 'after the flesh'. That is, 'They which are the children of the flesh, these are not the children of God: but the children of the promise are counted for the seed', Rom. 9:8.

Not all the carnal seed of Israel, born of the flesh, are 'of Israel'. Only those chosen out from that number as the children of the promise. These alone are the true Israel, a very much smaller number than the total number of outward, natural Israelites. This is the first part of the mystery. And for lack of owning that it is a mystery—despite the apostle's direct statement that it is so—many have stumbled. It is a *mystery*, nothing obvious about it: the reality is concealed beneath the form that stumbles the carnal. But God unlocks the mystery to the spiritual. And to none other.

The second mystery is like unto it, namely, the mystery of how to account for the 'all' Israel that is to be saved, Rom. 11:26. How can the word 'all' suit the case, when only a part of the totality is to be taken out of Israel after the flesh? Then who, and what, is the other part, to make up the total number implied by the word 'all'?

Why, evidently, the remainder of 'the children of the promise'. That is, the residue of Abraham's spiritual seed over and above those chosen and called out of Israel after the flesh.

But who are these? How can Abraham have children other than those which came out of his own loins? By a mystery. What mystery? The mystery that Abraham 'might be the father of all them that believe', Rom. 4:11, 'though they be uncircumcised'. That is, of the Gentiles.

For, surely—however mysterious—if Abraham be their father, they must be his children. And, if so, of the seed of promise, the spiritual Israel.

Here is a seed that is of the faith of Abraham, 'who is the father of us all', Rom. 4:16, even 'the father of many nations', Rom. 4:18. Not just the believing in Israel, but the believing out of every nation, these are counted for the seed, and are Israelites indeed, as it is written, 'I will make thee the *father* of many nations.'

Why should it be thought a thing incredible with brethren, that God should raise up seed unto Abraham from these Gentiles? What do they expect of mysteries? Premillennial banalities? Nay, for Paul the apostle calls this a mystery.

Premillennialists, wise in their own conceits, cannot conceive of mysteries. Does that make the mysteries of God of none effect? God forbid! 'Know ye therefore that they which are of faith, the same are the children of Abraham'? Gal. 3:7. And if of Abraham, shall they be less of Israel?

And if of Israel, then, added to that number out of the circumcision who were of the faith of their father Abraham, those of the uncircumcised nations who are of the same faith of Abraham, being counted for the seed, make up the total number of 'Israel' in a mystery.

Now, this opens the mystery of 'All Israel'. So that they, the believing Israelites, without us, the Gentiles which believe, should not be made perfect, that is to say, complete. This is the Israel of God, Gal. 6:16, 'All Israel', on whom, saith he, as upon new creatures, abides peace and mercy.

Here is that spiritual Israel, an Israel which stands in all the believing seed of Abraham in a mystery. Not only that elect number called out of Israel after the flesh, but that number called out from the Gentiles also, all that be of the faith of our father Abraham, the father of many nations, all the chosen seed.

Here is that number which shall be saved, and saved by grace alone, through faith only. And, though this is a great mystery, it is withal an absolute certainty, for it shall surely come to pass in that day that, Romans 11:26, 'all Israel shall be saved', and none other.

Romans 16:25,26 is the remaining passage in this epistle in which the word *mustērion*, mystery, occurs.

'Now to him that is of power to stablish you according to my gospel, and the preaching of Jesus Christ, according to the revelation of the mystery, which was kept secret since the world began, but now is made manifest, and by the scriptures of the prophets, according to the commandment of the everlasting God, made known to all nations for the obedience of faith.'

In this place not only are the words 'revelation'—the understanding of which is the ultimate objective—and 'mystery'—the present enquiry—directly connected, but, moreover, it is stated expressly that the 'mystery' itself is that which has been revealed: 'the revelation of the mystery'.

From this observation it becomes evident that he who would grasp the significance of the revelation must also understand the nature of the mystery.

Romans 16:25-27—the whole passage—is both a difficult and a complex place. One reason for this is the series of subclauses, each one of which enlarges upon its predecessor. The matter being of great depth, this apparent complication can leave the reader bewildered unless the object and structure of the passage as a whole is borne in mind.

In effect this place is like a box within a box within a box—each neatly fitting into the other—from the final opening of which the contents become clear.

A simple method by which one may grasp the purpose of the whole is to proceed from the first to the last clause without regard to the intermediary stages. If this is done the general tenor of the passage immediately comes to light.

The object of the apostle is to give glory to the everlasting, the only wise God, for the wonderful soul-establishing doctrine of the gospel expounded in the sixteen chapters of this great epistle. The apostle commences, 'Now to him that is of power to stablish you'—in this same doctrine—and he concludes, 'to God only wise, be glory through Jesus Christ for ever. Amen.'

All that lies between this opening and that concluding passage—in which the apostle gives glory to God—is by way of a series of unfolding sub-clauses, the one explaining the other.

This is achieved by the formula 'according to'. Three times this occurs as such, and once the word 'and' implies a fourth clause also 'according to'.

Observe this. Verse 25, 'stablishment' is, first, 'according to' Paul's gospel; 'and', second—it is also according to—the preaching of Jesus Christ. This in turn is 'according to' the revelation of the mystery. Finally, notice, there is a fourth 'according to', verse 26, 'according to the commandment of the everlasting God.'

However, it must be kept in mind that these four successive explanatory passages do nothing but enlarge upon that by which—and the way in which—the saints are established to the glory of God. This is brought out by the apostle Paul in giving glory to God for his power to do such a wonderful work of grace on their behalf.

Note firstly the apostle ascribes power to him who is able to stablish his people. But this power is not exercised without means, but through means. Then according to what means does God put forth his establishing power in and to the saints? According to three essential factors this power is exercised. Nor can there be any stability—much less looking to his power—without all three in due succession and equal proportion. Each of these three means or factors in the exercise of God's power must now be considered in due order.

The first means by which God puts forth his power, verse 25, is 'according to' *my gospel*. But what was it that was so distinctive about Paul over against anyone else that entitled him to use the personal pronoun 'my' gospel? It was the manner in which he received that gospel. It was this that was unique.

The eleven apostles had learned from Jesus on earth, and, the Holy Ghost being given after his ascension, the work of that same Spirit was 'to bring all things to their remembrance' whatsoever he, Jesus, 'had said unto them' whilst on earth. But Paul never knew Jesus on earth. He did not know Jesus until after he was glorified. All that Paul received, he received from the glory.

There was nothing for the Spirit to bring to Paul's remembrance, because he had nothing to remember.

The first acquaintance Paul had with Jesus was that of a light above the brightness of the sun shining in its strength at noonday. This was blinding, impossible to behold.

Here was the glory of the Lord, 'above the brightness of the sun.' This was the Lord, shining in glory, resplendent in light unapproachable, the light of his own Person, glorified in heaven. A voice sounded from this radiant glory in heaven. Paul cried 'Who art thou Lord?'

Then came an answer from the excellent glory, a response from the radiance of the divine Being, which replied 'I am Jesus'. That revelation showed *just how glorious* was the Lord Jesus. It made clear *just how glorified* Jesus had become. And it manifested *just how the glory of God* above all heavens had received the very one whom Saul had denounced as an impostor on earth. That blinded Saul. The light of the glory streaming from Jesus blinded Saul. It also gave rise to 'my gospel'.

Here was revelation. It was light from heaven. This was revelation from heaven, even from the throne of glory above the heavenlies, from the excellent glory, from light unapproachable, from the very presence of God.

This was a revelation of righteous judgment, a revelation of wrath from heaven, yes, but it was a revelation of righteous wrath *quenched.*

For the revelation manifested the presence of Man in the glory. A glorious Man in heaven, by whom, and in whom, and through whom righteousness of God was revealed in the gospel, freely imputed to the ungodly by grace through faith. Because atonement had been wrought on the earth.

This was, according to Paul, 'my gospel'. He saw it, he received its doctrine, and, though at first it blinded him, he came to it 'not after man'. He 'neither received it of man', 'neither was he taught it', but 'by the revelation of Jesus Christ.' It was light from heaven. And light every ray of which radiated from the glorified Son of God.

This is the gospel of God, the gospel of the grace of Christ, particularly expounded in the epistle to the Romans. Here, first, Christ is seen as having died in the place of his people. Then, they are seen as having died with him. Next, his people are viewed as risen with him in newness of life. Finally, a company, the assembly, the *ecclesia*, appears as one body, united as members with the Head.

Paul closes this epistle by giving glory to God that he is of *power* to establish the saints at Rome—and in every place and in all ages—in that same truth of the gospel. Indeed, God's power, put forth in stablishing his people, was of divine necessity 'according to my gospel', and in no way otherwise, despite the pretensions of those who would—in their lying schemes—separate the Holy Ghost from the doctrine of the apostles, and interject the law into a gospel that from first to last was wholly of grace.

But not solely 'according to my gospel', this power, it is also exercised through a second means in conjunction with the first.

Not only is the power of God to stablish the saints exercised through Paul's gospel of the glory, but also according to —'and'—the means of 'the preaching of Jesus Christ', verse 25.

The word 'preaching' here is not 'evangelizing' it is 'announcing'. It is the 'proclamation of Jesus Christ'. Here is a mystery: the mystery of Christ. Great is this mystery of godliness: God was manifest in the flesh. The Son, one with the Father and with the Holy Ghost from eternity in everlasting deity, in due time took human nature into union with his divine nature, becoming incarnate, being born of a woman, in a humanity at once perfect and sinless.

It was God who was in Christ reconciling the world unto himself, not imputing their trespasses unto them. He that saw him, saw the Father. The Father's will was his meat and drink, the Father's works were his life and breath, and the Father's speech was his word and doctrine.

And at last the Father's commandment—which was everlasting life—was the consummation of his pathway in the mystery of sacrificial death. For the death of the Prince of life was a mystery, a mystery of divinity, in which the one who was without sin was made sin; the one who did no sin bare sin; and the one who knew no sin became sin.

Yes, and he through whom all this was effected was the Father, who loved the Son of his love with love immeasurable, from eternity to eternity.

This is the mystery of vicarious atonement, wrought by the Father, through the eternal Spirit, in his only begotten Son. And this, further to nothing but the divine will, counsel, and eternal purpose of the everlasting God, determined before the heavens were framed, the world was formed, or the mountains were brought forth.

The third day God raised him from the dead, glorified in the body. But not alone. 'For both he that sanctifieth and they that are sanctified are all of one.' All his people—in the counsel of God—rose with him, yea, and ascended in him: being quickened together with Christ, raised up together with him, and being made to sit together in heavenly places in Christ Jesus.

And this is the mystery: his people called out of Israel were either already dead, or yet alive on earth at that time. As to his people called from among the Gentiles, these were not yet born. But in Christ, in his death, resurrection, ascension, and reign in glory, all were and are one with him and in him in the sight of God. So that where he is, there they are also.

'This is a great mystery, but I speak concerning Christ and the *ecclesia*.' For Christ loved the *ecclesia*, and gave himself for it; that he might sanctify and cleanse it with the washing of water by the word.

Moreover, in a mystery, this same Jesus, which was taken up from the first disciples out of their sight into heaven, shall so come in like manner in the sight of the last disciples from heaven. He shall come again, thereupon raising the dead, changing the living, and catching up the *ecclesia* in the clouds to meet the Lord in the air. Dissolving the heavens and the earth in flaming fire, he shall send forth his angels, raising all nations from the dead, all peoples from the beginning of the world to the end of it, judging Israel, yea, judging the world in righteousness.

Furthermore he shall separate for ever light from darkness, sheep from goats, heaven from hell. He shall create a new heavens and a new earth. He shall bring in the new Jerusalem, the holy city. And he shall establish his own assembly, his *ecclesia*, as his bride in the everlasting inheritance of eternal glory.

Now this is the mystery of Christ, and Paul calls the setting forth of it 'the proclamation of Jesus Christ'. By this, together with 'my gospel', and the revelation of the mystery, and by nothing else, God's power is put forth to establish his assembly.

The third, last, but concurrent means by which God puts forth his power to stablish the saints, without which neither power is committed nor establishment follows, is that of the 'revelation of the mystery'.

The power of God is not only according to 'my gospel', nor simply according to 'the preaching of Jesus Christ', it is also 'according to the revelation of the mystery', verse 25.

This means of the exercise of God's power, and of the saints being rooted, grounded, and settled thereby, is yet another, a third means, parallel with but distinct from both 'my gospel' and 'the preaching of Jesus Christ'.

From which it follows of necessity that the 'revelation of the mystery' is not the written record of Paul's gospel in the epistles. That answers to 'my gospel'. Nor is it the apostolic proclamation of Jesus Christ in the new testament scriptures. That is called 'the preaching of Jesus Christ'. These two factors are essential, however, in concert with 'the revelation of the mystery', for the power of God to be put forth in the stablishing of the saints.

Just as 'my gospel', and, 'the preaching of Jesus Christ', are separate and distinct means, so likewise 'the revelation of the mystery' is to be distinguished from each singly, and from both together.

It is quite true that the apostles' preaching and writing of the gospel itself, announcing the Person, life, and work of Jesus Christ, were in themselves revelation, just as they were mystery. But they were the record, the written record, the testimony received and set down in scripture by chosen apostles.

In their day the apostles preached this record, and began the work of writing that which they had received in what was to become, collected, the new testament scripture.

Apart from this scripture, however, and quite distinct from —though altogether in concert with—that apostolic preaching, there was a work of God immediately on the heart and directly upon the soul of such as were to be saved. That work was a mystery.

Now the apostles have long since gone. Nevertheless, thanks be to God, their writings remain in the new testament scriptures, that is, in the text and version ratified by the Holy Ghost,* a text and version commensurate with 'my gospel' and 'the proclamation of Jesus Christ' from the beginning.

But just as in the lifetime of the apostles, when they themselves preached that gospel, and proclaimed Jesus Christ, *that was not enough in itself* without the revelation of the mystery, so now.

To this day, the preaching of the gospel, together with the proclamation of Jesus Christ, must be accompanied by 'the revelation of the mystery', to be effective.

*Read 'The Great Deception', Tract for the Times No. 12, The Publishing Trust. See advertising pages.

If the saints are to be established, then, even today, God, who commanded the light to shine out of darkness, must shine in their hearts also, to give the light of the knowledge of the glory of God in the face of Jesus Christ. To this latest hour the God of our Lord Jesus Christ must grant his people a spirit of wisdom and revelation in the knowledge of him.

Still the Spirit of truth must take the things of Christ—in the gospel and in the proclamation—and reveal them unto the saints. Still, despite the preaching of the gospel, and the proclamation of Jesus Christ, flesh and blood cannot fathom, much less receive, either gospel, scripture, or Christ, for this comes only from 'my Father which is in heaven'.

This inworking Paul here calls 'the revelation of the mystery'. Without it, there can be no power, no light, no life, no love, no union, no communion. For all the preaching, even apostolic preaching, without the light of revelation from heaven, everything remains but a dead and ineffectual letter. As dead as that which killed under the old covenant. That is why Paul insists on 'the revelation of the mystery'.

The gospel, Paul's gospel, is full of revealed mystery, and so is the proclamation of Jesus Christ. But both the preaching in that day, and the written record of that preaching in our own day, both, I say, give no more than the revealed *facts* about Christ and the gospel.

They tell the truth about him, and all the truth about him. But he, himself—his own Person—is infinitely more than the facts about him. One may know of the one yet remain oblivious of the other. The Person of Christ may remain a total stranger, whilst acquaintance with truths concerning his Person may well crowd and fill up the mind, even greatly affecting the life.

With 'the revelation of the mystery', however, the life of that Person himself is mediated to the interior spirit. The life that is in him is communicated spiritually by the Spirit to one's own spirit. 'He that is joined to the Lord is one spirit.' This is a great mystery, but, nevertheless, it is a revealed mystery, in fact it is 'the revelation of the mystery'.

This is the actual communication to the inner man of the light that he radiates, the life that he imparts, the love that he gives, of the essence that is his Being. This is ministered by the Holy Ghost, one with him and one with us in the inward spirit, so that union is joined, and communion sustained, within the hidden man of the heart.

This union and communion of and with the divine light, life, love and Being of the Son, commensurate with quickened faith in the gospel, and spiritual illumination from the Holy Ghost, is what is intended by the words 'the revelation of the mystery'. Without it there is no being stablished.

The power of God is put forth in revealing the mystery—together with 'my gospel' and 'the preaching of Jesus Christ'—to unite with his Son, stablish the saints, and build up the *ecclesia*. Without these things, and all of these things, there is no new testament work of God, no calling, saints are not stablished, and the *ecclesia* can neither appear nor exist.

Without such an interior work of God, I say, all that can exist, at most, is an illusory evangel, spurious evangelism, an empty profession, a false faith, blind zeal, and a so-called 'church' filled with the congregation of the dead, presided over by place-seeking, corpse-dressing undertakers in consequence.

But in truth the gospel of God is very far from the sickly drivel to which it has been reduced by modern evangelicals. The gospel—'my gospel'—is a *mystery*. But there is no mystery about the vain concoction of a soufflé of texts—from some commercially viable latter-day 'version'—larded with anecdotes, jokes, and appeals either to sentiment or exhibitionism, leading to some superficial 'decision' or 'commitment' from those who are taken in by this vanity.

How can they suppose that this will settle the issues of everlasting eternity, or answer for suited righteousness before the face of Almighty God?

But *the* gospel, Paul's gospel, the apostolic gospel, 'my' gospel, is a mystery, it is the *mystery* of the gospel, and therefore anything, but anything, that does not reflect this mystery *cannot* be the gospel. More: what contradicts the concept of mystery, by its trifling, humanising, entertaining, chaffy, and vacant emptiness, must be a downright *perversion* that will become utterly and eternally disastrous to those who, willingly ignorant, turn their itching ears from the truth to embrace it.

It was the mystery of the gospel that was made known by the apostles. It was the revelation of the mystery that was made known by the Father from heaven. Nothing less establishes the saints in the *ecclesia* of God, 'according to my gospel, and the preaching of Jesus Christ'.

This is that which was commanded of God, and made known by the apostles, sent from Jesus Christ, in the beginning of the new testament. This is that which had been 'kept secret since the world began', verse 25, though it was 'now made manifest', verse 26. Here it is evident that both the gospel, and the *ecclesia* brought in by it, are mysteries hidden from the foundation of the world: 'kept secret since the world began'.

Then, neither the giving of the law nor the existence of Israel had anything to do with the present revelation 'now made manifest'. Nor had the law or Israel to do with the apostolic disclosure in the new testament of the hidden secret brought to light by the glorifying of Jesus Christ and the sending forth of the Holy Ghost from heaven.

It is true, that this hidden secret was spoken of from ancient times as a veiled mystery which, in the fulness of the ages, God would make known. But it was spoken of in this way by the 'prophets'. If so, it was declared as 'prophecy', yet to be fulfilled.

Now, declares Paul, it is fulfilled. The secret kept from the beginning of the world is 'now made manifest'. And with this manifestation, the scriptures of the prophets—who wrote things which they themselves could not understand—suddenly were made explicable.

The prophets prophesied of things really obscure to them. They prophesied of secrets which were quite veiled to them. They searched diligently to understand the hidden meaning of what they themselves had foretold.

'Of which salvation the prophets have inquired and searched diligently, who prophesied of the grace that should come unto you: searching what, or what manner of time the Spirit of Christ which was in them did signify, when it testified beforehand the sufferings of Christ, and the glory that should follow. Unto whom it was revealed, that not unto themselves, but unto us they did minister the things, which are now reported unto you by them that have preached the gospel unto you with the Holy Ghost sent down from heaven; which things the angels desire to look into.'

So Peter tells you. To the prophets it was a secret, a divine secret, and they knew that it was a secret. Which is what Jesus himself taught: 'For verily I say unto you, That many prophets and righteous men have desired to see those things which ye see, and have not seen them; and to hear those things which ye hear, and have not heard them.'

Here was a secret, kept even from those that prophesied, kept from the foundation of the world. And yet the prophets, not knowing what they meant, prophesied before of the sufferings of Christ, and of the glory that should follow. There it is in their writings, in their scriptures. How poignant that they themselves searched into the meaning, yearning, longing, rising up early and seeking diligently.

But none, no, not even the prophets, the seers, or the righteous men of old time, none could open God's secrets. 'But now'—all this—'is made manifest by my gospel, and the preaching of Jesus Christ, according to the revelation of the mystery'. 'And', continues Paul, 'by the scriptures of the prophets', verse 26.

Suddenly the key is there. It is turning, the door is flung open, the veil is rent, the hidden things are made manifest, they blaze with light: 'and by the scriptures of the prophets.'

All this, the calling and establishing of a people for his name, according to 'my' gospel, and the preaching of Jesus Christ, according to the revelation of the mystery, all this, I say, is 'according to the commandment of the everlasting God, made known to all nations for the obedience of faith', verse 26.

Even as Paul was commanded to preach the gospel to the Greek nation in Achaia, at Corinth: Paul did not know, the very people did not know, but the Lord knew that he had much people in that city, and therefore Paul was sent. He preached 'my' gospel, he proclaimed Jesus Christ, and, 'according to the revelation of the mystery' the Son was revealed in that people by the Father from heaven. 'The testimony of Christ was confirmed in you', I Cor. 1:6.

All was by God's commandment. From the beginning Paul did not choose Christ, the Father revealed him. 'When it pleased God to reveal his Son in me.' Paul did not choose to preach, God called him. 'Paul, an apostle of Jesus Christ by the commandment of God our Saviour, and Lord Jesus Christ which is our hope', I Tim. 1:1. 'Paul, an apostle of Jesus Christ by the will of God, according to the promise of life which is in Christ Jesus', II Tim. 1:1.

Paul did not prepare and send himself, God prepared and sent him. 'I was made a minister, according to the gift of the grace of God given unto me by the effectual working of his power', Eph. 3:7.

'But rise, and stand upon thy feet: for I have appeared unto thee for this purpose, to make thee a minister and a witness both of these things which thou hast seen, and of those things in the which I will appear unto thee; delivering thee from the people, and from the Gentiles, unto whom now I send thee', Acts 26:16,17.

All, all, all was of God, first and last, nothing was of man, man was ruled out, God ruled by Jesus Christ through the Spirit. The flesh was kept utterly mortified, there was no room for the flesh. All was by God's commandment.

'According to the commandment of the everlasting God', Romans 16:26. This agrees with the beginning of the epistle, 'By whom we have received grace and apostleship, for obedience to the faith among all nations, for his name', Romans 1:5.

What a revelation is this! Hidden from the foundation of the world, as high above Israel as the heavens are above the earth. So far transcending the law as the Son is superior to the angels. The hidden secret was to be made manifest by 'my gospel and the preaching of Jesus Christ', which was to go forth among all nations, for his name.

Preached among all nations, yes, but withal that preaching, nothing but revelation could manifest the mystery. Nothing but revelation could open the mystery. And nothing but revelation could impart the mystery. And that is what the ministry sent from Christ is intended to fulfil according to the commandment of the everlasting God.

And this must hold good even to this day. The preaching of the gospel must be 'by the commandment of the everlasting God'. 'How can one preach, except he be sent?' This is the ministry God will own, 'according to the revelation of the mystery.' All other ministry is spurious. It is of man.

'Take heed whom ye hear.' 'Take heed what ye hear' 'For many antichrists are gone out into the world.' 'Many deceivers are entered into the world.' The apostasy has run on apace. We are almost at the end, when deception abounds, and must abound.

As to the remnant that is left, this remnant itself will be 'hated of all men for my name's sake'. As to the ministry sent down from Christ, it is foretold, 'he that killeth you will think that he doeth God service.' Oh, how we need to pray and cry for a return to the gospel and the ministry that was in the beginning.

With God all things are possible. And all things are possible to him that believeth. 'To God only wise, be glory through Jesus Christ for ever. Amen', Romans 16:27.

Five times over the word *mustērion*, 'mystery', occurs in the first epistle to the Corinthians. Firstly in I Cor. 2:7. 'But we speak the wisdom of God in a mystery, even the hidden wisdom, which God ordained before the world unto our glory.'

Evidently this answers to the apostolic preaching of 'my' gospel, and the proclamation of Jesus Christ, according to the revelation of the mystery, which was kept secret since the world began, Rom. 16:25.

In I Cor. 2:7 'we' refers to the apostles, sent forth by Jesus Christ according to the commandment of the everlasting God, Rom. 16:26. Just as the 'hidden wisdom', agrees with the reference in Romans to 'the mystery kept secret since the world began, now made manifest.'

This is the Word which was in the beginning, which was with God, and was God. 'All things were made by him; and without him was not any thing made that was made. In him was life; and the life was the light of men. And the light shineth in darkness; and the darkness comprehended it not.'

And so matters stood, hidden, secret, uncomprehended, from the foundation of the world. Until 'The Word was made flesh'. That was the beginning of the opening of the secret kept since the world began, but 'now made manifest'. It was the beginning of the disclosure of the hidden wisdom.

For now, by the commandment of the everlasting God, the apostles have been sent forth to preach with the Holy Ghost sent down from heaven, to declare not only that the Word was made flesh, but also to proclaim everything that followed in consequence. This, his birth, death, resurrection, and ascension, his glorious Person revealed by the Father from heaven, this, I say, was to be preached among all nations, for the obedience of faith.

This was the doctrine of the apostles, sent to preach the gospel, to proclaim Jesus Christ, according to the revelation of the mystery.

This is 'the wisdom of God in a mystery, even the hidden wisdom, which God ordained before the world unto our glory.' This the apostles, sent from Jesus Christ on high, spoke forth with power.

Observe, I Cor. 2:7, they 'spoke' the wisdom of God in a mystery. If 'spoken', then it was the mystery of Christ in the faith of the gospel, as it is written, 'I believed, and therefore have I spoken; we also believe, and therefore speak', II Cor. 4:13. This mystery, first taught directly by Jesus to the apostles, then revealed within and brought to memory by the Holy Ghost from heaven, is called 'the mystery of the gospel'. This the apostles thereafter believed, spoke, preached, recorded and wrote. This is to 'speak the wisdom of God in a mystery.'

The revelation of this mystery, which the apostles and ministers of Christ taught, preaching and proclaiming Christ by the gospel, I say, the revelation of this mystery was wrought by the Father from heaven through the Holy Ghost on earth.

This was the glorious revelation of the Son by the Father. The Holy Ghost disclosed the reality of the things preached within the heart of the saints, by the light of divine revelation from heaven. This was a divine mystery: unfathomable, immeasurable; beyond all imagination, every dimension, past any comparison, outside of all human comprehension.

At once divine, heavenly, supernatural, spiritual, here is the mystery kept secret from the foundation of the world, now manifest, 'the hidden wisdom in a mystery'. But it is the revelation of that mystery, by the Father, not just the preaching of it by the apostles, that brings fruition to the purpose of God in his people.

The mystery is preached, yes, but being preached, it is revealed by the Father from heaven, as it is written, 'Eye hath not seen, nor ear heard, neither have entered into the heart of man, the things which God hath prepared for them that love him.'

Then, these things being incomprehensible, how can those who love him receive them?

They can receive them because 'God hath revealed them unto us by his Spirit: for the Spirit searcheth all things, yea, the deep things of God. For what man knoweth the things of a man, save the spirit of man which is in him? even so the things of God knoweth no man, but the Spirit of God.'

'Now we have received, not the spirit of the world, but the Spirit which is of God; that we might know the things that are freely given to us of God', I Cor. 2:9-12.

I Corinthians 4:1 refers to the apostles, the ministers of Jesus Christ, as 'stewards of the mysteries of God'. 'Let a man so account of us, as of the ministers of Christ, and stewards of the mysteries of God.' But how could these, but men, dispense divine mysteries?

Because God wrought by them, Christ spoke in them, and the Spirit worked through them.

Precisely because they were nothing in their own eyes, spoke not of themselves, preached not themselves, were empty of self-interest, void of self-seeking, God, in Father, Son, and Holy Ghost, used these chosen vessels, filling and emptying them out to others in the preaching of the word. And, even as they spoke, the Spirit came on them that heard.

Therefore it was not them that spoke, but the Spirit of their Father that spoke in them. It was not their administering the stewardship, but the Spirit of Christ administering through them.

Christ through the apostles administered to others the ministry of the new testament; the ministry of the Spirit; the ministry of righteousness; the ministry of glory; the ministry of the word; the ministry of reconciliation; and the ministry of the gospel. And who was sufficient for these things? But these divinely called and sent ministers had this treasure in earthen vessels, and thus their sufficiency was of God.

Next, I Corinthians 13:2 speaks of one's understanding all mysteries, and all knowledge, yet, lacking charity, being nothing. In view of what has been said about mysteries, how is this?

Consider Balaam, the son of Bosor, who loved the wages of unrighteousness, called by Peter a prophet, if a mad one. Now of this Balaam it was said, 'God came to Balaam, and spake', and, 'Balaam answered God'.

Yet again, 'The LORD opened the eyes of Balaam'. Then, 'Balaam said unto the angel of the LORD', and, 'The angel of the LORD said unto Balaam.' Once more, 'The LORD put a word into Balaam's mouth'. Further, 'And the LORD met Balaam, and put a word into his mouth.' Balaam had the sight: 'Balaam lifted up his eyes, and he saw.'

Consider this man, for he saw mysteries, and, moreover, understood them. 'Balaam the son of Beor hath said, and the man whose eyes are open hath said: He hath said, which heard the words of God, and knew the knowledge of the most High, which saw the vision of the Almighty, falling into a trance, but having his eyes open.'

'I shall see him, but not now: I shall behold him, but not nigh: there shall come a Star out of Jacob, and a Sceptre shall rise out of Israel. Out of Jacob shall come he that shall have dominion.' These are the words of Balaam.

And he said, beholding as in a glass, darkly, the mystery of justification: 'God is not a man, that he should lie; neither the son of man, that he should repent: hath he said, and shall he not do it? or hath he spoken, and shall he not make it good?'

'Behold, I have received commandment to bless: and he hath blessed; and I cannot reverse it.'

'He hath not beheld iniquity in Jacob, neither hath he seen perverseness in Israel: the LORD his God is with him, and the shout of a king is among them.' 'According to this time it shall be said of Jacob and of Israel, What hath God wrought!'

Now, here is prophecy with a witness, here is the understanding of mysteries in truth, and here is all knowledge comprehended briefly in a vision. But here is no charity.

Balaam saw visions, he prophesied, he understood all mysteries. But 'though I have the gift of prophecy, and understand all mysteries, and all knowledge; and though I have all faith, so that I could remove mountains, and have not charity, I am nothing', I Cor. 13:2.

And Balaam was nothing. Balaam was lost.

His eyes were open, he understood all mysteries, yes. But for all that, he had not the faith of God's elect; much less had he the indwelling of God's Spirit. One may see mysteries as did Balaam, yet remain void of the experience of the mystery of Christ, peculiar to the heirs of promise.

None receive this, save that the Father in heaven reveals the Son by the Holy Ghost sent to his chosen people, redeemed by the precious blood of Christ, and justified by grace. And what could Balaam say of this? Nothing.

He knew much, but he felt nothing.

He saw much, but he experienced nothing.

Such a man may, spiritually, behold a scene, a view, a vision, a concept, yet remain entirely outside of it and objective to it. And what Balaam saw, Balaam never entered into, and never experienced, for he had neither part nor lot in the matter concerning that about which his vision was so clear.

It is one thing to see a spiritual matter, but it is another thing to have experience of the matter seen.

It is one thing to understand a divine mystery, but it is quite another thing to participate in what is understood. One may watch a company eating and drinking, but starve to death from failing to partake of the meal oneself. So one may understand all mysteries, yet enter into none of them.

Those who have the interior teaching of the Spirit are led into all truth, not simply to view it, but to experience it. Not merely to understand it, but to be transformed by it. The understanding may come from sight, but the experience must come from participation.

Mysteries may be inexplicable, but they are not altogether indescribable. But such a description, however helpful, can give neither participation in nor experience of the heavenly mystery. Nothing but the revelation of the Father, the gift of the Spirit, the ministry of the Lord, and the operation of God, can do that, bringing into union and communion.

To receive such grace from God is not merely to have understanding. It is to add experience. If one does no more than understand the truth that there is such a thing as a revelation of the Son from the Father in heaven, to a chosen company on earth, that is not to be of that company. It is to understand what brings—others—into that company.

However, only that company in itself considered is called by Christ, 'My *ecclesia*'.

Next in order comes the use of the word 'mystery' in connection with 'tongues'. Under the ministry of the apostles, at the first, many miraculous signs and gifts appeared. This is acknowledged in the epistle to the Hebrews: 'How shall we escape, if we neglect so great salvation; which at the first began to be spoken by the Lord, and was confirmed unto us'—a later generation—'by them'—the first generation—'that heard him; God also bearing them'—not us, notice: them—'witness, both with signs and wonders, and with divers miracles, and gifts of the Holy Ghost, according to his own will?' Heb. 2:3,4.

One of the earliest miraculous signs was 'tongues', given also—though the record of this is exclusive to the first Corinthian epistle—as a gift in the very early *ecclesia* together with the distinct provision of a separate interpreter.

The gift, as such, was neither recorded as having been given to nor was it permitted to be used by women in the congregation of the saints. Women were to be silent in the assembly. They were to learn in silence with all subjection. And this plain truth should shut up the Pentecostals and Charismatics, bold in their awful errors, pretending to such miraculous gifts when these no longer exist. Nor have they existed since the first apostolic times. As opposed to the later apostolic times: 'God bearing *them* witness', notice; not 'us', Heb. 2:3,4. Tongues are—barely—mentioned in a mere two of the—earliest—books, out of a total of twenty-seven. The regulation of 'tongues' is the subject of I Corinthians 14.

'Follow after charity, and desire spiritual gifts, but rather that ye may prophesy. For he that speaketh in an unknown tongue speaketh not unto men, but unto God: for no man understandeth him; howbeit in the spirit he speaketh mysteries. But he that prophesieth speaketh unto men to edification, and exhortation, and comfort', I Cor. 14:1-3.

In this solitary place out of all the epistles, notwithstanding the remarkable sign—not gift—of tongues two or three times in Acts, the apostle discourages the use of tongues in the assembly, the rather preferring its use—if at all—in private devotion. It is well known that solitariness soon damps the ardour of the flesh; whereas an audience much inflames it. It is equally well known that the flesh of the Corinthians was much inflamed by spiritual—pseudo or otherwise—impressions. This, however, was under their own control. 'The spirits of the prophets are subject to the prophets.'

On the other hand Paul much encourages prophecy. If tongues—given their special signification in the very first early apostolic times—were to be used in the *ecclesia*, two principles obtained. First, there must be interpretation miraculously given from a source other than the original speaker. And, second, women were not only forbidden to speak in tongues, or to interpret, in the assembly: they were forbidden to speak at all. 'Let your women keep silence in the *εκκλεσίαις*.'

As to the use of the word *mustērion* in this connection, I Cor. 14:2, the 'mystery' of tongues at Corinth was that no one had the slightest idea what this noise was supposed to convey. Verse 11, 'If I know not the meaning of the voice, I shall be unto him that speaketh a barbarian, and he that speaketh shall be a barbarian unto me.' It is perfectly clear what the apostle means.

The last use of the word 'mystery' in First Corinthians occurs in chapter 15, verses 51,52. 'Behold, I show you a mystery; We shall not all sleep, but we shall all be changed: In a moment, in the twinkling of an eye, at the last trump: for the trumpet shall sound, and the dead shall be raised incorruptible, and we shall be changed.'

This is the mystery of the resurrection of the dead. How can these things be? Inexplicable, beyond all known laws, outside rational explanation: in a word, a mystery. But none the less certain.

Here is a mystery in a mystery.

First, the dead shall be raised at the last trump: the power of God shall be put forth in a way unprecedented. Corruption shall put on incorruption, and mortal shall put on immortality. Dust shall be gathered from the ends of the earth, remains from the depths of the sea, elements from the four winds of heaven, and the dead shall be raised, soul to his body, incorruptible.

But yet another mystery. Next, in a moment, in the twinkling of an eye, the living saints shall be changed, their bodies shall be changed, from this vile body to the likeness of his glorious body. This shall be brought to pass in that last remnant of the *ecclesia* gathered in unity in the last day. These are the living that shall be changed.

But, in every saint, from the foundation of the world to the end of time, raised from the dead or changed in life, in that twinkling of an eye, the ancient saying shall be brought to pass: 'Death is swallowed up in victory. O death, where is thy sting? O grave, where is thy victory?' Death is swallowed up in victory, in that day of resurrection, in a mystery. Thanks be unto God which giveth us the victory through our Lord Jesus Christ.

The epistle to the Ephesians, concerned to reveal the *ecclesia* according to the eternal purpose of God in Christ, yields the greatest number of references to 'mystery' out of any book in the entire new testament.

Already it is abundantly clear that 'revelation' and 'mystery' lie at the foundation and heart of the *ecclesia* of Christ.

It is equally clear that neither has the least place in even the outermost periphery of the professing 'churches' of our day, nor is there the least 'mystery' in the superficial drivel that passes for gospel in the modern profession of evangelicalism. Much less is there any place for 'revelation'.

Yet in the new testament Paul's gospel was 'not after man', for he neither received it of man, neither was he taught it, but by the revelation of Jesus Christ. As to the assembly, the *ecclesia*, this was itself a mystery, its fellowship was by the revelation of the mystery, and, indeed, its union with Christ was called a great mystery.

What fails to reveal this, cannot be of Christ's *ecclesia*, or, therefore, of his building. This omission in itself shows the glaring discrepancy between the ministry, the gospel, and the assembly of the new testament, and that into which the divisions of Christendom have fallen in the apostasy.

And apostasy is the word: it is a 'falling away from' the original. And worse: with the falling away, there has developed an attitude of not caring enough—individually and collectively—even to bother about it. However it is not to the latter-day falling, but to the original standing, that our attention is now directed.

Ephesians 1:9 gives the first occurrence of the word 'mystery' in this epistle. Further to 'the riches of his grace', the context continues: 'Wherein he hath abounded toward us in all wisdom and prudence;'—then verse 9—'Having made known unto us the mystery of his will, according to his good pleasure which he hath purposed in himself.'

How marvellous is God's assembly! It is the place—a mystery of divine union in itself—in which the Father discloses his secrets. It is where the Spirit, pervading the very atmosphere of the assembly with his holy presence, makes known heavenly mysteries in the midst of and to all the gathered saints!

Here he makes known the mystery of God's will. What privileges therefore belong to the true assembly, that God should make known to us the things which he has purposed in himself, so that the mystery is conveyed by one Spirit to the heart of the whole company.

Mark that the making known of this mystery is in the past tense: 'having made known'. The mystery was—and to the world in darkness, still is—What is God's will? But to the saints in light there is no mystery. God's will has been made known to them, as one, by the interior teaching of the Holy Ghost: 'having made known unto us the mystery of his will.'

What is God's will? About what? About time, eternity; this world, the next; heaven, earth; about man, men; the Jews, the nations; the creation, history; inbred sin, outworking sin; lust, vice; avarice, covetousness; wrath, war; authority, government; knowledge, enlightenment; suffering, death; inheritance, succession: Where, what, is the will of God?

At these questions the world stumbles off in darkness. But the saints walk on in light. Why? Because with them is the secret. God has 'made known unto us the mystery of his will.' He has made it known unto us, it is a mystery. For grace has abounded towards us in all wisdom and prudence, and we all know it: What a place is this assembly!

Bathed in heavenly light; quickened in divine life; filled with everlasting love; aglow with the coming glory: an habitation of God through the Spirit. What is his will? It is to bring to pass the destiny of the Christ.

In Ephesians 3:3 Paul informs the saints from whence he obtained his ministry. That is, verse 2, if ye have heard of the dispensation of the grace of God given to him, for the *ecclesia*. Thus he obtained it: 'How that by revelation he made known unto me the mystery.'

He was not taught his ministry by men: 'not by man', saith he. He did not receive 'a biblical education' as a scholar: 'neither was I taught it.' Then how had he such light, such perception in divine mysteries? 'How that by revelation he made known to me'. Mark that, *he* made known to me. Not men made known to me, not academics, not professors, not doctors: '*He* made known to me.'

But how did God make known this ministry? Was it by causing Paul to study, memorise, use his intellectual talents, improve his scriptural knowledge, read the Rabbinical commentaries, observe the tradition of the elders, study the ministerial library books? No, all this was *utterly disqualified.*

'By revelation', saith he. That was the way, that is the way, and that shall be the way, by which Christ's ministers are given their ministry. Paul received it by revelation. Received what by revelation? The ministry that calls sinners, perfects saints, edifies the body, brings in the assembly, and which Christ uses to build his *ecclesia.*

What is this ministry? What was made known to Paul? 'How that by revelation he made known unto me *the mystery.*' What mystery? The mystery of Christ.

This follows, Eph. 3:4. 'Whereby, when ye read, ye may understand my knowledge in the mystery of Christ.' This agrees with what the apostle calls, Rom. 16:25, 'My gospel, and the preaching of Jesus Christ, according to the revelation of the mystery which was kept secret since the world began.'

Just so, speaking of the mystery of Christ, Paul declares 'Which in other ages was not made known unto the sons of men, as it is now revealed unto his holy apostles and prophets by the Spirit; that the Gentiles should be fellowheirs, and of the same body, and partakers of his promise in Christ by the gospel', Eph. 3:5,6.

Here the mystery of Christ is seen to be in one body, of which he is the Head, and in which the members are the heirs of promise called out from among both the Jews and the Gentiles.

The revelation of this mystery—which was hidden from the foundation of the world—was to be opened by his holy apostles and prophets, with the Holy Ghost sent down from heaven, according to the commandment of the everlasting God.

It follows that this is a spiritual revelation, the vision of which was first given to the apostolic ministry. Being sent forth of God in the power of the Holy Ghost the revelation of this mystery was to be made known through the preaching of the gospel both to Jew and Gentile. 'For by one Spirit are we all baptized into one body, whether we be Jews or Gentiles, whether we be bond or free; and have been all made to drink into one Spirit.'

By this inward and spiritual baptism all the members of Christ are constituted as one body, united in one Spirit to one Head—which is Christ—so as to dwell in him, and he in them.

Contrary to the guileful deceit of an 'invisible body' schemed up as an excuse for perpetuated denominationalism by the 'evangelicals', however, this inward, spiritual, and invisible baptism does not, and cannot, nullify the truth that 'your *bodies* are the members of Christ', I Cor. 6:15. And if our 'bodies' are 'the members of Christ', it follows of necessity that in the assembly of such members of the body of Christ, the *ecclesia*, there must be an external, visible, corporeal unity corresponding to that which is internal, invisible, and spiritual.

Unless, like the fabled 'invisible man', the 'evangelicals', divided asunder in denominations and various Brethren sects, suppose that the members of Christ have invisible bodies? If not, given that our 'bodies are the members of Christ', then the body of Christ, however inward, spiritual, and mysterious, *must have a corresponding outward appearance and visible unity.*

This is called, the mystery of Christ, into which all the heirs of promise, justified by faith, are baptized of the Holy Ghost.

This is the *ecclesia*, and it is a great mystery, but—contrary to what is no more than the feeble excuse of disobedient evangelicalism—it is not an invisible one.

Ephesians 3:9 follows. Paul had been made a minister of the gospel, verse 7. He had not made himself a minister, pursuant to his ambitions, desires for a career, or thirst to occupy a 'pulpit', as they call it. Men had not made him a minister. Christ had made him a minister.

This 'being made a minister', therefore, was not something that had occurred to Paul as a result of his having attended the academic institutions set up by men for the purpose. In the new testament there were no academic institutions set up for the purpose! He who made Paul a minister was divine, not human. The work was spiritual, not academic. All was directly from heaven. There was nothing at all of man in this work.

Hence Paul's 'being made a minister' had nothing to do with the degrees and honours awarded to 'divinity' graduates further to studying some syllabus conforming to the requirements of the religious education board. Such inventions were of the world, of the flesh, being introduced long after the close of the new testament. Paul reckoned himself dead to the flesh. The world was crucified unto him, and he unto it. He was dead to all the honours and rewards of man. Then how had he become a minister? He had been *made* one. By whom? By Christ glorified, and Christ glorified alone.

But how had Christ done it? 'According to the gift of the grace of God given unto me by the effectual working of his power.' And by nothing else. And by no one else. The hand of man did not appear in this work.

It was by the effectual working of *his* power. Any other pretended qualification or approval of or for the ministry must be, by definition, both spurious and in contempt of Christ's authority. Actually, in the light of the word of God, such things are *beneath* contempt. Why? Because 'That which is highly esteemed among men is *abomination* in the sight of God.'

In accordance with those divine principles, upon which the whole ministry of the new testament stands throughout the age, the work of God, and the work of God alone, without the hand of man, had made Paul a minister.

Christ had called him from heaven. The Spirit had empowered him on earth. The grace of God had sent him abroad. The effectual working of Father, Son, and Holy Ghost was magnified in the preparation, sending and working of this minister of the gospel, Paul.

Why? Why was this? To what end was this grace given? 'Unto me'—verse 8—'who am less than the least of all saints, is this grace given'—that is, this grace given to become a minister—for this purpose: 'that I should preach among the Gentiles the unsearchable riches of Christ.'

'And to make all'—all saints, that is: the translators' interpolation in italics, 'all *men*', is not only patently incorrect, it is impossible—'And to make all *saints* see what is the fellowship of the mystery, which from the beginning of the world hath been hid in God, who created all things by Jesus Christ', verse 9.

Once again the unprecedented nature of the *ecclesia* appears: here is a new thing, absolutely new. No precedent exists for this unique revelation. How could it, since it had been 'hid in God'? Who can prize out what is hidden in God? And hidden in God 'from the foundation of the world'. Until that time when Jesus Christ, risen and ascended, sent forth his apostles.

'To the intent that now'—not in eternity: in time; now—'unto the principalities and powers in heavenly places might be known by the *ecclesia* the manifold wisdom of God, according to the eternal purpose which he purposed in Christ Jesus our Lord.'

These things being proposed, how can the eternal purpose of God in Christ Jesus our Lord be magnified by the squabbling divisions, the complacent sects, the apathetic denominations, all content with the apostasy, all so indifferent to their perpetuation of this disintegration?

How can these divisions, I say, manifest such a revelation, move all heaven by this mystery, silence principalities and powers in the heavenlies through such divine unity, still even the hosts in the glory by the indwelling of Father, Son, and Holy Ghost, one God—one *ecclesia*—blessed for evermore? They cannot. Their very systems render it impossible.

But these things will happen, and must happen, when all saints are made to see what is the fellowship of the mystery. When, separated from the world by the gospel, the heirs of promise are drawn out from the sects, the denominations and the apostasy, by the preaching of Jesus Christ, who suffered without the gate. It will happen, I say, when all saints are united together in one assembly, 'My *ecclesia*'.

'The fellowship of the mystery.' What fellowship is this? It is the fellowship of the Spirit, and fellowship in the Spirit. It is that interior, experimental, and spiritual awareness of his divine Person and work, as altogether superior to our own personal measure and experience of it, or that of any one assembly. Then the fellowship is realised.

Yet it is hard labour to make all saints see it. But this is the labour of the ministry. 'To make all saints see what is the fellowship of the mystery.' This is to dwell as one assembly in God, Father, Son, and Holy Ghost. This is for God, Father, Son, and Holy Ghost, to dwell as one in that assembly, in one company, one body, one *ecclesia*.

This is the oneness that is to be experienced in the whole assembly, variously represented in the assemblies of the saints in every place. Thus wherever and whichever the assembly, there will be the common owning, experiencing and setting forth of the one body, the one *ecclesia*, in all the earth. It is the 'fellowship' of the mystery: the conscious experience of it. It is the immediate common consciousness in each of the assemblies, of what is true in the one assembly, of the indwelling love of God in one Spirit, one Lord, and one God and Father, inhabiting the one house of God. It is this fellowship that makes manifest the unity of all the assemblies as one assembly throughout the whole earth.

This is the fellowship prayed for by the Lord Jesus, John 17. Here Jesus 'lifted up his eyes to heaven'. For it is heavenly, this fellowship, it is a heavenly mystery. And he said, 'Father'. Because it stands in sonship, this fellowship, it is a communion unique to the 'adoption', chosen by the Father before all worlds, and given to the Son of his love as his own from out of the world, 'that he should give eternal life to as many as thou hast given him.'

It is not individual, this fellowship. Although all that are of it are called individually into the fellowship. It is 'the *men* which thou gavest me out of the world: thine they were, and thou gavest them me.'

'The men which thou gavest me out of the world' are the object of Christ's love, regarded as a company. 'I pray for *them*', plural. For there are two companies, and two only. 'I pray not for the world.'

The world has its own company, and its own dark and confused religion, a confounding together of law and gospel, works and faith, idolatry and worship. The world has its own 'churches' as it calls them, but these are neither the objects of Christ's prayers, nor of his love.

The elect are the object of his love, and the subject of his prayers, that by the ministry they might come into the fellowship of the mystery. 'I pray for them: I pray not for the world, but for them which thou hast given me.' That is, given to him from out of the world, to be separate from it, world without end.

As to the world, as soon as this company is manifested, and the fellowship of the mystery is made known in them, the world hates and detests them: how much more the ministry used by Christ to fulfil the will of God? 'I have given them thy word; and the world hath hated them, because they are not of the world, even as I am not of the world.' And again, 'They are not of the world, even as I am not of the world.'

This being so, such a people should be gathered to him, and by him, and in him, by his sending from heaven 'some, apostles; and some, prophets; and some, evangelists; and some, pastors and teachers.' What for? 'For the perfecting of the saints, for the work of the ministry, for the edifying of the body of Christ: till we all come in the unity of the faith, and of the knowledge of the Son of God, unto a perfect man, unto the measure of the stature of the fulness of Christ.'

This coming unto the measure of the stature of the fulness of Christ is what the ministry of the gospel—sent from Christ, empowered by the Holy Ghost—this, I say, is what the ministry of the gospel achieves 'according to my gospel, and the preaching of Jesus Christ, according to the revelation of the mystery.' This is that for which Jesus prayed: 'Sanctify them' —mark that, *them*; it is *together*; it is *corporate*; it is together in one—'Sanctify them through thy truth: thy word is truth.'

This sanctifying work is wrought through the gospel, 'my gospel', through the gospel and through the preaching of Jesus Christ according to the revelation of the mystery. Thus this union together in the fellowship of the mystery is accomplished: 'Sanctify them through thy truth: thy word is truth.'

The fellowship of the mystery is a fellowship that is in union with the Father and the Son, yes, but it is in union with all saints too. So-called 'mysticism' is so selfish; so is modern evangelicalism: because both make everything of the individual. Why? Because the appeal is to self. Self-interest is the basis. That is why the worldly admire and attend them, and the world hears them.

But once see the glory of Christ, the greatness of his Person, and nothing can answer to such glorious greatness, nothing less can be commensurate, than all the saints together in one. Not at all for their personal indwelling; nor primarily for their locally united indwelling; but for his indwelling in one universal unity: 'an habitation of God through the Spirit.'

'I in them'—*them*: all of them; in all the earth; visibly united —'and thou in me, that *they* may be made perfect in one.'

One body, many members, for the indwelling life of one Head, in all saints throughout the whole earth. Here is seen a visible unity setting forth in each assembly everywhere the one assembly in Christ, and the one assembly of Christ. 'That the world may know that thou hast sent me, and hast loved them, as thou hast loved me.'

This is the fellowship of the mystery. Nothing less. This was that on account of which the Spirit was so urgent in Paul to 'make *all* saints see'. Precisely this.

The union of Christ and the *ecclesia*, as that of the *ecclesia* and Christ, is not only a mystery: it is a great mystery. 'This is a great mystery: but I speak concerning Christ and the *ecclesia*', Eph. 5:32. 'For we are members of his body, of his flesh, and of his bones', verse 30. How can this be?

It cannot be save in a mystery, a great mystery, the revelation of which belongs to those of full maturity. For we have many things to utter of Christ, but we are not able, because ye are yet babes, having need of milk, and not strong meat.

'For every one that useth milk is unskilful in the word of righteousness: for he is a babe.' That is individual. 'But strong meat belongeth unto them'—mark that, *them*: that is corporate—'that are of full age, even those'—plural—'who by reason of use'—in the assembly—'have their senses exercised to discern both good and evil.'

'For this cause shall a man leave his father and mother, and shall be joined unto his wife, and they two shall be one flesh. This is a great mystery: but I speak concerning Christ and the assembly', Eph. 5:31,32. That is, Paul speaks these words, 'They two shall be one flesh', in order to explain that we are members of Christ's body, of his flesh and of his bones. This explanatory text concerning a man and his wife, quoted by the apostle, was first uttered by Adam in the spirit of prophecy at the beginning of the world, when the LORD God caused a deep sleep to fall upon Adam, and he slept.

'And he took one of his ribs, and closed up the flesh instead thereof. And the rib, which the LORD God had taken from man, made he a woman, and brought her unto the man. And Adam said, This is now bone of my bones, and flesh of my flesh: she shall be called Woman, because she was taken out of Man. Therefore shall a man leave his father and his mother, and shall cleave unto his wife: and they shall be one flesh', Genesis 2:21-24.

But what father and mother did Adam possess, that he should speak of leaving them? Or what fathers and mothers, or children born, were there in the world when he spoke? None at all.

Evidently Adam said this not of himself, nor for his own sake, but in the spirit of prophecy he spoke of Christ, and altogether for our sakes, upon whom the ends of the world are come. But did Adam speak of such things, in the first days of creation?

Yes, verily, for this secret was hid 'from the foundation of the world'. As an undisclosed secret, it was spoken of 'by the scriptures of the prophets' from the very beginning. And so Paul teaches: 'I speak concerning Christ and the *ecclesia*'. Then so did Adam.

But I repeat: What father and mother did Adam possess, that he should propose leaving them? I answer: He had none; he could not leave what he did not have. Therefore he spoke of Christ and the assembly, as Paul teaches.

But if he spoke of Christ, how then could father and mother be predicated of Christ?

It is true that the Son was sent by the Father: that is, into manhood. Likewise it is true that he came from the Father: that is, from deity. But what of his 'mother'? Could this refer to his mother literally? If so, how did he 'leave' his mother literally? But we speak of mysteries, the interpretation is mystical. Then what if his 'mother', mystically, embraced all that was conceived in the work of God which, spanning time, brought to pass the coming and birth of the seed of the woman promised in a mystery from the very beginning?

Observe, therefore, as to his mother, mystically, 'there appeared a great wonder in heaven; a woman clothed with the sun, and the moon under her feet, and upon her head a crown of twelve stars: and she being with child cried, travailing in birth, and pained to be delivered.' Will any say that this was his mother literally? For it was certainly his mother mystically. Given the immeasurable greatness of Christ, literalities, though never so true, cannot once transcend the temporal and material to express the infinite and invisible. Mysteries must be employed if this is to be realised.

'And she brought forth a man child, who was to rule all nations with a rod of iron: and her child was caught up unto God, and to his throne', Rev. 12:1,2 and 5. Now, here is his 'mother', mystically, and this is his leaving her—'caught up'—in a mystery.

Without doubt, the man child described is Christ, whose destiny is to rule all nations with a rod of iron, Psalm 2:7,8 and 9. But that man child was born of a woman. And that woman is here portrayed in a mystery evidently significant of much more than Mary.

Though this figure, Rev. 12:1, cannot exclude Mary, his mother literally, the heavenly woman—'I saw a great wonder in *heaven*'—soars symbolically to embrace all the work of God from the very beginning, continued through Israel, the entire work that brought him forth. For this is that in the womb of which—in a mystery—he had lain since the first promise. Thence, Ps. 139:13-17, brought to birth, immediately he is caught up. That is leaving his mother. What for? According to Paul, to be joined in one to his heavenly bride.

Who then is the woman, Revelation 12:1, the spiritual mother, of whom Mary was the literal, the actual embodiment? Clearly more than Mary is intended; yet she must be included. But it is evident that Mary was not in heaven at Jesus' birth, though this mystical woman was. It is further evident that Jesus was not immediately caught up when Mary bare him, though the man child was. Then who is the heavenly 'mother' of Rev. 12:1?

Observe, Gal. 4:26, that 'Jerusalem above' is the 'mother of us all'. That is, of all the freeborn sons. If so, of the Son in whom is seen the whole 'adoption'. The Spirit of Christ travailed in Israel, who appeared as the sun, with Rachel as the moon, and the children of Israel as the twelve stars, Gen. 37:9,10. Now this woman, mystical Israel, was clothed with the sun, and the moon under her feet, and upon her head a crown of twelve stars. She, in the counsels of God, by the Spirit of Christ, in the spirit of prophecy, travailed in Israel to bring forth him 'of whom Moses, and all the prophets spake'. And, the fulness of time being come, 'When Zion travailed, she brought forth.' This is Jerusalem above.

Shall the child be caught up, shall he leave her, shall he say 'Woman, what have I to do with thee?' He shall, when he takes to him his heavenly bride. Israel, of whom Christ came, was on earth, though viewed in Rev. 12:1 according to the heavenly counsels of God as bringing forth the man child. But Christ ascended on high, 'Caught up to God, and to his throne', leaving Israel, but bringing in the bride. This is a great mystery, but 'I speak concerning Christ and the *ecclesia*.'

Ignorant brethren who profess everything, and know nothing, must contend, for that is their nature: I would not that they should be ignorant, neither wise in their own conceits. Let them tell us out of their accumulated premillennial traditions, If this be not the Spirit's meaning, What is?

Who is the father and mother of Adam that he should so speak?

And if he prophesied of Christ, and Paul says he did, How did Christ leave his 'father' and his 'mother'? when? who were they? where did he go? to do what? who was the 'wife' to whom he was to cleave? and with what result?

When they can answer these questions, from their charts and book-learned notions, then shall the Ethiopian have changed his skin, and the leopard expunged his spots.

Again, what is the significance, the interpretation, of the words, 'The LORD God caused a deep sleep to fall upon Adam'? What sleep? and why? Since out of this came forth the woman, what is the meaning?

This sleep is the same as that which fell upon Abram, which he experienced, when he would know how righteousness should be imputed without works. Whereby should he know this?

Standing all bloody between the sides of the slaughtered sacrifices, behold, 'a deep sleep fell upon Abram; and, lo, an horror of great darkness fell upon him.' 'And it came to pass, that, when the sun went down, and it was dark, behold a smoking furnace, and a burning lamp that passed between those pieces' (of the sacrifice), Gen. 15:12,17.

This deep sleep of Abram answers to the deep sleep which fell upon Adam, and foretells in a figure what should fall upon the Seed of Abraham, which is Christ, in the justification of his people through his vicarious death on their behalf.

When Christ had hung three hours upon the cross, having spoken forth certain of the seven utterances which must sound from Golgotha, the darkness fell, and silence prevailed. 'Now from the sixth hour there was darkness over all the land until the ninth hour.'

This was the fulfilling of the time prefigured by the words 'And the LORD God caused a deep sleep to fall upon Adam'. Likewise, 'A deep sleep fell upon Abram; and, lo, an horror of great darkness fell upon him.'

The fulfilment of this mystery, set forth in ancient times by the sleep of Adam and of Abram, was of incalculable significance. It was immeasurable, unfathomable in Christ. In the event, the depth of darkness into which he was plunged, and the unspeakable horror that came upon him, when 'the LORD laid upon him the iniquity of us all' and 'made him to be sin for us, who knew no sin', can never be conceived. Though it is to be believed.

Then passed the smoking furnace of the wrath of God against iniquity, and the burning lamp of divine righteousness against sin, 'between the pieces'. That is, through the very midst of the sacrifice. Burning wrath went into the very heart of the sacrifice, throughout the hours of darkness, searching, and consuming. Thus the sacrifice of Christ was fulfilled.

Within those hours was compressed the everlasting judgment and indignation of the Almighty, until divine righteousness had rolled over and discharged an eternal weight of vengeance against the iniquity of Zion. This fell upon her substitute. So God her Saviour brought in everlasting righteousness on her behalf.

'For Zion's sake I will not hold my peace'—against her substitute on the tree—'and for Jerusalem's sake I will not rest'—pouring out everlasting vengeance on the atoning sacrifice—'until the righteousness thereof go forth as brightness, and the salvation thereof as a lamp that burneth', Isa. 62:1.

Thus Christ, the promised Seed, finished the transgression, made an end of sins, made reconciliation for iniquity, and brought in everlasting righteousness. 'For their sakes I sanctify myself', that is, to the death of the cross, 'that they also might be sanctified through the truth', that is, the truth of his atoning death, Jn. 17:19. For Jesus suffered without the gate, 'that he might sanctify the people with his own blood', Heb. 13:12. Yes, and so it was that, in the deep darkness, from that dreadful sleep of horror, the bride was taken out of his side, for, 'both he that sanctifieth and they who are sanctified are all of one.'

Both he that sanctifieth and they who are sanctified are all of one. All of one? Then there, at Golgotha, all that they were, was made his, so that they and he became one in the place of sin and death. And, from thence, all that he is, became theirs, so that he and they were made one in the place of righteousness and life.

All that stood against them, became his—as, 'all of one', he became identified with them—and all was taken away. Likewise all that stood for him, became theirs—as, 'all of one', they became identified with him—and all was freely bestowed. Even to 'bone of his bones, and flesh of his flesh', assured in the likeness of his glorious body at the resurrection from the dead.

His people, as one body, were seen by the divine counsels as in his side from eternity, before the heavens existed or the earth was brought forth. 'According as he hath chosen us in him before the foundation of the world.'

Indeed the saints were seen in Christ an eternity before Adam was created from dust in time. Seen from everlasting, 'according to the promise of life given us in Christ Jesus', before the earth was formed, or the mountains were brought forth. Here was a people determined from the ancient settlements of eternity 'According to his own purpose and grace, which was given us in Christ Jesus before the world was.'

The first man Adam, a living soul, was the first man created. But the second man Christ, the life-giving spirit—though second to appear—was the first chosen, even from eternity, upon whose hand was bound the scarlet thread of an everlasting election. For he is before all things, and by him all things consist. And he is the Head of the body, the assembly, who is the beginning, the firstborn from the dead; that in all things he might have the pre-eminence. He is the first begotten from the dead, Head and members in a mystery, the new man, which after God is created in righteousness and true holiness.

As Eve was in Adam before she was yet formed, only thereafter to be taken from the flesh and bone out of his side, likewise the bride, the Lamb's wife, was in Christ in divine purpose from eternity. Thereafter, in time, out of the 'deep sleep' of the death of the cross, she was taken out of his side, to be formed by the sending forth of the Spirit of Christ from the ascension.

His bone, her bone; his flesh, her flesh: 'bone of his bones, and flesh of his flesh.' His life, her life; his Spirit, her spirit: 'he that is joined unto the Lord is one spirit.' Taken out of his side: 'forthwith—from his side—came there out blood and water.' So came forth the bride of Christ, redeemed by blood, washed in water, one spirit with the Lord, according to the purpose of him who worketh all things after the counsel of his own will.

Seen in divine counsel from eternity. Redeemed by blood at the cross. United in reality from the glory. Taken out of his side in time. An help meet for him: 'This is now bone of my bones, and flesh of my flesh.' 'For we are members of his body, of his flesh, and of his bones.'

And so it shall be made manifest in glory at the resurrection. And so it should be made manifest now in the *ecclesia*. 'This is a great mystery: but I speak concerning Christ and the *ecclesia*.'

The word 'mystery' appears for the last time in this epistle in the final chapter, Eph. 6:18,19.

'Praying always with all prayer and supplication in the Spirit, and watching thereunto with all perseverance and supplication for all saints; and for me, that utterance may be given unto me, that I may open my mouth boldly, to make known the mystery of the gospel.'

Here the mystery is that of the gospel. Then the gospel reveals mysteries, and brings to the mystery, itself being a mystery. A mystery, for it is attended by the power of the Holy Ghost. A mystery, for a heavenly ministry is sent to preach it. A mystery, for the revelation of the Father from heaven accompanies it. A mystery for it declares the mystery of Christ.

These things being so, let the reader carefully consider what, if anything, answers to such a description today? And ponder likewise how much has been lost, not only in terms of doctrine and power, but in terms of revelation and mystery?

Given the lack of separation from the world; the failure to face the issues of division and denominationalism; the cult of individualism at the expense of the gathering of the assembly; the compromise of 'evangelism' to accommodate every form of opportunism; the substitution of sentiment for doctrine on the one hand, and of historical 'theology' for the gospel on the other; the setting up and perpetuating of a system of hired employees in direct defiance of the ministry of the new testament—not to mention the fashionable departure from the Greek text and English version owned and used by the Holy Ghost for centuries past—I say, given these things, is it any wonder that there is no *mystery* in the modern perversion of the gospel?

But *the* gospel is that gospel which was from the beginning, the only gospel, the gospel of our salvation, the gospel that brings to the mystery, and brings in the mystery, and is itself a mystery. 'My' gospel. This ever was called, and ever shall be called, the *mystery* of the gospel.

In the epistle to the Colossians the word 'mystery' appears four times. And since the gospel is a mystery, and the assembly is a mystery, and the Father reveals the mystery, and by the revelation of the mystery Christ builds up his *ecclesia*, due importance must be given to these references if we are to understand the nature of the *ecclesia*.

The first two occurrences of 'mystery' in Colossians run together in the twenty-fifth and twenty-sixth verses of the first chapter. The context of these verses takes in the whole of Colossians 1:24-29.

Paul, made a minister of the gospel, writes of himself, 'Who now rejoice in my sufferings for you, and fill up that which is behind of the afflictions of Christ in my flesh for his body's sake, which is the *ecclesia*: whereof I am made a minister, according to the dispensation of God which is given to me for you, to fulfil the word of God; even the mystery which hath been hid from ages and from generations, but now is made manifest to his saints: to whom God would make known what is the riches of the glory of this mystery among the Gentiles; which is Christ in you, the hope of glory: whom we preach, warning every man, and teaching every man in all wisdom; that we may present every man perfect in Christ Jesus: whereunto I also labour, striving according to his working, which worketh in me mightily.'

Here, the fulfilling of the word of God appears as Paul's preaching of the gospel, which he describes in turn as the preaching of the mystery, the preaching of Christ within, and the hope of glory.

Evidently therefore the apostolic preaching of the word, ministered in the Holy Ghost, received by revelation, brought the saints into the fellowship of the mystery. Christ was revealed in them, not simply in terms of individuals, but as a company in unity.

What they received as individuals was for themselves; but what they were as a company was for Christ.

The pronoun in verse 27 is plural, not singular. It is not 'Christ in *thee*' but 'Christ in *you*'. It is Christ in *the assembly*. It is *his* assembly: not *theirs*. He is the individual, not them; they are the company for his individuality.

And not only so: such is the greatness and glory of Christ that nothing less than *the* assembly, the *whole* assembly, adequately reflects his glorious Being. That to which *each* assembly answers, is that glorious whole, in turn a reflection of the bride, the Lamb's wife, in the day of her espousals.

It is not simply a question of the unity of all the saints, of the body, at any one given place, as if that were an end in itself. The truth is that this but reflects the unity of the whole assembly, the entire *ecclesia*, all saints in every company, the sum of the companies in unity. Thus the one body in its entirety answers to the indwelling of the one Person of the Holy Ghost—in turn answering to the Person of Christ—throughout the whole earth.

The immediate expression of this unity is that which the saints experience in any given locality, gathered together in the unity of the one body in that place. The ultimate expression—though made known to the heavenly vision of all saints—Christ himself sees from the heavenly glory, from his own place on high. And, at rest in that unity, in his own Person he indwells the one body in its entirety, by one Spirit in his fulness: Christ in *you*, the hope of glory.

The mystery of his will was that this was predestined from eternity, but was kept secret from the foundation of the world, from ages and generations, but now by the apostle, was made known. The heavenly mystery has been revealed in one body.

Called by the gospel, as pilgrims and strangers on the earth, abiding afflictions and persecutions, the saints, being justified by faith, redeemed by grace, have received the 'adoption'. Christ is formed in the whole assembly, the entire body, as united with all the members in one indwelling Spirit.

This unity is not that of some saints seen in a given locality by us from below, but of all saints seen throughout the earth by him from above. All saints: not simply those saints seen and known to oneself where one assembles. All saints seen and known by Christ from where he reigns in heavenly glory.

The Head indwells nothing less than the whole body by one Spirit. This is the indwelling which spiritually constitutes the visible unity of that one assembly in all the earth. This remains to be recovered and realised in our day. So does the gospel which brings it in. So does the ministry sent to fulfil this work.

Thus it is not love only to the saints at Ephesus, if one dwelt at Ephesus; or to those at Colosse, if one met in that assembly: it is one body, loved for Christ, his sake, in all saints *everywhere*. Paul's thanksgiving at Ephesus was because of their 'faith in the Lord Jesus, and love to *all* the saints', Eph. 1:15. And at Colosse he rejoiced, because he had heard 'of your faith in Christ Jesus, and the love which ye have to *all* the saints', Col. 1:4.

They had received the revelation of the mystery. Not only far above their individual blessing; but even further above the blessing of that visible number locally assembled. This was not what was for *them*, it was what was for *him*. One body for *Christ*. One body *for* Christ, and one *body* for Christ: '*my* assembly'.

That was what was destined for glory, which now showed forth his glory in one body: 'Christ in *you*, the hope of glory.'

There are certain emphases that stand out in this passage. If repetition appears, it is because matters dealt with elsewhere are taken up here also. Nevertheless the passages in Colossians must be considered equally in due order to obtain the proper proportion and balance of the truth throughout all the epistles.

The first emphasis is Paul's ministry. Here principles proper to all ministry—sent from Christ on high—are exemplified. He speaks, verse 23, of 'the faith' and 'the gospel', adding, 'whereof I Paul am made a minister'. This is repeated, verse 25, 'Whereof I am made a minister'.

He did not make himself a minister; others did not make him a minister. Nor did the 'church', so-called, or some denominated division of it, make him a minister. Christ made him a minister—first and last—by divine exterior providences, and by supernatural interior teachings; by long painful disciplines, and by intense living experiences.

Christ called him; Christ taught him; Christ prepared him; Christ gifted him; Christ empowered him; and Christ sent him. And where was the hand of man in that? Conversely, where is not the hand of man in what is called 'the ministry' today?

The second emphasis to which attention should be drawn in this passage is Paul's afflictions. Such afflictions are common to the ministry in all ages. Not of Paul only, but of each one whom he sends, Christ says, 'I will show him what great things he must suffer for my name's sake'.

Of course, every child of God must learn suffering from the hand of God. 'If ye endure chastening, God dealeth with you as sons; for what son is he whom the father chasteneth not?'

But Christ's ministers are made to suffer more than they all, that such might be able to minister consolation and comfort to every scourged and chastened son. 'I sat where they sat.' Hence Paul says of himself, 'Who now rejoice in my sufferings for you, and fill up that which is behind of the afflictions of Christ in my flesh for his body's sake, which is the assembly.' Afflictions and sufferings. 'Bonds and imprisonments await me.'

How much more so now. Christ's ministers *cannot* go the way of the world, the denominations, of the traditions of man. That is, they cannot go into a sectarian 'ministry', false in principle, and fallen in exercise. They cannot. Though were they to do so, this would be something that the world would be prepared to tolerate, if not downright approve. But those sent from Christ find this intolerable; they will neither approve of, nor enter into the divisions of fallen denominationalism. What a price, what sufferings, what afflictions, the consequent pathway brings!

Christ's ministers cannot contract for hire, much less to a mere segment of a fragmented 'church'. They will not confine themselves to a mere sectarian building—for that is what men call the 'church': a building—filled with unbelievers, a mixed multitude, and a few cowed saints.

The body of Christ is the vision of his called and sent ministers. The *ecclesia* is their object. To them the mystery has been revealed. And—despite the isolation from denominational, independent, and organised apostasy—reviled, jeered, ostracised, slandered, libelled, counted as the offscouring of the earth, they will not be disobedient to the heavenly vision.

Their life, their labour, is all for the body, for the *ecclesia*. Nothing less. This is to 'fill up the afflictions of Christ, for his body's sake', with a witness.

The third emphasis is upon Paul's doctrine. That is, the content of his ministry. Paul ministered 'the faith', verse 23. Not the law, not works. All was of faith, and all by faith. The content of his ministry was nothing but the faith of Jesus Christ, the faith of the Son of God, and the faith of God's elect.

Paul ministered 'the gospel', verse 23. That is, the doctrine of the gospel in its sum. Every truth in balance and proportion to the whole: *the* truth. Every doctrine radiating from Christ, his Person and his work, all fitly framed together to constitute the doctrine of Christ. 'The gospel'.

By definition this was not the philosophical arrangement of some so-called systematic theology. That is, the forcing of biblical truths into a philosophical framework, foreign to the mind of the Spirit of truth. There was no such thing in the new testament.* Nor was it 'reformed' doctrine, a mixture of law and gospel; tradition and text; Moses and Christ; rationalism and nationalism, a mixture which, for all that may have been of worth, obscured the pure faith and the heavenly vision of the *ecclesia* as it was in the beginning. Whatever may have been of value in such a system, and from such a period of history, that value stood only in the measure of its faithfulness against the corruptions of popery. But, purged and purified from all tradition, the Holy Ghost would lead the saints to what was in the beginning, to the gospel in its entirety, to the recovery of the body of Christ.

Paul was made, and made by the Son of God—verse 26—a minister of the *ecclesia*. The 'agreement to differ' of denominationalism, the delusive myopia of evangelicalism, the uneasy truce of Christendom, knows *nothing* of this. But Paul knew of it! Separate from the world, dead to the flesh, crucified to the pride of life, his ministry was from heaven, and was heavenly. He was a minister of *the* assembly. He would never have debased his ministry to serve some broken fragment of the apostasy that was to come. He would have devoted himself to the recovery of what that assembly, the one body, had been at the beginning. He would never have been disobedient to the heavenly vision in order to accommodate ecclesiastical corruption to his own advantage.

Paul consistently and selflessly ministered 'the mystery' verses 26,27, utterly apart from man, or from the mind of the flesh imposing itself upon divine things, or from the corruption this brought to pass in consequence. By faith he countered that—and all other—corruption, wherever it appeared.

This is another emphasis. Such a ministry of the gospel, of the faith, of the mystery, Paul's ministry, therefore, by the

*Read 'Foundations Uncovered', The Publishing Trust. See advertising pages.

power of God, brought in and maintained the divine, spiritual, heavenly mystery, and did so by revelation. By this ministry God called the saints out of all nations, separating them for the inheritance of the world to come, being predestinated to everlasting glory.

Observe therefore the words, verse 23, 'Whereof I Paul am made a minister'. A minister of what? Of the gospel. Note again the repetition of these words, verse 25, 'Whereof I am made a minister'. Now, in the second case, Paul's being made a minister answers to verse 24, 'his body's sake, which is the *ecclesia*'. Paul here refers to himself as a minister of the body of Christ, of Christ's assembly.

It is the same ministry, the same minister. Observe, however, that this ministry extends from the gospel to the body of Christ, the assembly. Why? *Because that is what the gospel inevitably brings in when it is rightly preached.* Hence Paul is a minister of the gospel, and, by definition, Paul is also a minister of the body, the *ecclesia*. The same ministry encompassed both, and accomplishes both.

It must accomplish both. Because those who are gathered as saints in Christ, and to him by the preaching of the gospel, are gathered by the revelation of the mystery into the *ecclesia*, just as they are baptized by one Spirit into one body. If that is not the effect then the man is not sent, and, it is not the gospel.

Where the man is sent, and it is the gospel, first sinners will be saved and saints perfected; next, the body of Christ will be manifested and the *ecclesia* built up under that one and the same ministry. When Paul speaks of himself in the same breath as a minister of the gospel and as a minister of the body, equating both with one ministry, it is futile to argue that the gospel can do anything less than bring in the body of Christ, the assembly. It is equally pointless to argue that such a gospel can be separated from the body of Christ, the assembly.

But this is exactly what has been done by and in modern evangelicalism. It is done on the one hand by holding the preaching of the gospel to be consistent with a denominational—or an independent—position. And it is done on the other hand by an 'evangelism'—so-called—which, whilst having no responsibility to any one denomination nevertheless submits to and craves the favour of all. This, on both hands, totally ignores the unity of the *ecclesia* of Christ, the one body, which still remains to be gathered.

But if Paul's gospel, *the* gospel, the apostolic gospel, the gospel of our Lord Jesus Christ, inevitably led to the one body of Christ, the one assembly—so that both are encompassed in one ministry—*what they call the gospel today cannot be the gospel as it was in the beginning.* At the very least, it must be a truncated version. If not, where is the one body, the visible and singular unity of Christ's gathered assembly?

The gospel which was preached in the beginning *inevitably* led to the one body, Christ's *ecclesia.* Hence that *ecclesia* was as much in the beginning as was the gospel. That gospel, the apostolic gospel, *cannot* lead to denominationalism, nor can it lead to independency. It *can* only lead to 'all saints' being united in 'one body', with none other in that body, no saints outside of that body, and no other bodies in existence.

This is that visible unity, separate from the world. Nothing less than this one body, filled with the Holy Ghost, can bring to pass the saying, 'that the world may know that thou hast sent me'.

Hence it follows with inexorable certainty that if the gospel which was in the beginning were to be preached again in its original purity and fulness, with the Holy Ghost sent down from heaven, in a denomination, or in independency, then its effect would be to contradict that denomination or that independency. It would be to challenge the entire basis upon which such congregations are gathered.

If such preaching were to be continued, one of two things must happen.

Either the entire number will repent of division from the unity of the body, a division leading to the formation of that particular denomination or independency, renouncing it thoroughly, returning to the unity of the one body by faith and in practice. Or else both the minister sent by Christ, and those who receive that ministry, will be cast out by the majority. In such a case both will be cast out into the unity of the one body. And cast out by sectarianism, however that may be the greater numerically.

If the denominations and independents claim to preach the gospel, but what they preach in fact proves to be consistent with the peace, amity and continuance of their system, *their claim must be false.* The gospel, as it was in the beginning, cannot subsist with what it could never have originated or formed. What has been produced and formed contradicts the gospel, and the gospel contradicts what has been produced and formed.

The only thing that the gospel does originate and form is of necessity the *one* body, and the *one* assembly. As it was in the beginning, is now, and ever shall be. The ministry of the gospel *must* result in the unity of Christ's body, that is, the gathering of all saints out of the world, and worldly religion, into the one *ecclesia* of Christ.

Whether men will hear or whether they will forbear, whether the minister be embraced or whether he be rejected, whether none receive this ministry or whether all receive it: no matter. 'Results' are irrelevant. 'What is that to thee?' Saith Christ, 'Follow thou me.' One gospel: one body; one ministry: one *ecclesia.* All for Christ, Christ for all, with

Christ all and in all. Otherwise, it is nothing but empty talk, it is consistent with nothing but hypocrisy, apathy, complacency, and indifference to the word of God.

The third use of the word 'mystery' in the epistle to the Colossians appears in the following context.

'For I would that ye knew what great conflict I have for you, and for them at Laodicea, and for as many as have not seen my face in the flesh; that their hearts might be comforted, being knit together in love, and unto all riches of the full assurance of understanding, to the acknowledgement of the mystery of God, and of the Father, and of Christ; in whom are hid all the treasures of wisdom and knowledge', Colossians 2:1-3.

Here the apostle labours, striving according to the working of God, which worked in him mightily, for the comfort and edification of the saints.

This however entailed great conflict against the powers of darkness, and of this present world. The apostle laboured in prayer, word, and doctrine, to perfect all saints—whether he had seen them, or they him, no matter, his labour was spriritual, heavenly, and, first, performed upon his knees.

Thus he strove to fulfil the work of the ministry, the perfecting of the saints, the edification of the body of Christ. First in each place, then as a whole, till all came in the unity of the faith, and of the knowledge of the Son of God, unto a perfect man, unto the measure of the stature of the fulness of Christ.

Constrained by the love of Christ the apostle laboured for those whom he had never met, for all were but one body. In the ministry for that body he strove: praying, labouring, writing, seeking to come to them, ever diligent, according to God's working, which wrought in him mightily.

He desired that in all their afflictions, persecutions, trials and temptations, their hearts would be comforted by the comfort wherewith he himself was comforted of God in all his tribulations. That as saints separated from the world they might be knit together in love.

What unity is this! Hearts knit together in love. As Christ had loved them, that they might love one another, being joined in heart each one in the fellowship of his love.

Finally, that these things might be unto all riches—not less! so abundant: all, all, riches—of the full—not less! so bounteous, so overflowing—the full assurance of understanding. Not just the understanding; not simply the assurance of it. The full assurance of it. Nothing floating in the head, or garnered in the intellect, no mere instructed judgment. Neither half-hearted nor transient assurance. This Spirit-taught work was infinitely deeper: it was 'the full assurance of understanding'.

Of understanding what? All the gospel; all the proclamation of Jesus Christ; all the revelation of the mystery.

This was to be taught in the power of the Spirit outwardly by the holy apostle, whilst they were led inwardly in light, life and love by the interior work of God, in Father, Son, and Holy Ghost. What assurance, what establishment, such divine instruction affords: 'the full assurance of understanding.'

This in turn led to the acknowledgement of the mystery of God, and of the Father, and of Christ.

First, the mystery of God. This mystery is that which could not be penetrated save by revelation.

There must be an unveiling. It was the divine secret. Then, only the deity could open it. This mystery had been kept secret since the world began, but now was made manifest, and by the scriptures of the prophets, according to the commandment of the everlasting God, made known to all nations for the obedience of faith.

Experiencing, believing, they were to acknowledge the revelation of this mystery, the disclosure of the secret.

In other ages it was not made known to the sons of men, as it was now revealed unto his holy apostles and prophets: it was a mystery kept from the beginning of the world, hid from ages and generations, but which was now to be made known.

Whereunto Paul was sent to them, and laboured for them, and wrote to them. Hence his earnest desire that they might acknowledge this mystery, hidden in God heretofore, but now preached unto them by the commandment of the everlasting God, who would send forth his Spirit to reveal the same within their hearts.

The saints were to acknowledge this mystery of God, hidden from the foundation of the world, and acknowledge it according to all riches of the full assurance of understanding. How could they understand and acknowledge such a mystery? Because the word of truth had come unto them, and, by Paul, the gospel of Christ had been fully preached.

They were therefore to acknowledge the mystery of his will, for the light of the glorious gospel had shined unto them. Their eyes had been opened, the veil had been taken from their hearts. They had been turned from darkness to light, from the power of Satan unto God, they had received forgiveness of sins, and inheritance among them which are sanctified by faith that is in Christ.

For when the mystery was preached, the revelation was made known. When the secret was disclosed, the glory was revealed. What glory, now to behold things hidden from the foundation of the world!

For the veil had been rent in twain from the top to the bottom. The sanctuary was opened. Christ, with his own blood, had entered into the tabernacle made without hands, made higher than the heavens, that which the Lord had pitched, and not man. Now, in the new testament, the deity was—at last—fully revealed. They acknowledged this? Then they acknowledged the mystery of God.

For he that had seen the Son, had seen the Father. Descended from on high, the promised Comforter had fulfilled the promised ministry. The mystery of God had been opened, and the revelation of that mystery was seen to be the very essence of the new testament, that which gave character to the *ecclesia*.

The revelation was of nothing less than the Father, the Son, and the Holy Ghost, three Persons, one God, blessed for evermore. And—grace beyond measure—of God, in Father, Son, and Holy Ghost, dwelling in the assembly of his people. Peter saw it: 'Thou art the Christ, the Son of the living God.' Flesh and blood had not revealed it, for the vision came from the Father in heaven, by the Holy Ghost on earth.

Thus the mystery of God was disclosed in the assembly by the Holy Ghost from heaven, through the revelation of the Son by the Father.

The mystery of the gospel was preached among all nations throughout the whole world by the commandment of the everlasting God. But the mystery of the revelation of the Son from the Father in heaven, was revealed by the Holy Ghost within the heart of every chosen vessel of mercy, gathered in the *ecclesia*, and none other.

This is what Paul calls, 'the mystery of God, and of the Father, and of Christ.' In fine, it is the revelation of the mystery of God in the gospel. This is the mystery of the Father, and of Christ, the revelation of which appears in the Spirit of sonship. The Father reveals the Christ, the Son of the living God; the Son reveals the Father; and the Spirit administers the revelation. This is to make known the mystery of God with a witness.

Colossians 4:3 is the last place in this epistle in which the word 'mystery' occurs.

In this context the apostle exhorts the saints to continue in prayer—not just to commence in it—and watch in the same —not simply to request and forget—with thanksgiving. That is, in a frame of faith, of thankfulness for such a God, such access, such an high priest over the house of God, such promises. Thanksgiving, perseverance, yes, but with trembling.

'Withal praying for us'—the ministers of the gospel—'that God would open unto us a door of utterance'—for the world and its religion will not—'to speak the mystery of Christ, for which I am also in bonds: that I may make it manifest, as I ought to speak.'

The mystery of Christ therefore was to be made manifest, and made manifest by the speech of the apostles.

Being sent of God, the apostle was to speak the mystery of Christ's everlasting deity, and of his eternal sonship. He was to declare the mystery of his taking human nature into union with his divine nature, in one Person, at the incarnation.

The apostle was to make manifest the unique and impeccable manhood of Christ; his birth; growth; life; the days of his flesh; his temptations and trials; besides the character and traits seen in his human nature. Withal he was to declare the mystery of his self-emptying, as touching the unapproachable, the glorious light of his everlasting deity in manhood.

The minister of the gospel must speak forth and open the mystery of Christ in his advent; his baptism; his transfiguration; his visitation; his crucifixion; his resurrection; and in his ascension. The apostle must describe his Galilean ministry; his ministry in The way; and his Jerusalem ministry. Paul, sent of God, must declare all Christ's words, discourses, deeds and signs. Moreover he must do so in such a manner as to open the spiritual meaning and the heavenly reality of these things, as disclosed respectively in the gospel according to Matthew, Mark, Luke, and John.

The minister of Christ must open the mystery of Christ's death in particular. He must show what occurred in the light, and what happened in the dark. And when, relative to both the light and the dark, Christ sounded forth his seven utterances, in what order, and with what hidden meaning.

The apostle must disclose the nature of the substitutionary atonement. What passed between the Father and the Son; and the Son and the Spirit; what was peculiar to his manhood; and what was distinctive of his deity.

The minister sent of God must be able to show the difference between sin and sins; bread and wine; flesh and blood; blood and water. He must distinguish between the way in which Christ was made sin, and how he bare sins. He must declare how the LORD laid on him the iniquity of us all, and what, precisely, is meant by 'all' in this place. He must show what was done for the elect in particular, and for the world in general, well instructed from divine teaching as to how to address each in turn.

The minister of the gospel must declare the distinction observed between the body and blood of Jesus in the sacrifice;

the shedding and the sprinkling of blood; how our old man, the body of sin, was crucified with him, and in him; why it was that blood was not shed until after death; and how all took place without the camp.

The apostolic ministry sent from above must make manifest the mystery of godliness as it concerns the three days in the tomb, up to and including the day of Christ's resurrection. Such a ministry must open, clarify, and expound in order how that God was manifest in the flesh; justified in the spirit; seen of angels; preached unto the Gentiles; believed on in the world; and received up into glory.

This ministry must expound to us how Christ was put to death in the flesh; quickened by the Spirit; and how in the Spirit he went and preached unto the spirits in prison, which sometime were disobedient, when once the longsuffering of God waited in the days of Noah.

By the power of God, by the anointing of the Holy One, by the teaching of the Holy Ghost, according to the word of God, this ministry must show to us how, when, and to what end, Christ descended into the lower parts of the earth, before he ascended up far above all heavens, that he might fill all things. Besides this, we are to be taught the significance of this descent and ascent to his present glorious ministry.

The minister sent of God to preach the gospel must reveal to us why on the day of resurrection Matthew records the angel of the Lord sitting on the stone outside the tomb, but Mark, Luke, and John do not. Why Mark describes a young man in a long white garment sitting on the right side inside the tomb, but Matthew, Luke, and John do not.

He must inform us to profit why Luke sets forth two men standing in shining garments inside the tomb, but Matthew, Mark, and John do not. And why John depicts two angels in white sitting, the one at the head, the other at the feet, where the body of Jesus had lain within the tomb, but Matthew, Mark, and Luke do not.

And let the minister of the gospel make clear from the gospel why no man—no apostle—saw any one of these visions. And why the women who did see them, with Mary Magdalene, were different in each case.

The good minister of Jesus Christ, nourished up in the words of faith and sound doctrine, must show us the significance of the forty days; of the ten days; of the fifty days; of those to whom the Lord appeared after he was risen from the dead; and of those to whom he did not appear.

Such a minister will instruct us as to the nature of Christ's risen body; that it was of flesh and bones; that he ate broiled fish and an honeycomb; that he could appear in another form; and that he could and did materialise in the midst of the disciples, the doors being locked; and that he could and did as easily disappear from their sight.

This ministry will inform us why the ascension of Christ is recorded in Mark, but not in Matthew; and why not in John, and yet in Luke.

Such a ministry will not forget to tell us why a cloud received Jesus out of their sight; and why Stephen saw the Son of man without a cloud, standing on the right hand of God.

Certainly the good minister of Jesus Christ will not neglect to enlarge upon the vision of Paul, revealing the Son of God —without a cloud—seated on his Father's throne above the heaven of heavens.

These are the mysteries of Christ, but not yet about his bringing in the righteousness of God by his faith at the cross, in order that such righteousness might be imputed unto all and upon all them that believe. Nor yet about his being a propitiatory, whilst making propitiation. Nothing so far about expiation; remission; ransom: neither yet about reconciliation; redemption; nor justification by faith.

Nor of the things in the heavens, the heavenlies themselves, into which Christ entered with his own blood, even the blood of better sacrifices than those once offered under the law on earth. Nor of his receiving and sending the Holy Ghost: of his Person, and work. Of his washing; regeneration; renewing: of the quickening; the baptism; the earnest: of his anointing; his filling, his sealing. All from Christ ascended, in the sending forth of the Holy Ghost from heaven. Nor is this yet to declare the power of Christ's ruling with the rod of his strength, sent forth out of Zion.

And what shall I more say?

For time would fail me to speak of Christ's heavenly work in sanctification; of his building his *ecclesia*; of his being the mediator of the new testament; of his having obtained eternal redemption for the people; of his being made Head over all things to the assembly, which is his body, the fulness of him which filleth all in all.

Nor is this yet to mention Christ's return; his inheritance; or his everlasting glory. Yet all these things are included in speaking of 'the mystery of Christ'.

Now, time may fail me to speak of these things here, but time will not fail every true minister of the gospel in the season appointed, upon whom it is encumbent 'to speak the mystery of Christ'.

But if those who claim to be ministers, pastors, evangelists, or any such like thing—whether they take false refuge in 'simplicity' or not—I say, if they cannot speak of such things, then it is evident that God never called them, Christ never prepared them, the Spirit never taught them, the Father never revealed his Son in them, and that they were never sent from heaven.

Had they been sent, they would have been able to do what every able minister of the new testament, every minister of the gospel, every steward of the mysteries of God, can do, and must do, that is, 'speak the mystery of Christ'.

II Thessalonians is the next epistle in which the Greek word *mustērion*, 'mystery', appears, though in this case the word is not used of God, neither of the gospel, nor yet of Christ. This place points to another kind of mystery altogether.

In II Thess. 2:3-6 appears the man of sin, the son of perdition, the latter title being the name given by Jesus to Judas, one of the twelve, who apostatized at the last. This is the character who will exalt himself above all that is called God, or that is worshipped, sitting in the temple of God, and showing himself that he is God.

But whoever could be deceived by such outrageous presumption? Everyone except the very elect. But surely such a thing must be too obvious to deceive anyone? No, for a mystery shrouds the reality, and that mystery deceives everyone except the very elect.

For—mark well—this is the will of man asserting itself in place of the will of God, whilst retaining the name of all the things by which the will of God is expressed. Only it is not the will of God commanding his own things. It is the will of man commanding the outward appearance of them.

In its very essence this is called 'Arminianism', and it is a mystery which—in its limited or curtailed form—has deceived everyone. That is, again, except the very elect. This did not commence with Arminius. It commenced at the beginning, inasmuch as Paul, even in his own day, informs us that 'the mystery of iniquity doth already work'. Here was the beginning of the will of the flesh at work in God's things. But it was restrained, and the man of sin, the false apostle, the son of perdition, was 'let' or 'prevented', from taking over the form of everything that was godly.

It is not that the form of godliness changes—not at first—but that through it there is the expression of the will of man, carrying mankind in approval whilst denying the prerogative, the power and the presence of God in his own things.

Yet all this, deceitful enough heretofore, will be as nothing compared to that which will come to pass when once the hindrance has been removed. Then, although the hidden powers of darkness that lay behind the restrained apostasy will be set free to work unhindered, the deceitful subtlety will be far worse. All will be shrouded in even greater mystery. So that the world, and the vast profession of Christianity, will not believe that this apparent renewal of power is not of God.

That is what is now beginning to take place. The expression of the will of man in the things of God and of Christ, of the gospel and of the 'church', meets with universal approval from mankind. This will grow and will prevail. It will fill the earth. It will be called a revival, a restoration, a reformation, a renewal.

In fact this is the deception following the taking away of the restraints. The angels who restrained, and the boundaries imposed by the commandment of the only wise God, will be let go. And in these last days they have been let go. So that—for those with eyes to see—the final unfolding of things at last comes to light. That is what has begun to happen in the last few decades.

It is a 'mystery' of iniquity. What presents itself to the sight is certainly not 'iniquity'. On the contrary, what appears in

Christendom, what is seen in evangelicalism, the vision of the Christian profession, the concern for the old standards and traditions, all this is the very opposite of iniquity. It is a vision of 'hope' of 'renewal', and of 'reformation', as they suppose. That is where the mystery lies: not in the well hidden iniquity.

The mystery itself is that none of all mankind, none born of the flesh—however religious, moral, devout, evangelical, reformed, fundamental, scriptural—none without the revelation of the Son, no, not one can tell it, save the elect, save those born from above. They can tell it. By the Holy Ghost, the very elect alone can tell it. But only just, and only after great searching of heart, sore trials, and through much confusion. For all the world, and all the 'church', think it a blessing. It is clear to them it is not iniquity—they can see no iniquity whatsoever—to them it is obviously a blessing. For the iniquity is hidden behind the 'blessing': it is a *mystery* of iniquity.

From the context it is obvious that this mystery stands in the subtle usurpation of divine things and places. That is, the taking over by the will of man of the gospel; of evangelism; of the ministry; of the bible; and of the names of divine things and works. The very name of Christ, of the Holy Spirit, yea, of the name God, of the 'temple of God', will subtly, imperceptibly, be transferred from the divinity which the names actually describe, to that which the whole outward 'church' wishes they would describe.

This will come *after* a great apostasy, verse 3. Mark that: *after* the apostasy. After the reaction to that apostasy has passed, when the generations that first perceived it—and protested against it—have ceased. Then, a 'balance' of 'normality', that is, apathy, will ensue. Next, new generations will arise to whom this original apostasy, and the first reaction, will be but history. There will be no sense of shock. The 'norm' of the generation into which they have been born will obtain, and will be that to which they are naturally accustomed. Only after this—imperceptibly—will come the loosing, the revealing, the outworking, of the *mystery* of iniquity. Such a time has already begun. It has come. But far worse is to follow.

This mystery is one of immense and ancient subtlety, of long and well-laid preparation. It will not appear upon earth save as the last bright hope of mankind, the salvation of an abused and decaying world, the embodiment of all that is good, drawing universal approval. This will be accompanied by the exertion of vast and invisible power, of forces swaying the very soul of humanity, of profound expectation moving the nations, which, as one, will greet each new unfolding of the 'mystery of iniquity' with immense gratitude and thankfulness.

This power, that energy, and those spiritual forces will bend the spirit of races and peoples as the wind inclines the fields of standing corn. This is not merely of Satan, it *is* Satan. But in a mystery. To men, it is not merely of God. It *is* God. The world, the worldly 'church', all in the 'outer court', all will be deceived. Hence Jesus called Satan, 'the prince of this world'. And the apostle named him, 'the god of this world'. And so it will appear: through the taking over of the things left to posterity by the apostles and the early *ecclesia*.

Only the elect will be undeceived.

It is a taking over of the form, the letter, and of the structure of Christianity; a taking over of the mantle of the reformation, of evangelicalism; yes, and finding the power and the results overwhelmingly confirmatory. At the last, Satan will be permitted to use supernatural working—though hitherto prevented—to complete the illusion.

Because this mystery had begun to work, the apostle Paul wrote this epistle. Then, it was exposed. This work of exposure was granted with light and power to the holy apostles.

By the commandment of God through Jesus Christ to his angels, and by the prophetic word in the mouth of his ministers, the mystery was kept in bounds. And so matters would stand until 'he be taken out of the way'.

Then—though God will surely awaken his elect, and warn an ungrateful and resentful world rejoicing in every expression of its own will—the whole world shall wonder after the beast. Yet to the very end God by Jesus Christ shall send faithful ministers with the prophetic word. These shall be hated, ostracised, reviled, slandered, and persecuted as never before. Thus shall the mystery work on apace, deceiving the whole earth, till—as it was in the days of Noah—the very last day.

Then shall that Wicked be revealed, whom the Lord shall consume with the spirit of his mouth, and shall destroy with the brightness of his coming: even him, whose coming is after the working of Satan, with all power and signs and lying wonders.

This is that man of sin, that son of perdition—John 17:12; Acts 1:16,17 cf. II Thess. 2:3—even that 'apostle', sitting in the apostolate, whom nothing but the coming of Christ shall unseat and bring to the light of judgment.

What of the elect? Their safety stands in separation from the world, from worldliness, from worldly religion, and from the apostasy. Of necessity this separation must be the negative rule of the saints. Likewise their abiding in the unity of the body of Christ, returning to that which was in the beginning, attending 'my' gospel, the preaching of Jesus Christ, and the revelation of the mystery, must be their positive precept.

Withal, this shall prove hard labour enough to hold fast, seeing the power, signs, lying wonders, false workings, besides the discouragement from those who have departed to follow the world. Especially those that seemed to be pillars.

Many will be more than content with mere posturing. Especially that multitude which holds for religion head notions concerning past history, such as the Reformation, or Brethrenism. I say, it will be hard enough, elect or not. Hard enough to resist 'all deceivableness of unrighteousness'.

But those who fail to resist the mystery of iniquity to the end, shall certainly perish. For the word is 'all deceivableness of unrighteousness in them that perish'.

Why will they perish? 'Because they received not the love of the truth, that they might be saved.'

'And for this cause God shall send them strong delusion, that they should believe a lie: that they all might be damned who believed not the truth, but had pleasure in unrighteousness.'

Then shall no faith at all be found in the earth when Christ comes? Verily; however little, or in however few.

For, 'We are bound to give thanks to God alway for you, brethren beloved of the Lord, because God hath from the beginning chosen you to salvation through sanctification of the Spirit and belief of the truth: whereunto he called you by our gospel, to the obtaining of the glory of our Lord Jesus Christ.'

Next follow the two passages in the first epistle to Timothy.

First, I Tim. 3:9. 'Holding the mystery of the faith in a pure conscience.'

That is, the deacons, or rather, servants, of the assembly, among other things, are to 'hold' the mystery of the faith, and not to dissipate it. Moreover the place in which it must be held is the conscience. Which, observe, should be preserved in a state of purity.

This distinctiveness of character, going before any elevation to office, must mark deacons, or servants, to the degree that if such traits are not apparent in persons, they are not fit for the appointment. Then let this be the degree for which they study. And let that be the motive for their studying. If in purity of conscience they are to 'hold' the mystery of the faith, then the revelation of that mystery must first have been made manifest to them. Moreover, the mystery must have been revealed in them. Otherwise, they are no more 'deacons' than dustmen.

Further observe that it is 'the' faith that is stressed, not their faith. Their faith may hold it, but what is held in their pure conscience is 'the' faith.

This refers to what is to be believed, and all that is to be believed, in the gospel, which is a mystery. It was hidden, but it is now made known by 'my' gospel, and the preaching of Jesus Christ, according to the revelation of the mystery. This is what is received in the inward man by the Holy Ghost from heaven, to be held and retained in purity of conscience.

Moreover 'the' faith is all faith: from the faith of Jesus Christ to the faith of God's elect. What is preached and what is held. From faith to faith. From which it is evident that this is nothing to do with the legal system, with the law itself, with works, with any forensic system of justification, or with the law as a 'rule of life', as they call it. Only that the faith wonderfully opens and enlarges the manner of our full and complete deliverance from the law through Jesus Christ our Lord and Saviour.

Next, I Tim. 3:16. 'And without controversy great is the mystery of godliness: God was manifest in the flesh, justified in the Spirit, seen of angels, preached unto the Gentiles, believed on in the world, received up into glory.'

Because of the—apparent—lack of sequence between any one statement and the next, this is a place which baffles the wise and prudent. But then these things, far from being revealed to the wise and prudent, are hidden from them. They are revealed to babes.

What things are revealed? Mysteries are revealed. It is the revelation 'of the mystery'. The 'mystery of godliness' is a mystery, by definition. Nothing but the revelation of this mystery can possibly bring in true godliness, acceptable in the sight of God.

The faith is not attained by intellectual processes, it has nothing to do with or say to religious education, it can never be the subject of a curriculum, it is not a discipline. *It is a mystery.* It is the *mystery* of the faith. Therefore it is impenetrable save by revelation. Nothing so much as this subdues the flesh in man, levels intellectual conceit, and stains the pride of all glory. Nothing other than revelation can bring in such deep humility, or such solemn reverence, acceptable as worship to God and the Father. In a word, nothing else can bring in 'godliness'.

Just as the 'mystery of godliness' was given by revelation, so it must be received by revelation, because it is a mystery in its very nature.

The mystery of godliness concerns the Son of God. It is the revelation of what happened to Christ in his deity—mark that; in his deity—from the incarnation to the ascension. Whenever and wherever this mystery is revealed, a holy awe, a heavenly stillness, a profound sense of the majesty of God, falls upon those to whom the mystery has been disclosed. This occurs under the ministry of the word, by the Holy Ghost from heaven. Both cause and effect are called, 'the mystery of godliness'.

This mystery comes to light when the preaching of Jesus Christ in his divinity sounds forth from those ministers sent of God in the power of the Holy Ghost from heaven. Then the Spirit mysteriously inworks piety. It is in this way that the mystery is revealed.

The mystery deepens in that the more objectively Christ's Person and work are set forth, the more subjectively the consequences appear in those brought to fear God, to tremble in his presence, and to bear the fruit of godliness. This mystery of godliness is made manifest in the saints united as one in the house of God, which is the assembly of the living God, the pillar and ground of the truth.

Lastly, the word 'mystery' occurs four times in the book of the Revelation of Jesus Christ.

The first occurrence is in Revelation 1:20. 'The mystery of the seven stars which thou sawest in my right hand, and the seven golden candlesticks. The seven stars are the angels of the seven assemblies: and the seven candlesticks which thou sawest are the seven assemblies.'

In the series of seven parallel visions given to John by revelation, the appearance of one like unto the Son of man, described in terms of seven features, precedes the first vision.

Being in the Spirit in the day of the Lord, John heard behind him a great voice, as of a trumpet, saying, 'I am Alpha and Omega, the first and the last. What thou seest, write in a book, and send it unto the seven assemblies which are in Asia; unto Ephesus, and unto Smyrna, and unto Pergamos, and unto Thyatira, and unto Sardis, and unto Philadelphia, and unto Laodicea.'

John turned to see the voice that spoke with him. What he saw was seven golden candlesticks. In the midst of the seven golden candlesticks stood one like unto the Son of man, clothed with a garment down to the foot, and girt about the paps with a golden girdle. The sevenfold description follows, mystically depicting his head and his hairs; his eyes; his feet; his voice; his right hand; his mouth; and his countenance.

Verse 20 shows first the mystery of the seven golden lampstands, then proceeds to that of the seven stars in the right hand of the 'one like unto the Son of man'. Here are two mysteries, each intimately connected with the *ecclesia* of Christ, as, of course, with Christ himself.

Seven—the numeral signifying perfection—is the sum of both the candlesticks and of the stars. Perfection is in the Lord's mind, and in his judgment. But, alas, the assemblies were short of it, save Smyrna and Philadelphia; nevertheless all alike are brought to and judged by the standard of the candlesticks of pure gold.

Perfectly, it was one candlestick with seven branches. Already, however, the vision was lost, the unity obscured, and all had come into individual trial. This appears in the sentence of judgment passed on each assembly against a respective candlestick. Judgment must begin at the house of God.

The garment of the one like unto the Son of man signifies judgment. Identical garments clothe the seven angels of judgment in chapter 15:6.

The mystery of the seven golden lampstands and of the seven stars is that of the righteous judgment of one whose eyes are as a flame of fire, passing sentence upon the already divided though—outwardly—locally united assemblies. The assemblies, even at this the very beginning, had left their first love. Little strength was left. But the Lord would judge, and did judge. With a view to the recovery of his own things.

The Lord judged by nothing less than a golden candlestick multiplied sevenfold. There was no other, no less, standard for divine judgment. And no less a criterion for the seven stars in his right hand. That standard, the angels must perceive, and by it, judge. Where there was gold, corresponding to the vision, there was approval. Where there was dross, I have somewhat against thee.'

The angels brought the judgment, for good or ill, and were held accountable, as if they themselves were the candlestick. That is judgment. For the seven angels are for judgment. But it is the Lord's judgment. Already dross was mixed with the gold. As to the revelation of the mystery, little appeared that was not confined to each limited and earthly sphere. No heavenly vision of one glorious *ecclesia* lighting with divine radiance each united assembly setting forth no less than the whole.

Nevertheless, whatever the lack of correspondence to the divine vision, there was still but one assembly in each place.

Yet not for that, but for what had been lost, the Lord judged, and judged by the angels. What, then, when in each place the assembly should fragment itself into divisions, denominations, schisms, one after another, till—each claiming to be the *ecclesia*! —there should be as many divided bodies as there are gods and idols in the world?

And what, when each of these splintered and irreconcilable divisions becomes more and more full of unbelievers than believers, until at last in most cases not one individual would be found who could account for any real and divine work of God upon his soul? What mystery is this?

And what judgment shall come forth, passing sentence against this standing denial—perpetuated by complacent apathy—of the nature and unity of the Godhead, in Father,

Son, and Holy Ghost, entrusted to the one *ecclesia* from the beginning?

Take notice, that a woe sounds from heaven, at the which the denominations, sects, and divisions should tremble. Whilst yet there is time, let the saints repent with a broken heart, and a contrite spirit, with mourning and weeping, coming out of what denies the existence of one God, to be brought by the Spirit under the headship of one Lord in one body.

Let all that name the name of the Lord hate the flesh with bitter self-condemnation, amazed with joy unspeakable and full of glory, that God, the living God, in a mystery of love, should restore the years that the locust and cankerworm have eaten, when all seemed irrevocably lost and under judgment.

This is the tempering of mercy with judgment with a witness, as it is the mystery of the seven golden candlesticks, and the seven stars in his right hand.

Revelation 10:7 follows: 'But in the days of the voice of the seventh angel, when he shall begin to sound, the mystery of God should be finished, as he hath declared to his servants the prophets.'

Again and again the seven angels are sent forth from the presence of the Lord, whether in relation to the seven golden candlesticks, the seven seals, the seven trumpets, the seven thunders, the seven voices, the seven judgments, or the seven vials of wrath.

Everything, but everything, in heaven and on earth, in the assembly and in the world, is brought to the righteous sentence of him to whom all judgment is committed. And every judgment is executed by the seven angels sent forth from his presence. When the seventh angel sounds the last trump, the mystery is finished. Time shall be no more. The last day, the day of judgment, shall have come to pass.

For the trumpet shall sound, and the dead shall be raised incorruptible.

'Behold, I show you a mystery; We shall not all sleep, but we shall all be changed, in a moment, in the twinkling of an eye, at the last trump: for the trumpet shall sound, and the dead shall be raised incorruptible, and we shall be changed.'

The prophets declared the mystery: 'Thou, Lord, in the beginning hast laid the foundation of the earth; and the heavens are the works of thine hands: they shall perish; but thou remainest; and they all shall wax old as doth a garment; and as a vesture shalt thou fold them up, and they shall be changed.'

'And the nations were angry, and thy wrath is come, and the time of the dead, that they should be judged, and that thou shouldest give reward unto thy servants the prophets, and to the saints, and them that fear thy name, small and great; and shouldest destroy them which destroy the earth.'

'And the temple of God was opened in heaven, and there was seen in his temple the ark of his testament: and there were lightnings, and voices, and thunderings, and an earthquake, and great hail.'

When these things come to pass, and they shall come to pass, then the mystery of God will be finished.

All conditions will be revealed; all states shall come to light. For in that day God will bring every work into judgment, with every secret thing, whether it be good, or whether it be evil.

He himself, the Lord God, will sit upon the throne. There will be no mystery, for all the books will be opened, every secret revealed, the heart of each one made naked and open, and the whole of humanity, from the first soul to the last, be exposed to the light of divine judgment. Indeed the mystery will be finished, for the dead, small and great, shall stand before God, to be judged every man according to his works, by the judgment of the everlasting God and of the Lord Jesus Christ.

'And death and hell were cast into the lake of fire. This is the second death. And whosoever was not found written in the book of life was cast into the lake of fire.' Here the mystery is finished of a truth.

The next passage, Revelation 17:5, must be taken together with the seventh verse, the last place to mention the word *mustērion*, 'mystery', in the new testament. Both places together show another kind of mystery than that of the mystery of God referred to in Rev. 10:7. In chapter 17 it is the mystery of iniquity. Yet it is part of the mystery of God that, in divine counsels, such mysterious working is permitted, and, indeed, used to increase the trials and afflictions of the saints.

Often the people of God are sorely perplexed and tried, in divers temptations and wonderings, thrown into dark places and gloomy confusion at the rise, force, spread and establishment of the mystery of iniquity. Often, they can barely make this out: and were it not for their afflictions, they could never make it out. Meanwhile, to their dismay, at the same time the mystery of the gospel, and of Christ, seems to languish and almost to perish from the earth.

Nevertheless God permits such perplexities, and uses them, that the saints should pass through the purging of fire. Without such soul-searching experiences, the people of God would never come to strong meat, neither would they learn to have their senses exercised to discern good and evil.

However, in that last day, that great day of the Lord, all mysteries shall be finished, whether of God, or of iniquity, whether of man's apostasy, or of Christ's *ecclesia*. All mysteries shall be finished, the day of wrath shall reveal it, and everything shall be made manifest according to divine judgment.

Revelation 17:5-7 reads: 'And upon her forehead'—that is of the visionary woman riding upon a scarlet coloured beast, which John saw when he was carried away in the spirit into the wilderness for the purpose—'was a name written, MYSTERY, BABYLON THE GREAT, THE MOTHER OF HARLOTS AND ABOMINATIONS OF THE EARTH.'

'And I saw the woman drunken with the blood of the saints, and with the blood of the martyrs of Jesus: and when I saw her, I wondered with great admiration. And the angel said unto me, Wherefore didst thou marvel? I will tell thee the mystery of the woman, and of the beast that carrieth her, which hath the seven heads and ten horns.'

Now, every letter-learned bible student, every correspondence course Christian, every traditional Brother, having perused a commentary or two, having consulted their hallowed 'authorities', in a moment, in the twinkling of an eye, can tell us all about the meaning which they have borrowed.

However, John the holy apostle, full of the Holy Ghost; unique in apostolic ministry; full in years; rich in spiritual experience; having seen the Lord and walked with him; having laid his head upon Jesus' breast; having followed the work of God from the very beginning; having been chosen to write many books of the new testament; John, I say, unlike these latter-day bible students—who only read of it—actually saw the vision. He was transported by the angel in the spirit for the purpose. Yet he confessed that he did not understand the meaning of that vision, without the divine openings given to him in the word of the Lord.

For John to understand such mysteries, necessitated divine revelation. And yet, given that revelation; illuminated by the Holy Ghost; having been carried away in the spirit; seeing and hearing the angel; receiving the very word of God; nevertheless John 'wondered'.

But conceited, letter-learned, self-styled bible students—especially of the premillennial and dispensational ilk—never wonder. Without anything remotely touching John's experience—let alone his apostleship—without a shadow of self-doubt, sublimely confident, fortified by dogmatic certitude, assured of the possession of all knowledge, these do not wonder. They *know*. They take up their bibles, and hold forth.

Yet what they hold forth they never gleaned from that bible about which they make such a noise, but from their favourite commentaries, books, speakers, and traditions.

These fools and blind, being wise in their own conceits, are themselves deceived by the very thing that they think they can discern with such sublime perception. The truth is that—not only John—none of the saints can perceive or understand what is meant by 'MYSTERY, BABYLON THE GREAT', without immediate, interior, divine revelation, in which God opens the inward eyes to see the reality of what is written, to discern—not the bare description, but—the actual vision itself.

Hence it appears that whilst the Holy Ghost uses the scripture in the enlightenment, man's use of it without revelation is to double blind the eyes, puff up the fleshly conceit, and quite seal the fast-shut doors of ignorance.

However, with such a hidden 'MYSTERY'—Revelation 17:5—that is, such a total mystery, even the apostle John, though 'carried away in the spirit', though transported 'to the wilderness', though instructed by the voice of the very angel, still 'wondered'.

But the interior revelation of the Holy Ghost, and his inward teaching, besides the words of the holy angel, manifested the word of God. And shall we who are nothing, and of no account, shall we, I say, hold forth with a boldness anathema to the holy apostles themselves?

Spiritual mysteries—by definition—cannot be approached, much less unravelled, by the mind or intellect of man. Revelation is essential. Such mysteries can neither be perceived from the page of scripture, nor be discerned through the study of the dead letter, nor yet penetrated by the reading of many books with much diligence.

Nothing but divine revelation opens spiritual mysteries. Obviously. Mysteries in their nature are beyond natural perception. 'BABYLON THE GREAT' is invisible. Here is no physical city, neither is the 'whore Babylon' external in the flesh. All is spiritual, and if spiritual, inward. And if inward, inward to the reader of the book.

But self-conceited Brethren, waving their bibles, know-alls to a man, think they can see it outwardly. But they are in it inwardly. Neither can the outward scriptures, nor the dead letter, save them from the blinding deceit of the mystery of 'Babylon'. Nor from the evil heart of unbelief that supposes it can see everything, though always anywhere and in anyone other than themselves.

The truth is, all mankind is shrouded beneath the darkness of spiritual Babylon. Everyone is blinded by the mystery of this delusion. The whole earth is carried away in bondage to this interior captivity. That is, until God commands the light of revelation, together with the chastisement of providence; till the Spirit gives the power to open the eyes, and Christ brings illumination to the heart. Then one may see what John saw, which is what he wrote, and see it not only for, but in, ourselves.

Then we discover that Babylon, and the love of it, has been quite consistent with our outward religion. The whore, and the love of her, we discern to have been wholly commensurate with our letterish profession.

When God grants revelation to see 'MYSTERY, BABYLON THE GREAT', then we not only wonder, as did John, we are cut to the heart with conviction, filled with trembling at our duplicity. Then we are overcome with fear to discover our own vulnerability, having found that we ourselves had been quite taken in by the mystery. Now, however, we are wholly overwhelmed with gratitude for such deliverance.

The book of the Revelation of Jesus Christ sets before the eye of faith the inheritance of the saints, the hope of the *ecclesia*, and the promise of the holy city, new Jerusalem. Withal the bride, the Lamb's wife. These things shall appear in glory when this present world has passed away and when time shall be no more. They will be manifest when the world to come has come to pass, and when eternity ushers in the inheritance of the saints in light.

But there is another city in time, equally mystical, to which the eyes have just as much need to be opened. This is the city of this world, and of its worldly religion, spiritually called 'Babylon', in which can be found the earthly duplication of everything proper to that glorious city and to its heavenly religion.

Furthermore none but those who have received 'my' gospel, and the preaching of Jesus Christ, according to the revelation of the mystery—their eyes being opened to see things spiritual and invisible—none but these, I say, can see through the subtlety of this deceitful mystery of iniquity.

Deceitful, because in the affection, the warmth, the love, in the inspiration, the opportunity, the fulfilment, offered by the religion of this MYSTERY, BABYLON — apparently spiritual, seemingly biblical, perceptibly traditional—there exists the copy of all that is of Christ, and all that pertains to the holy city. Here there appears a seductive, earthly and visible alternative to the distant, heavenly, and invisible things set before the faith of the saints in the heavenly city, and in the vision of the Lamb's wife.

And who is sufficient for these things?

None but those whose eyes have been opened, who have been turned from darkness to light, and from the power of Satan unto God. None but those whom the Spirit cuts with an invisible sword, a two-edged spiritual sword, a sword sharper than any visible sword, piercing to the dividing asunder of soul and spirit, joints and marrow, discerning the thoughts and intents of the heart.

By this sword the saints, having been cut to the heart over their own state, are enabled to see the blinding subtlety of the world's city, and the world's harlotry, precisely because in such wounded souls there is revealed the glorious light of the heavenly city, and the divine beauty of the bride of Christ.

The light by which the Father in heaven reveals the Son, the radiance of the glory of God in the face of Jesus Christ shining into the heart, this, this alone keeps the saints in a holy and separate pathway. This alone preserves them as pilgrims and strangers in their straight and narrow way through this present evil world, despite all the subtle working of the flesh, and notwithstanding the blinding and deceitful duplication of spiritual religion.

Nothing but such a revelation keeps this company on the way to everlasting glory. And the name of the company? The *ecclesia*, or, the assembly, of Christ, to whom 'my' gospel has been preached, the proclamation of Jesus Christ heralded, and the revelation of the mystery made known.

The mysterious city Babylon, and the woman riding upon the beast which carries her, called the harlot Babylon, have as their objective the destruction of the saints, the marring of the heavenly testimony, the confounding of the glorious gospel, and the ruinous division of Christ's own *ecclesia.*

The means chosen to achieve these ends appears in the evolution of two systems, the one social, and the other religious, with which to beguile the people of God. A mystery lies in the apparent discrepancy between the end and the means. For the means seem to bear no relation whatever to the end. It is a mystery.

The city, and particularly the woman, Babylon, present a mystery. Within this Babylon there is discovered a meticulous duplication of all that is holy, all that is of God, all that is of Christ, all that is of Jerusalem above, all that is of the bride of Christ, and all that is biblical, in a way believed on in the world. This is achieved by such seductive craft, such deceitful working, such confusing guile, that it made even the holy apostle to wonder.

But by the Spirit; by the word of God; by suffering afflictions; by chastening experience; by revelation from the Father; by light from the Son; by heavenly vision: thus at length the mystery is opened, and so are the saints' eyes, the elect being undeceived. Indeed, the elect, and all the elect, and none but the elect, are enabled wholly to overcome, by the blood of the Lamb, and by the word of their testimony, as they answer by the obedience of faith to the solemn cry, 'Come out of her, my people.' Amen.

Revelation 17:5 and 7 provide the last occurrences of the word *mustērion* in the bible. Thus, even to the end, to the very last, there are dangerous and deceitful mysteries brought in to deceive the saints. Acknowledging the divine mysteries, these mysteries of iniquity set out to duplicate and merge with all that is of God.

The symbolic use of 'Babylon' in the revelation, shows the fabrication of a diabolically subtle system which deceives the whole world, and all worldly religion, by the forms, signs, appearances and spirit of its imperceptible rise and insinuation into the consciousness, mind, and heart of mankind.

But clad with the whole armour of God—not merely individually; for this armour is not individual: it is for the whole *ecclesia* in unity—as one body, one new man, the faithful remnant shall stand firm.

By the girdle of truth; by the breastplate of righteousness; by the shoes of the preparation of the gospel of peace; by the shield of faith; by the helmet of salvation; by the sword of the Spirit; and by constant prayer, the assembly, through those ministers sent from Christ in heaven, brought to the unity of the faith, and of the knowledge of the Son of God, unto a perfect man, appears as a man of war. But this war is not against flesh and blood.

This war is against principalities, powers, against the rulers of the darkness of this world, against spiritual wickedness in heavenly places. Then divine vigilance, and heavenly militance, are essential to the assembly. The war is constant, and the war is spiritual.

The Mystery, the Mother of Harlots, Babylon the Great, insinuates much scripture, and many texts, into the head, judgment, and mouth of self-conceited individuals who avoid every issue of the faith and of the *ecclesia* of Christ. This fills them with self-importance, in order that they, in turn, may entice and beguile the simple with their fleshly pretensions.

Many truths and half truths are unlawfully wrenched from context, stolen from the *ecclesia*, to be placed in the mouth of every hireling. These ply their trade for the wages of unrighteousness, when neither they nor their sects have either part or lot in the matter.

But to the poor pilgrim people, the separated and holy assembly of Christ, to whom such scriptures actually pertain, to them, I say, the Spirit of truth brings home these same scriptures of truth as their own inheritance. This unmasks, within and without, the MYSTERY, BABYLON THE GREAT in all her devious and deceitful workings.

The bewildering, and, indeed, bewitching nature of Babylon—which means confusion and inspires babel—as it concerns Christendom and evangelicalism appears as that which is out of the unity. Albeit in their division and independency each sect professes the dead letter, wrongly applying to itself epistles belonging to Christ's *ecclesia*, still, all is confusion. It is babel.

All alike claim salvation, all in turn clamour their supposed knowledge of and deliverance from the very confusion in which together they are held. For denominationalism is confusion. Which, by definition, agrees with Babylon.

If not, if they object, why are they content to abide therein? Why not answer to the faith of God's elect and 'Come out of her, my people, that ye be not partakers of her sins, and that ye receive not of her plagues'? Rev. 18:4. Why not? Because they show not the marks of his people, neither have they the faith of God's elect. If they had, their obedience would be evident to all men.

For the assembly of Christ is not in confusion. On the contrary, together with all who have heard his voice, obeying by faith, all who are of this assembly go forth—or have gone forth—to him outside the camp, bearing his reproach.

These are Christ's separated people, his assembly, who have come out of confusion and division into the unity of one body, into the fellowship of the Father and the Son, into Christ's *ecclesia*. These are the people who have heard the joyful sound, who walk in the light of the glory, who have received the revelation of the mystery, being baptized by one Spirit into the unity of one body.

This is the people, the one people, indwelt by one Spirit, one Lord, one God and Father, to whom it is given to know the mysteries of the kingdom. They have been called out of the world by 'my' gospel, and the preaching of Jesus Christ, according to the revelation of the mystery.

Ministers sent by Jesus Christ from heaven in the power of the Holy Ghost speak to them the wisdom of God in a mystery, as able ministers of the new testament, stewards of the mysteries of God. They behold in vision the mystery of the coming again of Christ and the resurrection of the dead, when the whole *ecclesia* shall be raised by him to everlasting glory. This is their blessed hope.

To this hope—to walk by faith in the light of it—they are constantly exhorted by their ministers, to whom by revelation God has made known the mystery. They have entered into the mystery of Christ, they know the secret of the fellowship of the mystery, they are united in one with the Son, in that great mystery, which is Christ and the *ecclesia*.

Such a people—O blessed is that people—hold the mystery of the gospel, their servants hold the mystery of the faith in a pure conscience. As saints, with fear and trembling, they receive the revelation of the mystery hid from ages and generations, being filled with the riches of the glory of this mystery, which is Christ in them, the hope of glory.

Ever growing in grace and in the knowledge of God, they attain together in one unto all riches of the full assurance of understanding, to the acknowledgement of the mystery of

God, and of the Father, and of Christ, in whom are hid all the treasures of wisdom and knowledge.

They are comforted, their hearts being knit together in love, both with one another and with all saints throughout the assembly—the whole being made manifest by the gathering into one in each place—united in the mystery of Christ.

Holding the mystery of godliness with all reverence, this is that company on whose behalf Christ commands his angels as flames of fire, as ministering spirits to the heirs of salvation. These heavenly and angelic ministers are in the likeness of seven stars in his right hand. Under their providence, as pure gold, the saints keep themselves in the love of God, praying in the Holy Ghost, looking for the mercy of our Lord Jesus Christ unto eternal life.

Such a spiritually minded, heavenly assembly waits patiently for the mystery of God to be finished, earnestly expecting the manifestation of the sons of God at the coming of Christ. Meanwhile they triumph over sin, Satan, the world and the flesh, by the cross, keeping their raiment white in the blood of the Lamb.

With keen watchfulness this little flock, this united assembly, preserves righteous judgment, with a holy separation keeping themselves from the mystery of iniquity, detesting the very garment spotted by the flesh.

With a godly hatred—but with fear, trembling, and a deep self-distrustfulness—they loathe as their deadly enemy the mystery of the woman, and of the beast which carrieth her, and of the city Babylon. Thus it is that this assembly, Christ's *ecclesia*, the people of God visibly united, but separate from the world and the worldly profession, abide in one Spirit, looking for the coming of Christ from heaven. Their language is one. The Spirit and the bride say, Come. Even so, come, Lord Jesus. Amen.

3. The 'Adoption'

'Blessed art thou, Simon Bar-jona: for flesh and blood hath not revealed it unto thee, but my Father which is in heaven', Mt. 16:17. Here the revelation of the Son is ascribed expressly to the Father, and exclusively to his divine work from heaven.

In consequence of this heavenly illumination from the Father, the Son—who all along had been clearly visible to Peter's eyes on earth—was revealed in a way undreamed of before that moment. The Son appeared in a manner inconceivable to the natural senses, unintelligible to the rational faculties, and removed from any amount of understanding gleaned from the diligent study of the scriptures.

This revelation of the Son came by an interior illumination from the divine and uncreated light that God is in and of himself, a light directly, but inwardly, radiating from the Father in heaven.

And where is flesh and blood, or where is the intellect of man, or where is anything under the light of the sun, in that? This is a light immeasurably beyond man, and inconceivably above the brightness of the sun.

Here is a light impossible for man—no matter how erudite in holy writ, how religious in practice—impossible for man even to begin to comprehend.

These are things which the Father has put in his own power: 'The world seeth me no more; but ye see me.' 'No man can come to me, except the Father which hath sent me draw him.' 'All that the Father giveth me shall come to me.' 'Every man therefore that hath heard, and hath learned of the Father, cometh unto me.' 'No man knoweth the Son, but the Father.'

Here, Peter had learned of the Father; the Father had revealed the Son. Peter *saw* him. Upon which revelation the *ecclesia*, the true assembly of God, is built by Christ. And in this place concerning Peter, that revelation, and the doctrine touching it, is set forth in the clearest possible manner.

i. The Father

Just as no man sees the Son—and therefore believes upon him—but by the revelation of the Father, so it is equally true that no man sees the Father—and therefore receives the Spirit of 'adoption'—save by the revelation of the Son.

'No man knoweth who the Son is, but the Father; and who the Father is, but the Son, and he to whom the Son will reveal him.'

'All things are delivered unto me of my Father: and no man knoweth the Son, but the Father; neither knoweth any man the Father, save the Son, and he to whomsoever the Son will reveal him.'

No man can know the Father except the Son reveal him. That is, inwardly and spiritually, by divine light and life. Without such a revelation no one can come to the Father. How can a man come to one whom he cannot see, whose nature and whereabouts are a mystery?

It is upon the revelation of this mystery that the assembly is built: 'the acknowledgement of the mystery of God, and of the Father, and of Christ.' It is this that brought in the *ecclesia*: 'Which is *in* God the Father, and *in* the Lord Jesus Christ.'

The name of the Father, once a hidden mystery in the deity, undreamed of under the old testament, was made manifest by the coming of the Son into the world, and declared by him to his disciples. 'I have manifested thy name unto the men which thou gavest me out of the world.'

'While I was with them in the world, I kept them in thy name.' That is, kept them in the name of the Father, who gave them to the Son, that he should keep them for him. 'I have declared unto them thy name, and will declare it.'

In the Son, the disciples saw the Father: 'He that hath seen me hath seen the Father.' In the Son's deeds, they beheld the Father's works: 'My Father worketh hitherto, and I work.' In the Son's speech, they heard the Father's voice: 'The words that I speak unto you, I speak not of myself, but the Father that dwelleth in me.' In a word, 'I and my Father are one.'

This oneness the disciples saw in the Son, it was manifested in the Son, and the name of the Father was declared unto them by the Son.

Thus the coming of the Son into the world revealed the mystery of the deity, hitherto shrouded in darkness behind the unrent veil, preserved from the eye of mortal man. 'He made darkness his secret place; his pavilion round about him were dark waters and thick clouds of the skies.'

'No man hath seen God at any time; the only begotten Son, which is in the bosom of the Father'—mark that; of the Father—'he hath declared him.'

Fatherhood was unique to the Son. It subsisted in the everlasting glory which the Son had with the Father before the world was. It abode in the eternal and divine relationships of Father, Son, and Holy Ghost, one God blessed for evermore. Amen. It was that Fatherhood which became manifested by the coming of the Son into the world at the incarnation. The Son declared the Father. Otherwise Fatherhood in God had remained unknown.

'For the life'—hidden from man in unrevealed deity since the beginning of the world—'was manifested, and we have seen it, and show unto you that eternal life which was with the Father' —if eternal life with the Father, then eternally with the Father; if eternally with the Father, then as Son with the Father from eternity; if as Son with the Father from eternity, then eternally Son—'and was manifested unto us.'

It was therefore the incarnation of the Son, his coming into manhood, that brought to light the mystery of God, Father, Son, and Holy Ghost, three divine Persons in one God, one God in three divine Persons.

It was the incarnation, yes. Nevertheless the ascension was that which manifested the full radiance of the revelation of the Father by the Son, just as it manifested the full radiance of the revelation of the Son by the Father. Because it was from the ascension that the Holy Ghost was given.

The ascension. Though his Sonship could not be hidden in the days of his flesh, though his Sonship was declared by the resurrection from the dead, still, even at the last, the language of the Son was this: 'Touch me not; for I am not yet ascended to my Father: but go to my brethren, and say unto them, I ascend unto my Father, and your Father; and to my God, and your God', Jn. 20:17.

During the days of his flesh Jesus instructed the disciples in the knowledge of that truth which, afterwards, the Spirit should bring to their remembrance. But the Spirit was not then given. Just as the Son was then exterior to them. The fulfilment of all that had been promised stood in the ascension of Jesus Christ on high, when he obtained for and gave to the disciples on earth that Holy Spirit of promise brought in for them through his death on the cross. 'It pleased God to reveal his Son in me', says the apostle. And, saith the Father, 'this is my beloved Son, in whom'—not with whom: *in* whom—'I am well pleased.'

Once ascended, the perfection of the atonement wrought on earth presented to God and the Father in heaven, there came to pass the words spoken outside the sepulchre, 'Go and tell my brethren'. And if his brethren, then his Father's sons. *That* is the surpassing wonder brought to pass by the Father, the Son, and the Holy Ghost, in the new testament. His Father's sons.

The Father having been glorified on earth, the Son having been glorified in heaven, in divine purpose the whole election is seen as having been brought in already justified before God. In consequence, the Spirit of sonship had been obtained and would be freely given to all the elect in point of time. Hence *an entirely new thing, a new creation had begun.*

This new creation stands in the revelation of the Son by the Father. And, equally important, of the revelation of the Father by the Son. Now, *that* is the new testament, and *that* is the character of the assembly.

Here a stupendous truth comes to light. With the ascension of the Son of God to the Father, a new order of manhood —mark that: *a new order of manhood*—came into being under his Headship. At present this is revealed inwardly—'as he is, so are we in this world'—but in that day it shall be manifested outwardly—'of his flesh and of his bones.'

This unique manhood is entirely different from that of and in Adam. 'The first man Adam was made a living soul; the last Adam a quickening spirit.' 'The first man is of the earth, earthy: the second man is the Lord from heaven.' And in him, and under his Headship, stand all the elect, the whole 'adoption', seen as 'the new man'.

In Christ the heirs of promise have obtained the forgiveness of sins, and have been justified by his blood. In the counsel of God they are seen as already risen, ascended, and glorified in the second Man. Already in his interior likeness, they patiently await his return, whence, in the resurrection from the dead, follows the glorious liberty of the children of God.

This new man in Christ, under one Head, and in one Spirit, this, I say, is what the ministry is sent to bring in for God and the Father through Jesus Christ our Lord, ascended on high.

'He gave some, apostles; and some, prophets; and some, evangelists; and some, pastors and teachers; for the perfecting of the saints, for the work of the ministry, for the edifying of the body of Christ: till we all come in the unity of the faith, and of the knowledge of the Son of God, unto a perfect man, unto the measure of the stature of the fulness of Christ', Eph. 4:11-13.

This describes the bringing in of the new creation, of the 'adoption of children'; that is, of sons to the Father in one new man. This is the new man. Joined by one Spirit to the Head, in the unity of one body, in the fellowship of the Father and the Son—for truly our fellowship is with the Father, and with his Son Jesus Christ—words cannot describe the unique *newness* of the one body in Christ.

As to the old man, our birth in the first man, our standing under the headship of Adam; as to this first creation, this present world, the old law and covenant: we are crucified. Dead and buried.

As to this old body, though reckoned dead, having been judicially condemned, nevertheless, still we feel its sinful flesh, its heavy burden. As yet we groan in it, being burdened. It is a vile body. But, our souls sprinkled with precious blood, washed by pure water, within dwells a new man in the Spirit of sonship, joined to the Lord in one Spirit, united with all the brethren, crying from within, 'Abba, Father'.

In the Spirit of sonship, together we wait for the coming of the Son from heaven, for we shall put on the likeness of his glorious body in rapture at his appearing. 'For we shall'—mark that, we *shall*—'we shall be changed', I Cor. 15:52.

From which it appears that the Father, by Jesus Christ, has brought in, and shall yet manifest, an entirely new creation. This was wrought at the cross, testified in the resurrection, and sealed in the ascension. When Christ entered into his Father's glory, receiving and giving the Spirit of promise in virtue of his finished work for all the 'adoption', then that which had been hidden from the foundation of the world became wholly unveiled, fully revealed.

The Father's house—that spiritual, heavenly house—is to be filled with sons, as by the Spirit the children of God are called and gathered in, to give thanks, praise, and worship to God and the Father by Jesus Christ the Son. 'Behold, how good and how pleasant it is for brethren to dwell together in unity!' By one Spirit the Son leads the praise in the midst of the assembly, saying, 'I will declare thy name unto my brethren, in the midst of the assembly will I sing praise unto thee', Heb. 2:12. This is no theory to the saints: it is their heavenly experience in their coming together.

Thus to bring the children from the north, south, east and west, out of false religion, delivering them from false ministry, from the sleight of men, from cunning craftiness whereby they lie in wait to deceive, to unite the sons of the Father as worshippers in his own assembly: this is the work of the ministry. 'One God and Father of all, who is above all, and through all, and in you all', Eph. 4:6.

The purpose of the work of the Son on earth; of his present ministry from on high; the intent of the work of the Spirit from heaven; of his present ministration on earth; the object of the brethren here below; of the heavenly assembly; all come together in one: that God and the Father should be worshipped in spirit and truth in the midst of the assembly.

To achieve this end the divine Persons of the Son and of the Spirit have become subject in time—though co-equal from eternity—to the Father in lowly service.

The Son, who, 'being in the form of God, thought it not robbery to be equal with God', nevertheless 'made himself of no reputation, and took upon him the form of a servant'. He emptied himself of the manifestation—mark that: only the manifestation—of his everlasting divine glory to take the place of humble subjection in manhood.

The Spirit, though eternal, Heb. 9:14, and, if so, divine, who ever subsisted in one divine essence with the Father and with the Son, nevertheless took the lowliest place of service, not only to the Father, but also in subjection to the Son. For 'he shall not speak of himself; but whatsoever he shall hear, that shall he speak.' Not speak of himself, no, but, yielding the manifestation of his own everlasting and proper deity—refusing to glorify himself—submissively he glorifies the Son. 'He shall glorify me', Jn. 16:14, 'For he shall receive of mine, and shall show it unto you.'

What lowliness! Not speak of himself? No, not speak of himself: 'He shall glorify me.' To be subject—who is equal—to the Father and the Son? Yes, for, 'All things that the Father hath are mine: therefore said I, He shall take of mine, and shall show it unto you.' Hence worship is in the Spirit, through the Son, from the brethren in the assembly, to God and the Father.

The overwhelming, the astounding truth of the new testament is that Fatherhood, unique to the Son in everlasting divine relationships from eternity, is that which is extended to the 'adoption'. How can these things be?

Because the righteousness of God, by faith of Jesus Christ, is unto all and upon all them that believe. Such a justifying divine righteousness, having been ratified in heaven, removes all distance between heaven and earth, God and man, time and eternity.* Such a righteousness, imputed to the justified, who are accepted in the Beloved, brings the whole number immediately into the very presence of God and the Father, even to the very throne of glory.

Brings whom? Who are the justified? Those, and those only, and all those, 'Predestinated unto the 'adoption of children' by Jesus Christ to himself', Eph. 1:5. Unto 'himself'? Unto the Father. And, if to the Father, then, as sons. That is what is so stupendous: sonship. 'Behold, what manner of love the Father hath bestowed upon us, that we should be called the sons of God.'

Sonship is divine; it is the everlasting relationship in deity between the Father and the Son. Yet from the ascension a new thing is revealed: *we* are called the sons of God. Fatherhood is revealed as having been extended to all in Christ. That is, in him, and by him, and through him, and from him, to the whole 'adoption'.

Staggering truth! Fatherhood unique to the Son and yet from the ascension to be bestowed upon all in him, even to all his members? Yes, for, 'we are members of his body, of his flesh and of his bones.' This is the fruit of his work in death for all those predestinated by the Father from eternity to the 'adoption of sons' by Jesus Christ to himself.

This the Son anticipated as he approached the cross: 'Now is my soul troubled; and what shall I say? Father, save me from this hour: but for this cause came I unto this hour.' 'Father, glorify thy name'—that is, of course, the name 'Father'— 'Then came there a voice from heaven, saying, I have both

*Read 'Justification by Faith', The Publishing Trust. See advertising pages.

glorified it'—that is, the name 'Father'; he had glorified it throughout the life of the Son on earth—'and will glorify it' —that is, the name 'Father', first glorified throughout the life of the Son on earth—'and will glorify it again.'

Glorify it again? When would that happen? When not the only begotten Son on earth alone, but now glorified in heaven, many sons in him, and with him, from the midst of the assembly, breathe with one voice the filial cry, 'Abba, Father'. Then his name, the name 'Father', will be glorified—magnified, extended—in the Spirit of sonship by Jesus Christ unto himself.

That is the assembly: the house of God. If so, it is the place of his children. There, one may hear the cry, 'Abba, Father'. The assembly is not a place of man's service. It is a place for the worship of sons. The house of God is not that place where a dumb and mute congregation—mixed with the world and the worldly at that—sits in semi-bored silence listening to some 'pastor'—'minister' or 'priest', call it what you will, it is the same in principle—hired by them for the purpose.

The assembly is at once heavenly, divine, mysterious, spiritual, filled with the Holy Ghost, awesome with the presence of Christ. It is a place of many brethren, of the service of sonship, of the voice of the Spirit and of the bride. A place of mutual, harmonious, soul-melting, heart-felt, Spirit-filled praise to God and the Father.

And this from the tongue of all the brethren as one, the voice of sonship as the sound of many waters ascending up to the Father by Jesus Christ, a sweet-smelling savour of Christ to Godward. This is the assembly, the place of the worship of sons to the Father.

Neither the bondchild, nor the bastard; neither the spiritually blemished, blind, lame, flat-nosed, or one having anything superfluous; neither the brokenfooted, nor brokenhanded, nor crookbacked, nor a dwarf; neither yet one that hath a spiritual blemish in his eye, nor one scurvy, or scabbed, nor one that hath his stones broken, nor yet one spiritually dead; no, none of these has any place here. As to the meaning of these things in the Spirit, he may run that reads it. For 'The living, the living, he shall praise thee, as I do this day.' For the living are whole: they are one.

But how can the living Father, who is One, be worshipped —and therefore represented in the unity of his Person—by dead and divided denominations, which are many, and signify malformed and blemished disunity? Does not this rather represent 'gods many, and lords many' as opposed to 'one God, the Father', I Cor. 8:5,6?

I say, How can the Father, who seeks sons to worship him in his own spiritual house, be honoured by some in this meeting-house; some in that meeting-house; more in their 'open' assembly; others in the local split from it; more still in the 'exclusive' meeting; others further down the same road in some house-meeting; many more in the denominations; still others nearby in their 'house of God', as they call it: how can this be? How? And all meeting at the same hour, all in a few paces of each other, and all augmented by, and mixed with, the unconverted and worldly?

How can these things be? How, if there be one body, and one Spirit; one Lord, and one faith; one God and Father of all, above all, and through all, and in all? How, if Father, Son, and Holy Ghost dwell in the one house of God?

Is this keeping the unity of the Spirit? Is this the unity of the faith? Is this the answer in one body to one Head? Is it the raising up of one house to the Father? And if not, *why go on wilfully ignoring it*? Why?

Say, is this the Father's house filled with worshippers united in the Spirit of sonship? Rather, by Christendom in general, and evangelicalism in particular, regarding the obedience of faith in response to the Father's house—as opposed to mouthing platitudes, theories, and texts—it might as well be said, 'We have not so much as heard whether there be any Father'.

Evangelists, pastors, ministers, workers, organisers, missionaries, plus a host of meddlers with youth and children, all these in practice have as their end not the worship of the Father by all the saints in one assembly, but themselves acting their part before the audience in their own denomination, organisation, or movement. What they think of is *themselves*, their work, their service, as they call it. All this is but making use of professing Christians, the 'church', as they name their divided denominations, as a means to their own selfish ends.

Whereas to the faithful the scripture is to be acted upon, to the hirelings the scripture is to be spoken from.

To the faithful, the Father, the Son, and the Holy Ghost are divine Persons to be rendered full right and due honour in the one assembly. But to the 'evangelical', to the 'church', such divine names are but words, ideas, to be included or excluded in their self-centred, self-important, self-glorying 'service', as they call it. If not, if they complain that this language is too strong, then where is the unity consequent upon the knowledge of divine Persons?

The same is true of their bible schools, their divinity colleges, their seminaries, and, indeed, of their 'theological' constructions. The same must be true. Such institutions are not so much as once named or mentioned in the whole of holy writ, old or new testament. Then they are nothing but inventions for the gratification of puffed up and inflated 'tutors' and 'students' full of the hot air of intellectual pride and ministerial pretension.

My experience is that they have not an original thought, put the lot together, add them all up, and multiply them over all their tedious generations, I say, not an original thought in all their empty heads. No, not one of them. Much less have they faith to act upon the truth. And they teach others?

They have a doctrine of this, a doctrine of that, a theology of the other. These things even the 'soundest' of them must look up in their books with the Westminster *imprimatur*, after the traditions of their fathers, testifying against themselves that they are void of experimental and divine revelation.

They have a Christology, a soteriology, an eschatology—to tell them what to 'believe'—they have hermeneutics, semantics, homiletics, if not dramatics—to teach them how to act in the 'pulpit'—yet not one of these artificial notions existed in the whole of scripture, first and last. And they have the impudence to call themselves 'evangelical' and 'biblical'? How can those that follow after them be so blind as to suppose that because they claim to be 'biblical', therefore they are so?

But worst of all appears their ignorance of God, in Father, Son, and Holy Ghost. At least at the time of the Reformation, though it was 'God the Father Almighty'—far from the consistent new testament usage—there was a real fear of God. But too much fear, wrong fear, a fear that hath torment: due no doubt to the mixture of law and gospel, nationalism and assembly, worldly authority and ecclesiastical power, inherent in the adoption by the crown and the nation of the Protestant religion.

But at least divine Persons were recognised, if viewed from an awful distance. A distance, that is, preferably to be kept in 'church', and necessarily reserved for the officiating clergy.

Now, however, 'God', a familiar friend, is 'you'd' on every occasion, reduced to 'Jesus'—first name terms obligatory—and treated with the gay abandon suited to banter with some door-to-door tout selling discount raffle tickets or cheap life insurance.

Everything is reduced to 'Jesus', except where form, abandoned as soon as possible, demands otherwise. Then where is God? Where is the Father? Where is his house? Who knows—by revelation—the Father? Who perceives the Father's will? Have they no knowledge? Do they not understand? To know the Father, to do his will, this is worship.

Jesus, the Son of God, came to *bring* us to the Father. He is not Jesus, but a false 'Jesus', who leaves us with himself. For Jesus said, 'My Father is greater than all.' Then why do they not worship the Father, in one assembly, as sons, in the Spirit of 'adoption', recognisably the united children of God in his own house?

Rather than do this, the tendency is to flatter Rome. From whence, incidentally, the 'you-ing'—calling God 'you' instead of 'thee' and 'thou'—came originally, swiftly to pass down the line through the Anglicans to all quarters. Not for nothing were Roman Catholics called 'papists' by a godlier, more serious, former generation.

The word 'papist' indicates one who bows to the authority of the *pape, papa* or *pope*—all of which mean 'father'. But do they not know that they are to call no man father upon earth; for one is our Father, which is in heaven, Mt. 23:9?

But the Roman Catholics and their fellow-travellers demand that millions—and their predecessors million millions—call the pope of Rome '*papa*', or 'father' upon earth.

So does Dr. Runcie, and so did his predecessor: they went to the 'father' on earth. Ramsay acted out the part of the prodigal son—on behalf of the entire Anglican sect—whilst the 'holy father' acted out the part of the Father.

At Rome the 'Father' received the returning prodigal of Anglicanism, after four hundred years, with open arms, a kiss, and a ring on the finger. Thus Rome's 'son' defied God's Son, and defied him knowingly, on behalf of the whole Anglican sect, casting God's words behind his back. And there those words remain—whatever the glib talk and slick juggling with scripture on the part of 'evangelicals'—until, individually, men and women come out, return, and seek them again.

By being 'father' on earth, by taking the name of the Father, by occupying the place of the Head of the 'church' withal, what is this but 'Opposing and exalting himself above all that is called God, or that is worshipped; so that he as God'—as Father—'sitteth in the temple of God, showing himself that he is God'—or Father?

But our Father is in heaven, and by the Spirit on earth, through the Son in glory, the children of God worship him only, in the unity of one assembly, which is the very opposite of the papist sect, and of all who fail to judge and separate from its evil.

The name 'Father' occurs some two hundred and sixty-four times in the new testament. Of this total, one hundred and eighty-six occurrences are in the four gospels, the remaining seventy-eight being in the epistles.

Three times the Father is referred to as 'Abba, Father'; six times as 'heavenly Father'; sixteen as 'Father in heaven'; and five as 'Father in secret'.

The term 'your Father' occurs nine times; 'our Father'—including seventeen references to 'God our Father'—nineteen times; 'my Father' occurs fifty-two times; and 'their Father' once. Six times we find 'his Father'; and once 'thy Father'.

The name 'Father', incorporated in various permutations—for example, O Father, Holy Father, God and Father—appears twenty-one times. And 'the Father'—again often with various permutations—occurs one hundred and twenty-five times throughout the new testament.

Of the appearances of the name 'Father'—in whatever form—in the gospels, the distribution is as follows: Forty-four times the name occurs in Matthew; five times in Mark; sixteen times in Luke; and one hundred and twenty-one in John.

Immediately the significance of this distribution will strike and illuminate the spiritual reader.

Matthew emphasizes the heavenliness of the Father, just as he is the one greatly to stress the kingdom of heaven. Of course, Matthew is the only gospel in which the word *ecclesia* occurs, falling three times from the lips of Jesus.

Only Matthew refers—five times—to 'heavenly Father'. And of the sixteen times that the Father is referred to as 'Father in heaven', fourteen of these references are to be found in Matthew.

Only Matthew speaks—or rather, only here Jesus speaks—of 'Father in secret'. Five times to be precise.

It follows that Matthew teaches a distinctive revelation concerning the heavenliness of the Father, unique to that gospel, as are his references to the assembly. This is emphasized by the proportion of his use of the name 'Father'—second only to John—compared with, say, Mark—five times—or Luke—sixteen times.

Of the one hundred and twenty-one times in which the Father is named in John—far and away the greatest number of any book in the bible—once it is said, 'thy Father'; once, 'his Father'; twice, 'your Father'; ten times, 'Father'; thirty-seven times, 'My Father'; and seventy times, 'the Father'.

Thus John teaches that Jesus' most usual way of speaking that holy name is 'the Father' and 'My Father'.

In John, it is only after the death of the cross, when propitiation had been wrought, when Jesus was risen from the dead, only then, I say, that Jesus refers to the Father, his Father, as the Father of the disciples: 'your Father'. 'Touch me not: for I am not yet ascended to my Father: but go to my brethren'—mark that: my brethren; and if brethren by union, then children by grace—'and say unto them, I ascend unto my Father, and your Father; and to my God, and your God.'

That is the place of peace for the assembly. And that is the relationship of grace. 'Grace unto you, and peace, from God our Father, and the Lord Jesus Christ.'

The work of God—so varied; so distinct; so consummate—is of the utmost importance in itself, considered in relation to the Son of man. But the work of God *as Father* is of the essence, if one is to understand the assembly, or, as we say, the *ecclesia.*

'My Father worketh'; and every one who names that name must be absorbed by what God does as Father. Of what he works as Father, most of all in relation to his own Son, and next in relation to the assembly. Least of all in relation to oneself.

How can any be called ministers—or even brethren—if they do not know these things and relationships by interior teaching and spiritual experience?

'But the hour cometh, and now is, when the true worshippers'—mark that: the *true* worshippers—'shall worship the Father in spirit and in truth: for the Father seeketh such to worship him. God is a Spirit: and they that worship him *must* worship him in spirit and in truth.' And, if so, then in the Spirit of sonship, and in the truth of the Father and the Son.

ii. The 'Adoption'

Evidently 'adoption' is the prerogative of the Father—as nature itself teaches—and must proceed on his initiative.

And proceed it does: so that the use of the very name Father, unique to the Son, is in him, and through him, and by him, granted to all the children of God.

Since the Father from eternity gave the 'adoption' to the Son; since the Father sent the Son into the world to bring that 'adoption' to himself; since by his substitutionary death the Son brought that entire 'adoption', already justified, to the Father and the Father to them; and since from his risen glory in heaven, by the Spirit of 'adoption' on earth, the Son gathers that 'adoption' together in one to worship the Father: it follows, when the Son speaks of the revelation to Peter from 'My Father which is in heaven'—Mt. 16:17—necessarily we are brought to a point concerning the 'adoption'.

The 'adoption'—as it has been translated—is that which, in, through, and by the Son, proceeds from the prerogative, initiative, and purpose of the Father. That is, of 'My Father which is in heaven', the God and Father of our Lord Jesus Christ, 'My Father, and your Father'.

To be taught this by revelation is to experience union with the Father and the Son, to perceive the mind of God, and to understand in what manner, and to what purpose, 'My Father worketh hitherto', in consequence of which, saith the Son, 'I work', John 5:17.

'My Father worketh hitherto, and I work.' The Father quickens the dead, bringing them to the Son, who, calling them forth to newness of life in and by himself, so that they are filled with the Spirit of sonship, presents them to the Father as worshippers in his house.

'For as the Father raiseth up the dead, and quickeneth them; even so the Son quickeneth whom he will.' And who are these? Those of whom he says, 'Behold I and the children which God hath given me.'

These children are called 'the adoption'. 'All that the Father giveth me shall come to me'—mark that, *shall* come to me—'and him that cometh to me I will in no wise cast out.' 'Every one therefore that hath heard, and hath learned of the Father, cometh unto me.'

Now this is to bring in the entire 'adoption' with a witness. Yes, but what does the word 'adoption' mean? And why keep putting it in inverted commas?

The English word 'adoption' is useless—worse than useless—to translate the meaning of the new testament Greek.

Any amount of sophistry and sly argument from other contemporary—profane—Greek usage of the word is wholly beside the point.

This is a question of words which the Holy Ghost uses, holy scripture; we are talking about the word of God, not about common usage, much less about the literary constructions of heathen in the dark.

It is impossible that the English word 'adoption' should convey the meaning of the Greek word *υἱοθεσία*, *huiothesia*, as it is used in the new testament. Impossible. And more: it is downright misleading, as will appear in the issue.

In language set apart by the Holy Ghost, the Greek *huiothesia* occurs five times in the new testament, being invested with that divine radiance, that unmistakable spirituality, peculiar to those words sanctified by the Holy Ghost that they might convey the mind and purpose of the Father, through the Son, in holy writ.

This is what the translation 'adoption'—so rendered three times out of five—has entirely obscured. 'Adoption' is precisely what divine *huiothesia* is not.

The remaining two occurrences of the word in the new testament both find the translators putting three separate English words to convey the one Greek word *huiothesia*!

Even then the translators have managed to make the two sets of three words differ one from the other, using the phrase —phrase!—'adoption of children' in one case, and 'adoption of sons' in the other.

Since *huiothesia* is but one word, and at that used merely five times, why do the translators render it so diversely? Which of their three renderings is correct?

Is it 'adoption', used thrice? If it is, why say 'adoption of sons' in the fourth instance? Or, if 'adoption of sons' is correct, why not use that on the previous three, or, indeed, on all five occasions?

Or is it really 'adoption of children'—the translators' other choice—after all? If so, why put 'adoption of sons' in the previous place, and merely 'adoption' in the three before that? Which of these confused alternatives is it? I will tell you. None of them.

It was this sort of thing that gave justice to the call for a revision of the bible in 1881. The revisers were given the brief of correcting no more than the 'plain and clear errors' of 'the English text of the Authorized Version'. A most laudable instruction, worthy of the approval and gratitude of us all. But when the translators first sat, Westcott and Hort,* rose up

*Read 'The Ministry of the New Testament', Vol.2 No.3, Autumn 1987, 'The Revision Revised' by Dean Burgon, The Publishing Trust.

immediately, dominating the whole body, blowing along those weak clergymen like men of straw, insisting on the substitution of their own—and false—Greek text instead of the inspired Greek text from which the Authorized Version had been translated originally.

Mark that, not correcting 'plain and clear errors' in the English translation as was their brief. But with sheer effrontery substituting their own Greek text for the original from which the English was translated, using *that* as the basis for revision.

Yet *their* Greek text, dishonestly insinuated, 'Falsified the inspired Greek text in countless places.' (Dean Burgon).*

This enormity, of truly staggering repercussions, resulted in a great boost for those trading in religious chattels, after the example of John 2:14-17. There followed ever-multiplying 'versions'—even to this very day—all based on the false, substituted Greek text of Westcott and Hort in 1881. Not one has returned to the faithful and tried original.

This enormity, I say, found its opportunity because of the occasional and obvious bungling of the original—1611—translators of the Authorized Version. As in the case of—for example—such mangling of the word *huiothesia*.

Only five times this word occurs, yet in their blundering ineptitude the translators have confounded themselves on each occasion, offering three alternatives, two of which are actually phrases. Even these differ. In every case, the use of the word 'adoption'—as we shall see—offers the worst possible contradiction to the mind of the Spirit.

*Read 'The Great Deception', Tract for the Times No. 12, The Publishing Trust. See advertising pages.

Only clergymen and religious academics could make so huge a mess in such a small compass, and get away with it, fawning all over King James in the process. There can be no question that moderate revision was called for, but what ought to have happened was that the errors alone should have been corrected, the text should have remained sacrosanct, and the great body of the Authorized Version—anyway Tyndale's labour—should have remained untouched.

It is right that the despicable 'Dedication to the King' from his sycophantic clergymen should have been torn out. Concerning the *ecclesia*, Christ alone is King. There is no room in the assembly for any flattery of earthly dignitaries, however exalted and worthy of respect in this present world. Christ's *ecclesia* is of an order separate from this world, and destined for that which is to come.

The Greek word *huiothesia* is a compound word derived from the conjunction of *υἱός*, *huios*, meaning 'son', and *τίθημι*, *tithēmi*, a complicated verb having the basic sense of 'set', 'lay', or 'place'. From this verb the Greek word *θέσις*, *thesis*, is derived, meaning 'setting, placing', as in 'setting' words and ideas in order. This of course is the origin of the English word 'thesis'.

The meaning of the Greek *thesis* ranges from 'giving' of a name, 'setting forth' in legal form, 'disposition', to 'laying down', 'deposit', 'payment'. *Thesis* may have the meaning of 'adoption' of a child, or of a citizen of a foreign state. It may mean the 'situation' of a city; 'position', or 'arrangement'. Of course, this sheds light on the meaning of 'thesis' in English, that is, 'position' assumed in argument, and requiring proof.

It is to the Greek word *thesis* that *huios*, 'son', has been joined, forming the compound *huiothesia*.

It is perfectly true that in Greek literature and on various inscriptions either before, or contemporary with, new testament times, *huiothesia* was used in the sense of 'adoption'. But then, this was true of the word *thesis*.

So that to use *huiothesia*—strictly meaning 'setting, giving, placing as a son'—for 'adoption' is no more than a loose application of a concept already defined and served by *thesis*.

Suppose the 'adopted' were a daughter: which would serve, *thesis* in the sense of 'adoption', or *huiothesia* in the sense of 'position as a son'?

It is evident that in itself, in its intrinsic meaning, *huiothesia* has a far greater potential—whether used or not—than the limited and loose sense of 'adoption'.

Hence, even from a balanced consideration of no more than profane Greek—not to consider the new testament Greek in and of itself—what kind of a conclusion is this, reached by a learned professor of theology of liberal German persuasion: 'The frequency of *huiothesian*' (in profane writings and inscriptions) 'lets us understand that Paul was availing himself of a generally intelligible figure'—adoption!—'when he utilised the term *huiothesia* in the language of religion.'

Here is this great doctor, had in vast repute, spiritually in gross darkness, the old veil thick and heavy on his heart, uttering words without wisdom. He sets men over God, the world over the *ecclesia*, earth over heaven, and would have Paul 'availing himself' of a 'generally intelligible figure' in order to borrow from the world ideas that make totally incomprehensible 'the language of religion', as he calls holy writ.

Is this 'holy men of God spake as they were moved by the Holy Ghost'? Is this 'All scripture is given by inspiration of God'? Is this 'It is not ye that speak, but the Spirit of your Father which speaketh in you'? Is this what the godly call 'Words which the Holy Ghost useth'?

The worst thing about it is that the learned doctor, having made a great name in religion, has climbed so high in the academic world of those universities which breed clergy, that he is quoted with deep reverence. Hence his inane mumblings must remain for ever petrified in innumerable theologies, lexicons, dictionaries, concordances, honoured over and over again by his peers and students.

Yet he is steeped in unbelief, pickled in modernism, and his utterances cannot compare in usefulness with the brayings of Balaam's ass.

Ah, but I must not judge! Oh? Must I then swallow this pernicious toxic waste and poison my system? No; but you must not judge! Oh? Then must I let others swallow it unwarned?

But it is not I that judge; it is Jesus who has judged, saying of all such doctors, 'How can ye believe, which receive honour one of another, and seek not the honour that cometh from God only?'

The scope of the *huiothesia*—so inappropriately translated 'adoption' in the new testament—the scope of the *huiothesia*, I say, is immense. Far from suffering the constricting definitions of man in time, here is a word known and set apart in the wisdom of God from everlasting. This is a word given a divine value, exploiting its inherent, potential meaning to the utmost. It is a word which has been given an infinitely suited construction by the Holy Ghost. A word of everlasting significance.

Now, for the understanding of this, one must be drawn into the mind of God by revelation. One must not debase oneself with musty tomes and crumbling inscriptions to grub a living. As it is written, 'He taught them as one having authority, and not as the scribes.'

Conceived in the mind of God from eternity, the *huiothesia* has its origin in the everlasting election of the Father; its fruition in the substitutionary work of the Saviour; its generation in the Spirit of sonship from the Holy Ghost; and its consummation in the rapturous resurrection and glorious manifestation of the children of God at the coming of Christ.

The arms of eternity embrace the *huiothesia*. From everlasting to everlasting it sounds. The glorious majesty enthroned above the heaven of heavens calls forth the *huiothesia*. From God to man, from heaven to earth, this mystery is brought to light.

Thence appears both the place and the Spirit of sonship. When Christ ascended into heaven and entered into his glory, seated in majesty as Son upon the throne of his Father, he requested, obtained, and sent forth the Holy Spirit of promise from heaven to earth.

This same Spirit of sonship from the first was poured out in a mighty baptism upon that people redeemed and justified by Christ's precious blood. So that, filled, with one accord they looked up to heaven, and with one voice cried out with joy unspeakable and full of glory, 'Abba, Father'.

This is not an 'adoption'. It is a generation. This is not a change of status in law. It is a relationship by birth. This is not taking a stranger born to others into the family. It is the bearing of children conceived from the Father to form the family. 'Adoption'? Not in the new testament!

In the new testament *huiothesia* is not the Father 'adopting' those of other, alien parentage. It is the Father begetting his own children, of his own life, by his own seed, through the Son of his love. These are not 'adopted' children of strange blood and stranger life. They are true born children begotten by the Father himself from his own life.

Because they *are* sons, God hath sent forth the Spirit of his Son into their hearts, crying, Abba, Father, Galatians 4:6.

None but a true born son can pronounce this Shibboleth. Bastards, adopted sons, foster-children, all stutter and splutter before such a test: they have neither the birth, nor the life, nor the Spirit, nor the language of Zion.

But the *huiothesia*, the truly begotten children, these have the Spirit of life in Christ Jesus, they are filled with the Spirit of sonship, theirs is the language of Zion: of them it is said, 'This and that man was born in her'. This is very far from the 'adoption' of one of foreign birth. The breathing of the true-born child gives utterance to the inimitable pronunciation, 'Abba, Father'.

'Abba, Father'. Words first uttered by the Son in the garden of Gethsemane. Afterwards to be breathed out by a vast multitude, which no man can number. But it is the same voice to the Father's ear. Because it is the same life that speaks forth the words. Now, this is both the life and the Spirit of sonship.

'Sonship's place'—or *huiothesia*—is held by those who are true-born children, of the Father's begetting, one with the Son. As one these shall rise from the dead by the glory of the Father, in the likeness of the glorious body of his Son, bone of his bones, and flesh of his flesh, out of whose side they were taken from eternity.

The full glory of this place, sonship's place, though now revealed by inward conformity to the spiritual image of God's Son, will not appear till the resurrection from the dead. Then the children of God shall be made manifest in glorious resurrection: that is, their full outward conformity to the body of the Son of God in glory.

'It doth not yet appear what we shall be: but we know that, when he shall appear, we shall be like him; for we shall see him as he is.' We shall be—the *huiothesia* shall be—in the full likeness of the Son, body and Spirit: 'in the likeness of his glorious body.' Now, that is 'Sonship's place', and is, indeed, the full assumption of sonship.

This 'placing in the condition of a son' appears in terms of the divine counsel and purpose of God in Ephesians 1:4,5.

In this chapter the apostle blesses the God and Father of our Lord Jesus Christ—his full ascended title: it is a question of what has been brought in by the ascension—who has blessed us with all spiritual blessings in Christ.

'According as he hath chosen us in him before the foundation of the world, that we should be holy and without blame before him in love: having predestinated us unto the *huiothesian*'—the 'adoption of children' as the translators will have it—'by Jesus Christ to himself, according to the good pleasure of his will.'

How the translators can justify even to themselves and their own sort their rendering of *huios*—son—by 'children', in the expression 'adoption of children'—for *huiothesian*!—will remain a mystery till the end of time. After that, they must answer at the highest tribunal to him who gave the word, whose word it remains.

Meanwhile, especially in a new testament in which the difference between 'sons' and 'children' is observed so strictly by very distinct and particular Greek words, let the reader mark and avoid the error. Let him do so however, in the margin of his bible, not falling into the trap of purchasing the false versions which secretly hide a thoroughly rotten and deceitful Greek text. Indeed a text that was nothing other than a sop to German scorners, and papist schemers, devised by the treacherous Westcott and Hort.

These deceivers, having set in train the lucrative business of publishing and selling what was to become the—then unthinkable—endless series of false, new versions, afterwards rested on the name that they had made for themselves in the academic—higher critical—world. And all this on account of the few mistranslations in the Authorized Version! Unlike others, however, the elect will never depart from that Greek text endorsed over centuries by the Holy Ghost. Nor will they deviate from the truth that no more is required of the labour of Tyndale, and the utilisation of that labour by the Authorized Version translators, than the correction of a small number of English errors. Meanwhile they note the few faults in time, but keep to the safe version for eternity.

Ephesians 1:4,5 shows that the elect, those chosen in the Son before the foundation of the world, were predestinated to the place of sonship for that glorious appearing when the world shall be no more. It is therefore the election which constitutes the full number of those called to sonship in Christ. The *huiothesia*—the 'assumption of sonship'—appears as that to which the election was predestinated from eternity.

This election in turn answers to Christ's *ecclesia*, whose destiny, in consequence of the work of the Father and the Son, is that of the glorious manifestation of the children of God in the day of Christ. Then, the election constitutes the *ecclesia*, and the *ecclesia* has been predestinated to the *huiothesia*.

This in turn illustrates the truth that sonship, in the mind of God, like so much new testament teaching, is not so much individual as corporate. Of course all are called individually, but all are called individually into that corporate entity.

Evangelicalism, however, among its other screening devices, deliberately hides this verity. It stresses the individual and individuality in order to cover up its wilfully ignoring the divisions and denominations—pretending that the *ecclesia* is invisible!—the issues of which it refuses to address.

Given that the election was predestinated to the place of sonship—the *huiothesia*—then all must be in the realm of what was purposed in the mind of God from everlasting. If so, before the world was. Then, not of it. It follows that Christ's *ecclesia*, which answers to the election, and which is predestined to sonship, was settled and determined before time began. It is not of this age, not of time. It is separate from the world and time, being above both.

The conception of the *huiothesia* springs from the Father in eternity; its existence issues from the Son in glory; its life flows from the Holy Ghost in deity; and its destiny pertains to the inheritance of the everlasting ages. And where is time in that? Where is the world, with its powers and authorities, in that?

Whilst walking blameless in submission to proper and lawful authority outwardly, nevertheless, inwardly and spiritually, the children of God, united in Christ's *ecclesia*, joined by one Spirit with the Head, own him alone as their authority: high above time, high over all, waiting for that coming day.

Again, if the election, predestinated to the place of glorious sonship, was chosen in him before time began, then it was chosen before the world existed, and, if so, before the creation of mankind generated in Adam. Then what manner of men are the children of God? They are a new creation. In the Son they are a new order of mankind, having no connection with Adam, or his realm, that Christ has not dissolved.

To the world and worldly religion this is preposterous. But to us it is certain. 'Behold, what manner of love the Father hath bestowed upon us, that we should be called the children of God: therefore the world knoweth us not, because it knew him not.'

The election was chosen in another, that is, in Christ, even from eternity, before the world existed, time began, or Adam was created. This election is not said to be chosen out of Adam—how could it have been? he did not exist—leaving 'the rest', about which the theologians blunder so grievously.

The election was seen in the Son from eternity, chosen in the Son from eternity, 'taken out of his side' from eternity, before the world was. Not chosen out of Adam in time, but chosen in the Son from eternity. The Father chose his own children in his own Son, as much and as wholly to be of Christ as ever Eve was of Adam. 'Chosen in him before the foundation of the world.'

Mark that, not chosen out of Adam in time, but chosen in the Son before time began. This is the purpose of God. And this is the origin and conception of the *huiothesia*. Blessed is he who receives this truth without reasoning or questioning, from the pure, divine spring of eternity, from whence it came. 'Sanctify them through thy truth: thy word is truth.'

Notwithstanding this high and glorious doctrine, hidden in God from before the foundation of the world, now revealed unto his holy apostles and prophets in the gospel, the election actually came to light in as contrary a state to the eternal purpose of God as can be imagined.

For, even as others, fallen in Adam, these were shapen in iniquity, and conceived in sin. As the children of disobedience, they were in slavery to the god of this world, bowed down beneath the old yoke, condemned by the legal curse, and under sentence of death. They were in bondage to the law of sin in their members, crushed underneath the heavy burden, blind, dumb, deaf, impotent, and shut up to wrath. And where is the purpose of God in that?

According to his purpose, God magnified his free grace in Christ so much the more because of the very worst conditions against it, overcoming all as if such a terrible situation had never arisen. He brought in his purpose from eternity, for eternity, as if nothing ever stood against it—or even appeared —in time, to the praise of the glory of his grace.

For God brings in his purpose in the elect as if time, the first man, the world, had never been. All will be precisely as he purposed and predestined in Christ before the world was. Here is grace abounding. How shall this be? It shall be because 'My Father worketh hitherto, and I work.'

The revelation of sonship was first to the Jews, 'to whom pertaineth the *huiothesia*', Rom. 9:4. This is what is taught in Galatians 4:4-7: When the fulness of time was come, God sent forth his Son, made of a woman, made under the law, to redeem them that were under the law, that we might receive the 'adoption of sons'—as the translators here render *huiothesia.*

'And because ye are sons, God hath sent forth the Spirit of his Son into your hearts, crying, Abba, Father. Wherefore thou art no more a servant, but a son; and if a son, then an heir of God through Christ.'

Here those predestinated to sonship from eternity have been redeemed—purchased, or even better, ransomed—beforehand. Before being called, they were ransomed. They had been ransomed because they were predestinated. The Father had chosen them from eternity, the Son had ransomed them in time, and the Spirit came to deliver them in consequence.

Though under the curse and bondage of the law, blind and enslaved, yet they were heirs. But they knew it not. God had predestinated them in his Son for glory, though they were sunk in the deepest mire.

In the fulness of time God sent forth his Son to ransom them, purchasing them out from under the curse of the law, being made a curse for them. Moreover he delivered them from under the law itself, so that they became dead to the law by the body of Christ.

All this was done for them. They had done nothing. They knew nothing. No change had taken place in them. But every change had taken place for them, and by the gospel of the grace of Christ, this is what the Spirit witnesses in their hearts in consequence.

They *were* sons—'because ye *are* sons'—from eternity. They *had been* ransomed in time. It was not that their ransom had been made possible provided they received it. They had already been chosen to sonship. They had actually been ransomed beforehand, that is, before they had even heard of the gospel. Now, that is grace.

And because the Father had chosen them, because the Son had ransomed them, God sent forth the Spirit of his Son into their hearts to declare to them this self-same thing. And where is man in that? It is all grace. There is nothing at all of man in it.

This is the character of the *huiothesia*. Because they were sons God sent forth the Spirit of his Son into their hearts. Mark that: they *were* sons before they had done anything, and before they knew that anything had been done for them.

They did nothing. God sent forth the Spirit. And when that same Spirit entered their hearts with his testimony, then, and only then, they knew that great things had been done for them, in connection with which they had done nothing, absolutely nothing, of themselves. Now, that is the *huiothesia*.

Everything, but everything, is by revelation from 'My Father which is in heaven'. Nothing was called for from man. No initiative was of man. God sent forth his Spirit. Yes, and it is 'into your hearts', plural, it is corporate, for this is that work by which in unity the sons of God are brought into the inward, spiritual, house of God.

Then they do something. Not of their own initiative: it is of his initiative. 'God hath sent forth the Spirit of his Son into your hearts, crying, Abba, Father.' He does it, the Spirit cries it, but they answer to it in consequence: 'Abba, Father.' Now, that is worship.

From which it is clear that God's *ecclesia* springs from eternity, was chosen in Christ, and answers to the election. This in turn agrees with the *huiothesia*, predestinated to glory. Predestinated to glory, yes, but the glory is even now revealed. 'Christ in you the hope of glory.'

This glory commences within. Despite this 'vile body', despite the body of corruption, despite the flesh—all of which have been crucified in the Son of man, a crucifixion reckoned to the people of God—'God hath sent forth the Spirit of his Son into your hearts, crying, Abba, Father.'

This crying is within. All glorious within. This is, 'We all, with open face beholding as in a glass the glory of the Lord, are changed'—inwardly—'into the same image from glory to glory even as by the Spirit of the Lord.' This is the revelation of glory by the Spirit of sonship.

But it is not the whole of sonship. It is the earnest of our inheritance. But it is not the inheritance. It is the pledge. But it is not yet the possession of that for which it is the pledge. It is the *huiothesia*. But it is not all that pertains to the *huiothesia*. It is the Spirit of sonship. But it is not the body of sonship.

This is precisely the teaching of Romans 8:14-23. In the first part of this passage everything is spiritual and interior. And of course, corporate.

'For as many as are led by the Spirit of God, they are the sons of God', Rom. 8:14. Evidently; because they are sons,

God hath sent forth the Spirit of his Son into their hearts. Hence, the being led—of course to the Father—by the Spirit is evidence both of sonship and purchase. Prior sonship and previous purchase.

Hence the sons of God are led by the Spirit to worship the Father in spirit and truth. Indeed, the Father seeketh—mark that, *seeketh*—such to worship him.

But it is all inward. The truth, the truth of the Son, sets free. 'Ye have not received the spirit of bondage again to fear; but ye have received the Spirit of'—what the translators call—'adoption, whereby we cry, Abba, Father', Rom. 8:15.

How can we fear? Were we not sons, we would not have the Spirit. Had we not the Spirit, we would not have been purchased. But we have the Spirit, we are sons, and we have been purchased. How then can we fear, or be in bondage? We have been delivered from fear and bondage.

But as yet it is inward. 'The Spirit beareth witness with our spirit, that we are the children of God', Rom. 8:16. Yes, with our spirit, that is spiritual and interior, but what of the body?

What of the body? We that are in this body do groan, being burdened. It is reckoned dead, because it was crucified with Christ, but it is not put off, and we suffer in it because it is a body of sin and death. Moreover the mortification of its members by the Spirit, together with self-denial of its desires by the cross, brings suffering and affliction.

But, 'I reckon that the sufferings of this present time are not worthy to be compared with the glory which shall be revealed in us', Rom. 8:18.

'Glory which shall be revealed in us', that is, as a whole, in the entire *huiothesia*, raised from the dead in the likeness of his glorious body, radiant beyond all conception. 'For the earnest expectation of the creation waiteth for the manifestation of the sons of God', Rom. 8:19.

'For we know that the whole creation groaneth and travaileth in pain together until now. And not only, but ourselves also, which have the firstfruits of the Spirit, even we ourselves groan within ourselves, waiting for'—the translators have again rendered *huiothesia* as 'adoption'—'waiting for the 'adoption', to wit, the redemption of our body', Rom. 8:22,23. But it is not 'adoption'. It is the consummation of sonship. It is the full 'assumption of sonship'.

First, the election was predestinated to sonship from eternity. Next, being purchased in due time, the Spirit of sonship is sent forth into the hearts of the ransomed. Finally, sonship shall be brought to consummation at the end of time with the assumption of the body of glory.

Sonship therefore is the destiny of the entire election in Christ, that is, Christ's *ecclesia*, and pertains to the new man, that body of which he is the Head. As such—bone of his bones, and flesh of his flesh—sonship necessarily involves a suited body, a body of glory, a body 'like unto his glorious body'.

This body of glory, created anew at the return of Christ, and the rapturous resurrection, answers to the destiny of the entire *huiothesia*. It answers to the present witness of the Spirit of sonship. And it answers to the everlasting purpose and good will of the Father in Christ.

In Romans, chapter eight, one sees the character of sons. Sons are together in the Father's house, united in one assembly, under the Son of his love. Their end and their desire is the worship of the Father, and thereunto they are called. They are an interior, spiritual people, meek, lowly, and broken of heart. They walk after the Spirit; they are spiritually minded. They do not walk after the flesh; they are not carnally minded.

The Spirit of God dwells in them; they reckon their body to be dead, though it feels far from it. But, by the Spirit they mortify the deeds of the body. They are led by the Spirit of God, they are the sons of God. They have the Spirit of sonship, and they cry continuously and unitedly from their heart by that Spirit, 'Abba, Father'.

They have the witness in themselves. They have the glory in themselves. Yes, but they suffer. They groan. They travail.

They groan within themselves, they wait, they yearn, they long. They suffer infirmities, they groan with groanings which cannot be uttered. Now, these are the infallible marks, the unerring characteristics, of the true children of God.

These are the sons of God. They belong to the Father. He is their Father. That is the meaning of Father: 'Abba, Father'. And that is the *ecclesia* of Christ.

V

The building of the Ecclesia

1. The Rock

IN the beginning the LORD God said, It is not good that the man should be alone; I will make him an help meet for him.

And out of the ground the LORD God formed every beast of the field, and every fowl of the air, and brought them unto Adam to see what he would call them: and whatsoever Adam called every living creature, that was the name thereof.

And Adam gave names to all cattle, and to the fowl of the air, and to every beast of the field: but for Adam there was not found an help meet for him.

Adam could see over every creature, but no creature could so much as see eye to eye with him. His life discerned all, and was over all, but no life could discern his life, for all was beneath him. There was no union, and there could be no communion.

Then the LORD God caused a deep sleep to fall upon Adam, and he took one of his ribs, and closed up the flesh instead thereof. And the rib, which the LORD God had taken from man, made he a woman, and brought her unto the man.

And Adam said, This is now bone of my bones, and flesh of my flesh: she shall be called Woman, because she was taken out of Man.

He knew—sleep, deep sleep, or not—he knew what had happened. He knew from whence she came. Soul answered to soul, heart to heart, and mind to mind. Because there was communion. There was union. They were one.

He felt within himself that they were one. There was a correspondence. He could communicate, he was understood. Deep called unto deep, the one to the other. This was life of his life, soul of his soul, being of his being: 'bone of his bones, and flesh of his flesh.'

This was no mere living creature. Nor was it man as such: this was *ishshah*—woman—for she had been taken out of *ish*—man—and the man recognised this immediately and infallibly. She was of him. Together they were one.

'And I say unto thee, That thou art Peter—*Petros*—and upon this rock—*petra*—I will build my *ecclesia*.' None in Israel had understood the second Man, the last Adam. No union, no communion.

'Whom do men say that I the Son of man am?' Some said this, some that, some the other. But there was none that understood, no, not one. Till the Father brought *Petros*, Peter, to Christ, as in a figure, before the time. Then there was recognition. There was correspondence.

The same light from heaven, the same inward Spirit, the same breathing 'Abba, Father', filled Peter. If so, here was a new creation. This was now bone of Christ's bones, flesh of his flesh. This was of himself; taken out of him; his own living order: a new creation.

The Father created from Christ what corresponded with him. This was taken out of the 'side' of the Son, from his deep sleep, in a figure. Immediately, brought by the Father to the

Son, there was the knowledge in Christ of what was of himself. This is the beginning of the creation of God. As it is the beginning of the *ecclesia* of Christ.

The name *Petros* appears over one hundred and sixty times in the new testament. Cephas, the Aramaic equivalent of *Petros*, occurs some six times.

It is Simon's new name, which the Lord wrote upon him when the Father brought him to the Son, and none shall erase it world without end. No, not even Peter himself, though in self-disgust and self-hatred, full of unbelief and despair, more than once he tried. But this is the new creation, not the old destruction, and, 'They shall never perish, neither shall any man pluck them out of my hand.'

'My Father, which gave them me, is greater than all; and no man is able to pluck them out of my Father's hand. I and my Father are one.' And in like manner the Son is one with all that which is taken out of his side.

The beasts of the field, and the fowls of the air, could no more communicate with the soul that was in Adam, than could man that was born of Adam communicate with the Son of God. 'For what man knoweth the things of a man, save the spirit of man which is in him?'

'Even so the things of God knoweth no man, but the Spirit of God. Now we have received, not the spirit of the world, but the spirit which is of God; that we might know the things that are freely given to us of God. Which things also we speak, not in the words which man's wisdom teacheth, but which the Holy Ghost teacheth; comparing spiritual things with spiritual.'

'But the natural man receiveth not the things of the Spirit of God: for they are foolishness unto him: neither can he know them, because they are spiritually discerned.'

This spiritual union and communion of divine life is very different from the miserable spectacle of dead old brethren muttering—and guessing—over the scriptures in some fusty meeting. To the contrary, this is the knowledge of divine Persons by way of *living union.*

This is what is seen in Simon being brought by the Father to the Son, who names him '*Petros*'. This is the beginning of God's creation in Christ. This is, 'If any man be in Christ there is a new creation.' This is, 'We are his workmanship, created anew in Christ Jesus.'

It is a new order: a new creation: the sons of God. Hence, a new name is required.

There is an obvious play on words between the name Πέτρος, *Petros*, and the substance *πέτρα*, *petra.* The name has been—virtually—transliterated into English as 'Peter'. Whereas the substance finds its way into our tongue under such forms as 'petrify', turn into stone; 'petrography', description of formation and composition of rocks; or 'petrous', of or like rock.

The Greek name *Petros* takes a part from the whole, *petra.* Some have translated *Petros*, 'a stone', as opposed to *petra*, 'rock'. But this is feeble, because the similarity inherent in the words '*Petros*' and '*petra*', is wholly lost by the disparity in pronunciation between 'A Stone' and 'rock'.

The equivalent continuity must be maintained in English to convey the force of the Greek. 'A Rock' and 'rock', if not perfect, certainly gives the impression conveyed by *Petros* and *petra.*

Jesus answered, 'And I say also unto thee, That thou art *Petros*, and upon this *petra* I will build my assembly', Mt. 16:18.

There is absolutely no possibility of this expression meaning that Christ would build his assembly upon Peter, that is, *Petros*. Only the most wilfully ignorant or perverted manipulators of the words of Jesus could twist his speech to imply such a thing.

Christ did not say that his assembly would be built upon '*Petros*'—Peter—but upon 'this *petra*'—this rock. Not upon a segment of rock, but upon rock *as a quality*, as that substance from which the segment was taken.

The *ecclesia* would be built by Christ upon the manifestation of that substance by his Father. Of that substance, and of nothing but that substance. As to that substance, it had been exemplified in the revelation of the Son from the Father in heaven. This is what was manifested in the spiritual, heavenly, and glorious confession: 'Thou art the Christ, the Son of the living God.'

Whenever this is repeated—not in word only but—in the same manifestation of the same substance, then and there the Son will confess the work of the Father, and the building of the *ecclesia* will increase accordingly.

To continue in the superstitious delusion of the papist sect, as if the 'church' were built upon *Petros*, is a ridiculous assumption made in the very teeth of clear Greek and plain English.

Moreover, the 'church' is built by Christ directly, not by the clergy: '*I* will build'. Nothing is delegated; much less to an invented hierarchy. Christ never delegates. He remains the Builder. And he builds, ἐπὶ ταύτῃ τῃ πέτρα, *upon this petra*. Not, *upon this Petros*!

To assume from an initially fabricated interpretation a series of successors to *Petros* in a position neither given to nor occupied by him, at a place not once mentioned by either Jesus or *Petros*, is a truly breathtaking presumption.

Where is anything said of it? Where is anything said—here above all—of Rome? Where is anything said—just once will do—anywhere in the new testament of Peter having so much as put one foot in the streets of the city of Rome?

And to cap it all, why be so stupid—if one must lie in the teeth of scripture—as to 'enthrone' with a spurious elevation *the wrong apostle* upon a seat that does not exist, and never shall exist, world without end?

Peter was the apostle to the *circumcision*, Gal. 2:7. To which, if ever any city corresponded, that city was Jerusalem. Rome, however, was of the *uncircumcision*! Paul was the apostle to the uncircumcision. Moreover of Peter, and the rest of the apostles, Paul affirms 'They saw that the gospel of the *uncircumcision* was committed unto *me*.' Hence Paul *did* go to Rome. Peter did not. However Paul, though in chains, went there to preach, not sit on his backside on an imaginary throne.

Since all is invention, why not a more plausible, less impossible, invention, and make Peter the pope of Jerusalem? The answer of course is that the inventors of this system of clerical supremacy were *already* established at Rome before they commenced this legend. And there they must justify their supremacy, or risk demotion. Hence the rather they would exhume the dead dust of Peter, in order to plant those remains where he never went in his life, much less in his death, that is, the city of their ecclesiastical takeover.

In truth, Rome was a city to which Peter never went—according to the scriptures —for all the laboured papist fables. On the other hand Paul *was* the apostle to the uncircumcised. And he *did* go to Rome. But not Peter. Couldn't they even get that right? But *right* never was a criterion in popery, and it never will be. Popery is as *right* as the Vatican bank; as *right* as Calvi hanging under Blackfriars bridge; as *right* as the fugitive financial 'archbishop' skulking from Italian justice—with the connivance of the pope—in the Vatican city.

How can otherwise intelligent and able men, some responsible for nations, conglomerates, companies, businesses, how can they, I say, be so *blind* about their immortal souls, when they are so far sighted about filthy lucre? How? Because the god of this world has blinded the minds of them that believe not. For in their superstitious fear they hope that popery can save them. But popery can save no one.

After all, when we speak of the false meaning given by the papists to Mt. 16:18, and their consequent fables, we are not speaking about some remote crumbling pinnacle of the Roman Catholic edifice. We are talking of that upon which *the whole edifice rests*. It rests upon a lie, and a lie so obvious that if the blind could not see it, at least they could not help falling over it. But because the papist clergy, and all who follow them, or those who seek union or communion with them, say, 'We see', therefore their sin remaineth, and they are in darkness even until now, John 9:41.

But Christ's *ecclesia*—that which he builds, and not man—rests upon rock. Not 'a Rock', but rock. And that rock is the revelation of the Son by his Father from heaven. 'On *this* rock I will build my assembly.'

On this rock? Is this Peter? No, that would be 'on thee'. On 'Πέτρος'. But it is not on *Petros*. Not 'on thee'. It is *πέτρα*. 'On this.' Upon the quality, the substance, *petra*. Upon 'it'.

Of course Peter is associated with that substance, he exemplified it, he was the figure and precursor of it, hence his new name. The connection is evident, 'Thou art PETROS and on this PETRA.' But the one is particular and the other is general.

The particular shows that Peter is built into the *ecclesia*, but the general shows that from which the *ecclesia* is built. One is the name by which Peter is called, the other the substance from which he is named. Upon the manifestation of such substance from the Father, the Son will build up his *ecclesia*.

Then what is this rock?

What is referred to by this figurative use of the substance 'rock', is the immutability, the indestructibility, the durability of what had been manifest in Peter: 'Blessed art thou, Simon Bar-jona: for flesh and blood hath not revealed it unto thee, but my Father which is in heaven.'

He may be *Petros*, but not upon that, but upon this *petra* Christ will build his *ecclesia*. This is the rock of the Father's everlasting election in Christ, an election manifested by the revelation of the Son by the Father from heaven in point of time on earth. This is what had just been revealed in Peter, and therefore it is that which he exemplified. Nothing in heaven or earth, time or eternity, divinity or humanity, can once compare with the durability of this immutable determination. Hence the suitability of the figure 'rock'.

Jesus had asked them, Whom do men say that I the Son of man am? All had their scriptural verses and opinions: the sacramentalists; the evangelicals; the fundamentalists; the modernists; the liberals; the priests; the scribes; the lawyers; the Pharisees; the Herodians; the elders; the Sadducees. But all, to a man, all were in the flesh, and all were in the thickest darkness.

And who can wonder? For 'No man knoweth the Son, but the Father; neither knoweth any man the Father, save the Son, and he to whomsoever the Son will reveal him', Mt. 11:27.

These things were *hidden*. But now they are revealed. Hence Peter declares, according to this rock, the revelation of the Son by the Father, 'Thou art the Christ, the Son of the living God.' Revealed? Revealed to whom? Whom the Father chose to beget, and none other. Hence, the election preceded the revelation.

Straightway Jesus pronounced Simon, the Son of Jona, to be blessed. For flesh and blood had not revealed this to him—

seeing it is hidden from flesh and blood—but 'my Father which is in heaven'.

Now, this is rock. And on this, and upon nothing else, Christ builds his *ecclesia.* 'All that the Father giveth me shall come to me, and him that cometh unto me, I will in no wise cast out.'

This is not the only figurative use of 'rock'. Christ is called 'that spiritual Rock'. Simon is named '*Petros*'. Obedience to Jesus' sayings is described as being founded upon a rock. Divine principles are referred to as rock.

In Matthew 16:18, however, it is the figurative suitability of the substance of rock, answering to the eternal election, the immutable counsel, the unchangeable oath, the everlasting covenant, the divine revelation, the glorious predestination, the heavenly illumination, in a word, to the manifestation of the eternal purpose of the Father in the Son. It is this, I say, that is the reason for the use of the word 'rock' in this place.

The substance of rock—because of its peerless durability—appears as the figure of the purpose and work of the Father in bringing the election to the Son. 'Rock'. Enduring substance, abiding world without end, when all, but all, all else has long since crumbled to dust, and turned to corruption.

On this, and on nothing else whatsoever, Christ builds his *ecclesia.* All that is of man—whether biblical, scriptural, fundamental, reformed, or whatsoever else religious men boast in—all that is of man is sand. But that which had taken place in Peter was not sand. It was not of man. It was of the Father. It was rock.

All that is of man is sand. No matter how biblical, how religious, how attendant upon divine things. Given that the origin and initiative in such divine things is of man, it is called 'sand'. But that which had taken place in Peter was not of man. It was of God. It was called 'rock'.

As to man, Simon was *Bar-jona*. But what had occurred was nothing to do with *Bar-jona*, any more than it was to do with Simon. Indeed it was nothing to do with flesh and blood. It was to do with 'My Father which is in heaven'. Utterly new, wholly different. Christ's Father in heaven by his own initiative had wrought that which had been made manifest in Peter. And that is what Christ calls 'rock'.

For what had come to light—O stupendous truth!—what had come to light was that Christ's Father was Peter's Father. The *huiothesia* had come to light. This in turn revealed the rock of eternal election.

It was not flesh and blood. Flesh and blood could deduce, rationalize, intellectualize, and yet for all that not one man could so much as recognise the Son of man. How much less the Son of God.

Here were things hidden from the wise and prudent, but revealed unto babes. And the conception, source and execution of such a revelation, exclusive to babes, Jesus calls 'rock'. This was what was revealed in Peter. This was the light that shone from heaven. 'My Father in heaven'.

If '*Father* in heaven', it follows, that here was a generation from above. This birth was of God, not men. Here was the rock of divine, heavenly revelation, of glorious predestination to sonship. The rock of sons chosen in Christ before the foundation of the world according to an eternal election, to stand sure in everlasting glory, when flesh and blood, when this world and time, had passed away for ever. Rock.

Some have supposed, because Christ is called 'that Rock', I Cor. 10:4, and the apostle states that 'Other foundation can no man lay than that is laid, which is Jesus Christ', I Cor. 3:11, that Christ is therefore referring to himself when he says, Mt. 16:18, 'On this rock I will build my assembly'. But this is purblind. It is an obtuse opinion born of the supposition that because a figure—that of 'rock'—is used for one thing, it cannot be used for anything else.

Obviously it was not Christ himself, it was Peter's confession of Christ as Son of the living God. This Jesus immediately ascribes to the blessing of the revelation from his own Father in heaven. That was the subject about which Jesus used the figure 'rock', Mt. 16:18. Not himself, but the work of his Father.

As a result of this revelation from the Father, Peter had said *that.* Jesus answers—mark that, answers, Mt. 16:17—'Blessed art thou, Simon Bar-jona: for flesh and blood hath not revealed it unto thee, but my Father which is in heaven.' He then comments as follows: 'And I say *also*'—observe that word, also—'unto thee.' Also? As well as what? As well as Jesus' answer to what had just been revealed to Peter by the Father.

'And I say also unto thee, That thou art *Petros*, and upon this *petra.*' What 'petra'? The 'petra' of the immutability, the durability, the unchangeability of the Father revealing his Son by the Holy Ghost from heaven to his own elect.

Had Christ been referring to *himself*, objectively, he would have said, 'Thou art Peter and upon *me*', or, 'Thou art *Petros* and upon myself, the *petra.*' But he did not. Because he was not referring to himself objectively but to the work of the Father subjectively in Peter.

The only other construction of which these words might be presumed capable—if one were blind, or ignorant, or both—is that imposed by the papists: that *petra* refers to *Petros.*

But then, Christ could not have proceeded from the *name* 'Petros' to the *substance* 'petra' without contradicting what these people say he was maintaining. To suit the papistical gloss this place must needs read 'Thou art *Petros*, and upon this *Petros*.' But that is a nonsense. Normal form of speech would require 'Thou art *Petros*, and *upon thee* I will build my *ecclesia*.'

That it does not so read, destroys the papist myth from a point of grammatical construction. If that were necessary. For, already, no more than an honest consideration of both text and context has quite annihilated this flimsy fabrication.

Nothing remains but to conclude that Christ refers to the work of the Father, revealing the Son to Peter from heaven.

Which is what the scripture everywhere asserts and implies upon the subject of Christ receiving from the Father those given to him, in order that of them—and none other—he might in consequence build up his own assembly.

2. The Building

Whilst the building which Christ builds is spiritual, it is ridiculous to assume that it is invisible.

This is the self-justifying conceit of 'evangelicals' who, in practice, defy Christ because of the worldly and material advantage to themselves in remaining within their denominational systems, as opposed to the pain and affliction—the cross—of leaving them.

To such hypocrites, the idea of an 'invisible unity' (sic) provides the ideal panacea for their occasionally troubled conscience. Of course coupled with their dire tales of the errors, calamities, and destructions that have befallen all those who have acted contrary to their worldly wisdom and fleshly prudence by 'leaving the denominations'.

These worldly 'Christians' are the spies—and there are many of them—who tell of walled cities great and high, of giants in the land, and of the impossibility of ever attaining in this life to such idealistic dreams as the land of promise.

Then why do these worldly-wise spies think that God ever brought his people out of the land of Egypt? To abide in the worldly and divided denominations, in which they think that they can have the best of both worlds, this one now, and that one hereafter? To avoid the daily cross, and real separation?

So we see that these have not entered in because of unbelief. And we are not to be surprised later to find the wilderness littered with their carcases. Why not? Because 'I sware in my wrath, They shall not enter into my rest', Heb. 3:7-19.

But Christ will build his *ecclesia* despite them, and though the building work be interior and spiritual, the building itself is neither, it is the outward and visible assembly of brethren dwelling together in unity. 'To whom coming, as to a living stone, disallowed indeed of men, but chosen of God, and precious, ye also, as lively stones, are built up a spiritual house, to offer up spiritual sacrifices, acceptable to God by Jesus Christ', I Pet. 2:4,5.

'Ye are built up'. Not 'Ye build yourselves up'. It is certainly true that very many have erred and fallen, leading others astray, who presumed to take the work upon themselves. So what? Does their presumption justify our defiance of Christ, doing despite to the Spirit of grace, casting his words behind our back, and nullifying the cause—in the present testimony of the unity of the one body—for which the Father sent the Son?

'That they be made perfect in one; and that the world may know that thou hast sent me.' Know? By what? By an invisible 'unity', the witness of which is actual sectarianism, and its testimony, permanent division?

The *only* way in which the world can know of our spiritual unity is by seeing our *actual assembly.*

'That the world may know that thou has sent me, and hast loved them, as thou hast loved me.' Loved them as thou hast loved me? That the world may know it? Know it by seeing it? What, when we are scattered all over a world-wide building site, covered with mire, rutted with the world's traffic, mixed with every base and offensive material, not even collected in heaps, and never actually constructed?

But Paul says, 'Ye *are* God's building.' Under the apostles the material was *gathered* and actually *built up together.* All together. And without any base material. 'Rooted and built up in him', Col. 2:7. 'In whom all the building *fitly framed together* groweth unto an holy temple in the Lord: in whom ye also are builded together for an habitation of God through the Spirit', Eph. 2:21,22.

Here—Eph. 2:21,22—the saints, and all the saints—brought to Christ by the Father—are built up by the Son into one visible unity. This applies not only to all the saints in any *one* given place: it applies also to all the saints together in *every* place. For that is what constitutes the only unity. And it applies *now*—'ye also *are* builded', present tense—now; not in eternity. It is a present testimony.

Nothing less honours the Son; nothing less glorifies the Father; nothing less answers to the Spirit; nothing less agrees with the doctrine. And nothing less is in the mind and intention of Christ about all those given to him by the Father *even at this very moment.*

And no amount of sophistry, of quoting so-called 'men of God' to the contrary, of going on about—usually short-lived, and always afterwards exhausted—so-called 'revivals', real or supposed, in the various denominations, or all of them together, I say, no amount of sophistry can alter the plain testimony of the word of God, or the clear expression of the intention of Christ throughout the age till he comes again: 'Upon this rock I will build *my* assembly.'

3. The Ecclesia

'Upon this rock', declared Jesus, 'I will build my *ecclesia*', Mt. 16:18.

Now notice that this is in the singular. Not *ecclesiai*, plural, but *ecclesia*, singular. Not, Build my 'churches', many; but, Build my 'church', one.

There are assemblies; these are called Christ's assemblies, or *ecclesiai*, certainly. But what he says here is in the singular, not referring to the assemblies, plural, but to the assembly, singular. 'On this rock I will build my *assembly*.'

For lack of this simple observation, vision has failed; sight has dimmed; the horizons have contracted; darkness has descended; and division has ensued. Whatever may be true of assemblies, of *ecclesiai*, of 'churches', *they are but part of one united, singular, and divine building*. 'My *ecclesia*', singular.

The singularity of the whole *ecclesia*; the unity of the one body; the fulness of the complete house of God; the oneness of Christ's entire assembly; *all must be constantly held before the vision of each assembly* if the whole is to be realised, and disintegration is to be avoided. When Christ says 'my *assembly*', singular, he *means* 'my assembly', singular.

Here we are not talking of the sin of schism, or the transgression of denominationalism. Here it is a question of the vision of the one assembly united in any given place, answering to the unity of the one assembly united in every place.

This is not therefore to descend to the question of the denominations, sects and cults separated into their divisions locally and therefore universally from the one true assembly. It is to ascend to the heavenly vision of that one true assembly in and of itself.

But if once that true assembly, though united as one in any given place, loses the heavenly vision of *the* assembly as a whole, it will lose the touch of the heavenly Builder; it will lose the sense of the unity of the Godhead; and it will lose the awareness of the one Person of the Spirit indwelling the one *ecclesia* of Christ.

Not only will it have lost the consciousness of one God and Father, who is above all, and through all, and in all, but it will have fallen from the vision of the assembly *as Christ sees it from heaven.* Just as it will fail of the sense of purpose *for which he views, and unites, all of the assemblies together in one.*

Not only that: sooner or later it will become cut off from gifts of the Spirit locally, and—what is even more serious—from those rare and essential gifts from Christ ascended, sent from the heavenly glory, not to any one of the assemblies, but to 'my assembly'. To the whole.

Hence observe, quite apart from the fact of his 'churches', Christ views his 'church'.

Or, as one ought to say, whereas we are inclined to speak in terms of Christ's various assemblies, Christ is accustomed to speak in terms of his one assembly. 'Upon this rock I will build *my assembly.*'

Our tendency is to look about us on earth, or, at best, from earth to heaven. But Christ looks from heaven to earth. It is the work of the Holy Ghost to bring to us this vision of the *ecclesia* as seen from Christ's heavenly elevation.

Likewise, in order to convey such a glorious vision, seen by the Head from those divine heights, Christ from time to time sends down particular—and unmistakable—gifts from heaven. These heavenly gifts from Christ are not sent to any one assembly, or group of assemblies, but every assembly—because it is to *the* assembly—in order that the glory of the divine concept of the *ecclesia* might find an answering radiance in the whole *ecclesia* as one upon earth.

This heavenly work of the Son of God belongs more particularly to the truth of the body of Christ, upon which, if God permit, I hope to write in a further volume.

But the question presses, What is Christ's assembly? If he builds *his* assembly, which is it, and where is it? How can we tell it?

How can we tell it? *Only by looking from heaven*! By that, one may tell to this day what it is to which Christ refers when he says 'Upon this rock I will build my *ecclesia.*'

The light is in heaven, the radiance is of heaven, the building is from heaven, and so is the heavenly vision. Without that, one can see nothing. With it, one can and will find his building, discover his assembly, and arrive at his *ecclesia.*

Upon this rock I will build—mark that, I *will* build—my *ecclesia.* Because the Builder has ascended, the building must be from heaven; the work must be a mystery; the power must be spiritual; the structure must be unified; the vision must be glorious; the revelation must be from the Father; and the living stones must be little children.

The mind of the flesh; the intellect of man; the criteria of the world; the work of the law; none of these will ever find out this work. It will be discovered by nothing save the revelation of the mystery. My 'church'. What is it? Which is it?

It is not the Roman Catholic 'church'. This does not bear one single mark of having been built by the ascended Head from the heavenly glory. It has none of the divine, mysterious, spiritual and distinctive characteristics of Christ's *ecclesia*. Neither of the *huiothesia*. Nor of the *eklogē*.

This is no meek, unworldly, spiritual, separated, melted, contrite, lowly, heavenly body, begotten through the gospel, sanctified by the Spirit, quickened by the Father, indwelt by the Son, justified by the blood, looking for the return of Christ from heaven, bringing in that city whose builder and maker is God.

Rather, it has the pope in place of Christ, the hierarchy in place of the apostolic ministry, the priesthood in place of sonship, the clergy in place of the brethren, the dogma in place of the doctrine, the college in place of the gospel, and the Vatican in place of the heavenly city.

It has its politics, its bank, its politicians, its bankers—dead or alive—its kings, queens, princes, rulers, presidents, lords. It has its countries, territories, properties, stocks, shares, treasures, investments. It has its cathedrals, abbeys, priories, 'churches', monasteries, convents, palaces, mansions, and its innumerable great houses.

But Christ's *ecclesia* has nothing. Nothing on earth. Nothing at all. Save Father, Son, and Holy Ghost. Nothing, that is, but what comes from heaven with the evangel.

The Roman Catholic sect has tradition in place of scripture, free will in place of election, imagination in place of revelation, superstition in place of faith, general atonement in place of redemption, universal charity in place of the love of Christ, Arminianism in place of free grace, Sinai in place of Zion, Esau in place of Jacob, Ishmael in place of Isaac, and, in practice though not in name, a Pilate for a Peter, an Annas for a John, and a Caiaphas for a Paul.

Here, the first man is put for the second, the first Adam for the last, time for eternity, money for glory, man for God, the carnal mind for the spiritual, and this world for the next.

This is an ancient system where philosophy is in place of prophecy, the flesh in place of the Spirit, the law in place of the gospel, a wafer in place of the indwelling Christ, and sacraments in place of the anointing. It has candles for light, clergy for life, and a box for love. It has vestments for appearance, a collar for show, and a title for pride.

But the apostles had nothing. Not a thing.

The assembly had none—but none—of the things essential to popery.

How then can this Roman Catholic system be called Christ's *ecclesia*? It cannot. In truth it cannot. He has not named it, he does not call it, and he will not own it. It is utterly the opposite to what he calls 'My *ecclesia*'.

The so-called 'Church of England', or, more properly, the Anglican sect, has as its head—further to an ancient argument with the pope over a divorce—the King, or, if you please, the Queen, of England. It has as its members the general population, based on geographical 'parishes'.

Christ's *ecclesia*, however, has as its Head the Son of God. His members are those of his body. His assembly is the *huiothesia*, that is, the heavenly and divine election. And where is the similarity between the Anglican sect and that?

Not very long ago the populace was forced by law— irrespective of belief—to pay 'tithes' to the 'clergy', as the erstwhile Roman Catholic priesthood preferred to be known after the king's divorce. But the 'clergy' were just as much 'priests' as ever. They were still bred up at Oxford or Cambridge. They were still clothed in 'priestly' garments of superstitious medieval invention. And they were still known by flattering titles invented by the old Roman Catholic sect. And they still extorted tithes.

But how shall this conveniently converted 'reformed' priesthood, in steeple-houses made of stone, wood, bricks, and mortar—called by them 'the houses of God'—make their parishioners members of Christ, seeing that the Father has reserved this heavenly privilege to himself, revealing Christ to none but his own chosen sons?

They shall do it by tap-water. And, lest it seem a thing incredible that gowned and robed 'priests', intoning some formula within their steeple-houses, could be equal to such a task, it shall be done only to the incredulous: that is, to the barest infants.

This strange work commences with the words, 'Sanctify this water to the washing away of sin'; and concludes with the breathtaking statement, 'Seeing now'—*now*: see?—'Seeing now that this child is regenerate and grafted into the body of Christ's church.'

And—if blasphemy be the ascribing to the creature what is proper to the Creator alone—what is this but blasphemy? And who would accept, much less practice it, but that priesthood, 'evangelical' and all, which leads the unthinking and superstitious multitudes into subscribing to their own—that is, the clergy's—sin?*

Then the 'Church of England' is not Christ's *ecclesia.* It may be the Monarch's sect, and a papistical kind of sect at

*Read 'The Gospel of God', Tract for the Times No. 1, The Publishing Trust. See advertising pages.

that—as events have more than borne out in the issue—but it is not Christ's *ecclesia.*

At its best, before events proved anything, the 'Church' of England's origins, its monarchical head, its national structure, its clerical system, its popish liturgy, its Arminian clergy, its sacramental basis; its confounding the world's force and heaven's power, human education and divine revelation, man's authority and divine sanction, earthly buildings and the heavenly *ecclesia*; I say, at best, this confusion showed that a system gendered by the wrath of the king was anything but reformed save for a sheet of paper with some thirty-nine theoretic articles written thereon.

In truth, the Anglican sect is anything but the divine, heavenly, mystical, spiritual, lowly, other-worldly and separated *ecclesia* of Christ.

The same in principle is true of Presbyterianism, another system allied to and supported by the worldly power. Unlike Christ and his apostles, Presbyterianism by no means disdains the use of the sword and war to impose its principles, and the use of the magistrate to maintain them. However, this earthly mixture resembles anything but the heavenly *ecclesia* of Christ.

Unable to extricate so much as the righteousness of faith from the old covenant system of justification by works, the sheer confusion of their 'theology'—as they call it—renders Presbyterian 'justification' unlawful. The same price for justification is, according to them, demanded, and paid, twice over,* and to effect such an injustice, they would force this pernicious system upon Christ.

*Read 'Justifying Righteousness', Tract for the Times No. 10, The Publishing Trust. See advertising pages.

Next, the Presbyterian 'church' member must keep the law as a rule of life! To make such an enormity acceptable, with Antinomian lawlessness Presbyterianism robs the law of its sanctions, pretending that this 'Christian rule' (sic) has no penalty! What? A sentence of death the rule of life? This is to be under the old yoke with a witness. But with what a setting aside of the cross of Christ.

Not only does such 'doctrine' contradict the faith once delivered to the saints, but it dishonours the law once given by Moses. The law must be the rule of the Christian, but—wonder of wonders—it carries no penal sanctions! Then it is not law. Law without penal sanctions is a contradiction in terms. It becomes impotent. It is reduced to advice. Then, if advice, there is no obligation to take it. Now, here is Antinomianism with a witness.

But woe betide—for example—the 'sabbath breaker' among the Presbyterians who fails of this 'advice', for sanctions enough shall be wheeled out from the Highland armoury to make the offender blanch. What hath he done? Woe unto him! He hath broken the sabbath; he hath desecrated the Lord's day!

But God calls the sabbath the seventh day of the week, which the poor man broke not. As to the Lord's day, it is a mystical figure, it is 'the day of the Lord'. The Son has ascended into the heavens, there to abide on high. This is the reign of the Lord in the unbroken light of the glory of heaven since the victorious ascension, about which the benighted offender learned absolutely nothing from these blind legalists.

No victory for the Presbyterian. Under an iron system of letter-learned clergy, the congregation must sit—preferably rigid with fear—silent throughout, under the law of condemnation and cursing as a 'rule of life' till death do them part. But the law is not a rule of life. It is called, the ministration of death, and life is what it cannot give, neither can it render advice on how it may be obtained.

Condemnation is the law's ministry, a killing letter is its character, and the sentence of death is all that shall ever be dispensed by it to every poor prisoner beneath its iron yoke—under whatever system—world without end.

And what in heaven or on earth, in time or eternity, before God or man, in the sight of devils or angels, I say, whatever has Christ's *ecclesia*—which is delivered from the law, and in nowise under it—I repeat, whatever has Christ's *ecclesia* to do with a mixed legal—and clerical—system such as this? Nothing. Nothing at all.

Partly the error lies in the nature of Protestantism. Protestantism is by definition a *protest*. It says—and quite rightly—Rome is wrong. But the gospel is an affirmation. The gospel was not based on a protest. The gospel—unlike the protest, 'No' and 'Never' to Rome—the gospel, I say, affirms 'Yea' and 'Amen' in Christ Jesus to every promise of God. The gospel is wholly positive.

The protest of Protestantism was, and is, both right and necessary in itself. But, by definition, it is not the affirmation of the gospel. That affirmation rang out long before the dark errors of the Romish sect existed.

The historical protest was surely right. It ought to have been made; and it ought to be made to this day. Because it is true. But that will not bring in the *ecclesia*. The protest must be continued. But that will not recover the gospel. The *ecclesia*, and the gospel, as revealed in the beginning, are other, different, matters entirely from the exposure of what is wrong.

The same applies to the Reformation. By definition reformation is the reshaping, or re-forming, of something already existent. So it was. But as it pertains to the 'ministry' and the 'church', the Reformation never purged out the old leaven, only reshaped the old lump, re-formed it.

However pure the articles of doctrine—and they were not *that* pure; they were really quite mixed: they were re-formed—those articles were quite another thing from the priesthood and the liturgy actually practiced and performed by the 'church'.

The 'reformed' creeds, confessions, and articles of the learned clergy were something other than that gospel preached in the beginning by those 'ignorant and unlearned', of whom men then took knowledge that 'they had been with Jesus'. Even as the learned clergy of that day said of Jesus himself: 'Whence hath this man letters, never having learned?'

But he spake as one having authority, and not as these scribes.

The gospel at the first began to be spoken by the Lord, and was confirmed to the saints by those that heard him, God bearing them witness. The faith was once delivered to the saints—not the clergy; not the pastors; not the ministers: the saints—and that gospel, in the purity of the doctrine of Christ, that gospel, I say, as delivered in the beginning, needs no re-forming. It needs recovering.

Independency is another system diametrically opposed to Christ's *ecclesia*.

In its nature, independency consists of a series of voluntary organisations, loosely bonded together denominationally but independent the one from the other.

It is a party system in which those subscribing to the rules of entry, or membership, of each respective 'church'—as its voluntary societies quaintly style themselves—are entitled to a say in its government.

That government is on the basis of one man one vote. Or one woman—it makes no difference—one vote. The Ayes have it. And, usually, they are feminine.

Here is the wholesale adoption of the polity evolved in ancient—and heathen—Greece. It is the system known as Democracy—from *demos*, crowd; and *kratos*, might: 'the might of the crowd'.

In the practice of independency the voting power of the many becomes the systematic contradiction of the singular rule of Christ. For his will is the disbandment of this sectarian adoption of heathen politics, set up in defiance of his absolute right to exercise government according to his own sovereign majesty.

On just such a 'democratic' basis the Baptist 'church' rests, as also does that of the Congregationalists. In effect, so does much—though not all—of the Open Brethren system. By *their* building *their* memberships, or 'those in fellowship', each of these sects in fact nullifies with total and devastating effect—whether or not true Christians be found in their systems—the building by *Christ himself* of his *own* assembly.

Unlike these sects, Christ builds those alone given to him by his Father, to whom the Father has vouchsafed the heavenly revelation. Independency, the Baptist, the Open Brethren systems, by their very existence, prevent this taking place. Their systems are an alien method of organising the religious —whether real or not—wholly incompatible with that which is built up by Christ from heaven.

Brethrenism *properly* so called—from which 'Bethesdaism', or Open Brethrenism, was a calamitous departure—is a different question.

Here was a sincere and earnest attempt to face the issues of denominationalism, and of the many divisions of the 'church', whether Anglican, Presbyterian, Methodist—an avowedly Arminian Society not intended at its inception to become a separate 'church' at all—papist, Baptist, Congregationalist, or other independents.

The commencement of the Brethren movement sprang from the conviction that denominationalism was a sin into which Christians had fallen, from which they should repent, and out of which they needed to be delivered, being brought into the unity of one body with their brethren.

Brethren never professed that the resultant assemblies *were* the 'church', or even *a* 'church'. Only that theirs was the position which, were all saints to repent and unite in the same way, would become commensurate with the assembly as it had been in the beginning.

It was never felt that such an ideal would be reached, but here was the path of obedience. At the least the position was being held for the Lord, and held on behalf of every other Christian in each locality, throughout the world, whether they answered to it or not.

This was a noble stance. As to themselves, whether but two or three, they would 'depart from iniquity'—the iniquity of sectarianism—and unite in nothing but the name of the Lord Jesus, gathering in the unity of the Spirit and of the one body.

Brethren refused to gather on any lesser ground, or on any partial ground, however true in itself. Creeds, forms of ordinance, differences of government, 'church' memberships, all these were grounds of division, and they were to leave such opinions behind, uniting only to the 'centre', the Lord Jesus Christ.

There was no question of claiming to be the 'church'—that was in irreparable ruin: it could never be recovered or built again. It was simply a question of 'coming out' to gather in the name of the Lord Jesus, and to await his return, as simple brethren, no distinctions.

There had been apostles in the beginning of course. There were their writings. The apostles, however, had no successors, although they did appoint 'delegates'. A strange word, without any scriptural precedent. 'Delegates' was an invention of Brethrenism to avoid otherwise impossible difficulties about the ministry.

Strange indeed, because the Brethren were such sticklers for their own selected jots and tittles of the letter of scripture. Or it was thought that they were. Then why such an alien sounding invention as 'delegates'? Could no more plausible excuse be found for dismissing what—to their embarrassment—was so obviously *there*?

Delegates, however, could not delegate. In the Brethren system. Hence, with the decease of Timothy, Titus, and the like, both delegates and delegations passed away. Long ago. Leaving only Brethren. Simple. Now all were brothers, and all were to unite as such. Office was anathema. Any 'ministry' was 'a brother with a gift'. And openness for every man ministry was *de rigueur* for a system already developing all the marks of a sect or cult despite themselves.

Quite apart from the precondition of dismissing the continuation of the new testament ministry, in Brethrenism, if one were not premillennial or dispensationalist, if one held justification to be by the imputing of righteousness, if one did not positively espouse Arminian 'love', if one sang psalms, or scripture only, and if one still wished to remain 'in', then one had better keep one's head pretty low, and hold one's peace with due prudence.

In short, by the noble principle of seeking unity, but on the ignoble basis of doing so as if in practice nothing were more important than submission to their own dispensational and other dogma, truth *had* been sacrificed, although Brethren would never admit it.

But truth was sacrificed. Obsessed with their own criterion of unity, or, rather, the appearance of that unity, whatever 'divided' the profession of Christianity must be refused. One sought out those who 'loved the Lord'; or who said they did.

Incredibly, Brethren supposed 'the Lord's people' to be everywhere and anywhere in the divisions of Christendom, irrespective of the decadence of the systems concerned. Roman Catholic, Greek Orthodox, outlandish sect, no matter. Since the great sin was 'division', the relative state of the divisions was immaterial. But the truth stands that evangelical belief was *impossible* in many of the decadent systems from which Brethren still looked for 'the Lord's people'.

Whereas whatever 'united' professing Christians, as long as there was a mere lip-service profession of 'loving the Lord Jesus'—never mind if from the darkest Romish or Eastern apostasy; no matter how void of the interior work of the Spirit; irrespective of how destitute of doctrine the confession —this was avidly embraced.

All were 'the Lord's people', dear brethren. Even if, for example, in darkest popery, Eastern idolatry, or blind sacramentalism. The vaguest claim of 'loving the Lord Jesus', even the wistful *thought* of it on the part of Brethren, this was sufficient to usher in the longing for their presence at their vacant seat around 'the Lord's table'.

Inevitably such an infatuation involved a jettisoning of the more unpalatable doctrines of grace, of divine sovereignty, as also the necessity of the interior work of the Spirit. There was by default a holding forth of what was universally acceptable in order to favour gathering at their table the maximum number without giving doctrinal or experimental offence.

Then, Arminianism, and levelling, were inherent in the system, which, unscripturally, began by *assuming* the existence of Christians, though divided. The apostles and their 'delegates' did not. They assumed the *gospel of God*, and that to be the means of converting and gathering the *ecclesia* of Christ.

For the Son of God himself builds up his own assembly from heaven. Not Brethren from the earth. And *builds* it. Not leaves it levelled flat, without form, order, or authority.

Moreover Christ does not build his assembly upon some theory of 'the ground of gathering', or of 'the ruin of the church'; much less upon the presumption of 'easy-believing'. He builds it by the commandment of the everlasting God, by the sending forth of ministers from on high in the glory, by the preaching of the gospel with the Holy Ghost sent down from heaven, by the proclamation of Jesus Christ, according to the revelation of the mystery.

This brings in Christ's *ecclesia*, and nothing else brings in Christ's *ecclesia*. No amount of subsequent theorising about dispensationalism, about the 'ruin of the church', about 'delegates', about 'the Lord's table', about 'the ground of gathering', alters this. All these Brethren theories are a substitute for the truth. That gospel, that apostolic gospel, which was in the beginning, once sent again in calling and power from heaven, that, I say, that will bring in what has been lost. Nothing else will; because nothing else can; even to the end of the age.

Since the very heart of Brethrenism was, and is, the question of unity, a 'simple gospel'—a euphemism for Arminian error—became its necessary periphery, the heart of the movement being centred about the Lord's table, the hallowed symbol of its existence.

This central event took place on 'Lord's day morning'. That is, it took precedence over the preaching or teaching of the word of God, or, indeed, of any worship at all other than in this devised form.

The Brethren felt themselves to be sublimely superior. They were conscious of being wholly 'scriptural'. But they were not so scriptural, much less were they so spiritual, in the first principles of the foundation and building of the *ecclesia* of Christ.

In fact Brethren were not scriptural even as to the name of their hallowed symbol. Because the Lord's supper is not called 'breaking of bread' at all in scripture. 'Breaking of bread' in itself refers to a simple meal. Certainly bread was broken as *part* of the supper, but only as a part. A part which never once, no, not once, lent its name to the whole. The name of the whole was, and is, 'The supper of the Lord'.

The Lord's supper is never once recorded—in the scripture—as having taken place on the first day of the week. The common meal—'breaking bread'—of Acts 20:7, took place after midnight, and, therefore during the early hours of Monday morning, the second day of the week. In any event, that common meal, or breaking of bread, was not called The Lord's supper. Neither in Acts 20:7, nor anywhere else. Again, this meal was taken after some hours of preaching, which, as always, came first.

Finally, supper, of course, is taken by normal persons in the evening, and not between breakfast and lunch.

Once examined by those who seek for the truth, the whole truth, and nothing but the truth, concerning Christ and the *ecclesia*, immediately the flimsiness of Brethrenism is exposed in its basic traditions and theories. And so is their characteristic of flitting from text to text, alighting as fleetingly, and as arbitrarily as a butterfly upon so many blooms, quite carried away with fanciful allegories. And all this in place of the solid, doctrinal, Spirit-filled and experimental exposition of the word of God.

It would be quite wrong, and unfair, to deny that much was right about Brethrenism that sorely needed to be stated. Likewise so much was faced that the denominations of Christendom perpetually avoided. But so much was wrong *in principle* from the very beginning.

The beginning did not last long. Due to interminable squabbles, and, of course, the *inherent* absence of authority in a system built on levelling, Brethrenism split up into more divisions and splinters than any of the sects which it proposed to remedy, and, in some cases, these divisions fell into very serious errors indeed.*

Brethrenism never was the divine and scriptural solution to the sin of schism and denominationalism which it supposed itself to be. But at least the early Brethren had the moral courage to face the issues of the assembly; at least they did something about the evil; and at least much was brought out and recovered that had long been lost.

Nevertheless, I repeat, Brethrenism was not then, and its innumerable splinters are not now, the answer to Christ's *ecclesia*, for the simple reason that Brethren *built themselves* into a system on different theoretic principles, and other bases, than that rock upon which Christ himself builds his own *ecclesia*.

It is customary for those with vested religious interests to attempt to justify the iniquity of denominationalism on the ground of past—so-called—'revivals'.

In revivals of religion, as they are named, after long periods of deadness and dryness, there comes a time of spiritual awakening. This is accompanied by an earnest spirit of prayer. But it must be recalled that revivals took place in 'churches' which

*Read 'Eternal Sonship and Taylor Brethren', Tract for the Times No. 3, The Publishing Trust. See advertising pages.

were, in those distant times, 'orthodox'. But where has this 'orthodoxy' gone now? Where is it today, that men should pass their time in dreams of the past? And when was the last 'revival', so-called?

'Revivals' did not—and do not—justify denominationalism. For short periods they transcended it, with all the awareness being upon the conversion of sinners: but as soon as it came to 'the perfecting of the saints', let alone 'the edification of the body', where then was the revival?

Turning away from the state—even the existence—of the denominations, revivals were concerned with sound conversions. First, of the affected congregations; then, of all round about them. That was the urgency.

But after that, what? After that, the unspoken and unfaced issues caused the sleep of death to fall again over the still divided parties. A sleep that was to remain unbroken for ages and generations, whilst each denomination succumbed in turn to modernism, indifference, affluence, and sheer worldliness.

This suited the clergy: they were not going to give up the position and power to which they owed everything. They would do nothing to destroy the structural existence of that denomination in which they had 'trained' and from which, in effect, they received both their stipend and their honourable status.

Saving souls was all very well. But enough was enough!

And do the heirs of these dead clergy justify their positions, and those of their denominations, because of some ancient 'revival'? Revivals justifying denominationalism? What are these clergy talking about? Sheer rubbish.

Revivals strove to overcome denominationalism. But vested interests and clerical jealousy choked them sooner rather than later, and hence the rarity was the revival: the norm, dead denominationalism.

The wane of revival came as soon as the initial turning of sinners passed on to the question of their growth. The end of revival came once the new converts sought a unity outside their denominational structures. Then the 'normal' state of deadness became again the rule of the denominations, as, alarmed, the 'clergy' swiftly asserted their authority over the 'laity'.

J.N. Darby once remarked that revivals were like pure water poured out on the ground: it became mud. And so it has proved. And that, when the ground was at least 'orthodox'.

Besides, the apostolic *ecclesia* did not proceed by such a process. One cannot find the word 'revival' in the mouth of an apostle. Nor of the Lord. One reads of sin reviving, or of the Lord 'reviving' from the dead. But the word 'revival' is not in the new testament. Pentecost was unique in every way. Look for a repetition of what was unique, and Satan will provide a duplicate. For God will never repeat what was done once and for all. 'Revival' was never a new testament process, any more than it was a new testament word. Hence, when awakenings have been genuine, their meaning and purpose has more often been misunderstood than not.

But things proceeded on quite another basis in scripture, which in fact records not the progress of denominationalism, but the prevention of it, as Christ built his own *ecclesia* by his own methods. Methods which certainly did not include a series of awakenings interrupting an otherwise perpetual state of deadness prevailing over the iniquity of unchallenged and unrepentant denominationalism.

Others love to justify their sectarian position by pointing to past men of God, especially of their own sect, much as do the Roman Catholics with their saints.

Witness how many point to the Reformation, or to the puritan period, or to the Westminster assembly, as though that were more than the scripture. In fact to them such periods, persons and things are stronger than scripture, because as far as they are concerned, here is the last word on scripture, and, if so, scripture no longer speaks for itself.

However, their patron saints, or sainted periods, speak to them instead of scripture, let them squeak as much as they will. The truth is, to these followers of men, scripture has no other voice than that of the dead men and past times which they idolize. Whilst, more often than not, they live carnal, worldly, empty, and lazy lives, not remotely squaring up with those whom they profess to admire.

At the very best they suppose that the faith of others is transferable to them. It is not. Woe be to those that thus glory in man, and hold the dead traditions of the fathers instead of the commandment of the living God. Where is the difference *in principle* between them and the Romanists who justify themselves and their sect on the basis of those whom they in their turn consider to be the saints? To the law and to the testimony! Isa. 8:20.

Far from such traditions, not even the dead letter will do for God's elect, for the letter killeth, but the Spirit giveth life. Living souls must have all their teaching from scripture, not out of themselves, not from the views of others, not through imbibing traditions, but by the revelation of Jesus Christ.

To use others, holy men, or special periods of history, to justify the sin of denominationalism is worse than justifying the rebellious ten tribes of Israel on the basis that prophets were raised up to testify against them for not returning to the unity of the house of David at Jerusalem.

Then there are those Tobiahs and Sanballats who would weaken the hands and discourage the hearts of God's elect from being built up by Christ in his *ecclesia* because, you see, they have seen it all before, it has all been tried, you know, and, of course, it all came to nothing. They can tell us.

Oh? so these wiseacres have seen it all before, have they, they have tried it, and know everything, do they? They can surely tell us that all is doomed to failure, can they? Then we are to lie complacent in failure like them, are we?

And have they seen a drunkard trying to get off the drink, and will they tell him, 'Ah, yes, we have seen it all before, you know, and it will all end in failure'? Oh, no, we must not say so of them, that be far from them so to speak.

From which one may discern plainly that their setting back and discouraging those who seek for whatsoever things are honest, just, pure, and of good report, applies only to those who seek thus for the things of Christ. Christ's building his own *ecclesia*, they will deride and discourage. Man and his worksmongering, do-gooding, blue-ribbon signing, they will applaud and encourage.

But what if there has been failure? What if there were mistakes? Have they never heard of Bruce and the spider, since a worldly fable seems necessary if one desires to speak to their condition? As to us, David suits our condition: 'Surely I will not come into the tabernacle of my house, nor go up into my bed; I will not give sleep to mine eyes, or slumber to mine eyelids, until I find out a place for the LORD, an habitation for the mighty God of Jacob', Psalm 132:3-5.

This is the Spirit of Christ in David, and it is the same Spirit in us, but it is very far from the spirit that is in them.

These are the selfsame people who stand for man and his sinful sectarianism, the very ones who deny Christ and his own *ecclesia*. They will encourage self-help, self-will, and all manner of self-righteousness, but let a man once seek Christ, his things, his *ecclesia*, his unity, his body, and, lo, there is a lion in the streets, they have seen it all before, it will all come to nothing, it is too hard, they can see it is no use. But they are the ones who are no use.

As to us, our language is this: Christ loved the assembly; and so do we. Christ gave himself for the assembly; and so will we. As to doing good to man, compared to upholding the cause of Christ, this is our speech: 'Whom have I in heaven but thee? and there is none upon earth that I desire beside thee', Psalm 73:25.

We will let these devil's advocates alone to work their own will. As to us, our language is 'Thy will be done'. Thus, for us, all is for Christ, and, to us, all of Christ's things are pre-eminent. Especially is this true of the assembly which he loved, for which he shed his precious blood, and for which he gave himself.

For this, for his continued, present, experimental building of his own one true *ecclesia*, we will count our own will, our own life, our all, as nothing but dung and dross, gladly laying down our honour in the dust for Christ's sake. And when we have done all this, and maintained it, what is it all, to count as sacrifice, beside his heavenly glory, his divine building, his own good pleasure? It is but nothing.

Then, so far from being discouraged, we will encourage ourselves in the Lord continually, let men do what they may. For, lo, he is with us alway, even unto the end of the age. And for what cause is he with us to the end of the age but to accomplish his own will? To the very end!

'Now unto him that is able to do exceeding abundantly above all that we ask or think, according to the power that worketh in us, unto him be the glory in the *ecclesia* throughout all ages, world without end. Amen.'

VI

The beginning of the Ecclesia

IT cannot be over-emphasized that the *ecclesia* of Christ, the assembly, is entirely new: nothing remotely like it existed prior to the day of Pentecost and the giving of the Holy Ghost. Christ's assembly is not in any sense a continuation of old testament Israel and its assembly.

In the one case Jehovah was veiled, and in thick darkness. In the other, the God and Father of our Lord Jesus Christ has been revealed in radiant light. One was earthly, the other heavenly. One was carnal, the other spiritual.

The one was temporal, the other is eternal. One was under the law, the other delivers from the law. In the one case the people were kept at forbidding distance by a mediatorial priesthood. In the other case the people have been brought within the sanctuary, and have become the priesthood.

One people was condemned by Moses through the legal commandment; the other has been justified by grace through the faith of Jesus Christ.

In the one testament God's wrath was kindled, the people were cursed, and the law was a ministration of death. In the other testament God has been appeased, the people are blessed, and the gospel is nothing but a savour of life unto life to all the heirs of promise. Just no compatibility between the two, no compatibility at all.

On every count the new testament *ecclesia* is a wholly new thing.

Yet the truth is, in most principles, and many respects, present-day Christendom appears closer to the legal system of earthly Israel, with its bondage to the priestly ministrations of man, than it does to the glorious grace of the heavenly *ecclesia*, with its liberty under the divine ministry of the Son of God.

Then, a new work is needed, and should be expected, recovering to our own day all that has been lost since the beginning.

When the Father revealed the Son to Peter at Caesarea Philippi, this brought to light a mystery which had been hidden from ages and generations, from the very foundation of the world.

This prophetic vision of the Son—although given before the cross—actually presumed his having been crucified, raised from the dead, ascended and seated as Son in the glory, in manhood, on behalf of his people. It presumed the Holy Ghost having been poured out from heaven to fill the *ecclesia* on earth.

That is the nature, as it is the character, of Christ's assembly: it is an entirely new, divine, heavenly, spiritual, supernatural, and glorious mystery.

Christ's assembly did not exist before, save in the eternal purpose of God, Father, Son, and Holy Ghost. But the atonement having been made, propitiation effected, redemption accomplished, justification wrought, righteousness imputed, the Spirit outpoured, the Father and his children—the *huiothesia*—were made one in divine and heavenly glory in Christ.

Christ being risen from the dead, the people for whom he died, seen as having died in him, necessarily were viewed in the counsels of God as raised up together with Christ from the grave.

The Son being ascended to his Father and their Father, his God and their God, he and his people being all of one, it followed also that they were viewed in God's purpose as ascended and seated together with him.

Before the *ecclesia* even began, therefore, this was its position, achieved vicariously by the death, burial, resurrection, and ascension of the Son of God. Hence, Christ ascended, the Spirit given, there came to pass the beginning of the fulfilment of the saying of Jesus at Caesarea Philippi, 'Upon this rock I will build my assembly.'

'Upon this rock'—that is, the rock of the revelation of the Son by his Father in heaven, drawing to the Son those whom he had chosen according to his own divine purpose and election in Christ.

'I will build'—not, 'I have built', or 'I continue building': which might have seemed to have applied to Israel, or to appear to have some continuity with what went before; but, 'I will build'. This refers to a future, new, different, work, about to begin in the manner made conspicuous by the Father's heavenly revelation to Peter.

'I will build my *ecclesia*'—then, this was the beginning of the *ecclesia*. This therefore must be the point, and the only conceivable point throughout time to the very end, I say, this must be the point of reference to which all must be brought, and by which all must be tried thereafter.

It was not that Jehovah had not wrought in Israel, or, indeed, throughout the old testament: he had. But he had not wrought this.

Now, through the Father's revelation from heaven of the Son by the Holy Ghost, a new work was to commence. An entirely new creation from God out of heaven would have its beginning.

This work would originate individually with the Father's revelation of the Son from heaven. The Son, recognising and receiving every one in whom this work had been wrought, would by the Holy Ghost from heaven build in, and build up, all those taught of the Father to come to him. The result of this building work he called, and calls, 'My *ecclesia*'.

The watershed was the day of Pentecost. That was the true beginning.

To that beginning everything that is subsequent ought to be true, for to it all must be brought, and by it every single word and work shall be judged at the last day.

It is therefore vital to understand the beginning of the *ecclesia*, and the *ecclesia* in the beginning. Everything since is totally irrelevant. Irrelevant? Yes, because everything since must itself be judged by the same one—and only—criterion.

Then what of the work of God before the existence of the *ecclesia*, in the days of the old testament?

Before, from the times of the patriarchs, God had wrought salvation in the earth. Before, God indeed had his people, just as much called his saints as those of the new testament.

He was their Saviour. By him they had been alarmed, awakened, convicted, and quickened. From him was their faith, their repentance, their righteousness, their obedience, their love, their hope, and their endurance. Of this the Spirit bears testimony in the eleventh chapter of the epistle to the Hebrews.

They were a regenerate people, Jehovah had quickened them to life. He was their light and their salvation. From him they received their help, for he was the Mighty One of Jacob. He was the saving strength of Israel.

All this is clear, never more so than in the psalms. But all this was either an individual work wrought in the patriarchs, or that wrought in the saints of Jehovah on earth in Israel within the confines of the old covenant and under the constrictions of the old law.

Now the veil of the temple has been rent in twain from the top to the bottom, the earth has been shaken, and the rocks have been rent. Now the darkness is past and the true light shines. Now even the dead have been raised to life again. If so, the *new* testament has begun.

God has gone up with a shout, the LORD with the sound of a trumpet. Heaven rings with the shouting of victory. God has triumphed gloriously, God sitteth upon the throne of his holiness.

Now Christ has ascended on high, all righteousness fulfilled. God's righteousness is declared for the remission of sins that are past. The Father has been glorified in the Son, and the Son has been glorified by the Father.

Christ is seated on the throne of his Father. The new work is wrought from heaven by the Son, glorified in manhood, a divine work, a heavenly work, an everlasting work: the work of Christ in building his own *ecclesia*.

The *new* testament has commenced, and it has proved new beyond all that eye could see, or ear could hear, beyond all that ever did, or ever could, enter into the heart of man to conceive. This is the beginning of the *ecclesia*.

The beginning of the *ecclesia* commenced with the baptism of the Holy Ghost.

This had been foretold by John the Baptist: 'He that sent me to baptize with water, the same said unto me, Upon whom thou shalt see the Spirit descending, and remaining on him, the same is he which baptizeth with the Holy Ghost. And I saw, and bare record that this is the Son of God.'

This baptism, which brings in Christ's *ecclesia*, and which brings into Christ's *ecclesia*, this baptism, I say, took place on the day of Pentecost. This was the day on which the Son of God poured out the Holy Ghost from heaven, who, descending, filled the whole company.

The baptism of the Spirit therefore is corporate.

The baptism of the Spirit is for the company, or to bring one individually into that company.

'For by one Spirit are we all baptized into one body, whether we be Jews or Gentiles, whether we be bond or free; and have been all made to drink into one Spirit.'

By this baptism the Holy Ghost himself fills the *ecclesia*. By the fulness of the Holy Ghost in the *ecclesia*, Christ indwells his own assembly. By the indwelling of the Son within that assembly, the habitation of God and the Father is made complete.

Here is the fulfilling of the house of God, which is the *ecclesia* of the living God, the pillar and ground of the truth.

It is the oneness of God in Father, Son, and Holy Ghost that is manifest in the *ecclesia*. God dwells in his assembly, and only his assembly, the world being void of his presence.

By this divine indwelling—from which the whole world is excluded—the entire *ecclesia* has the testimony of being the only habitation of God. But the whole world has nothing at all that is of God.

The world is therefore convinced by the power and witness of the Spirit come down from heaven to dwell in Christ's *ecclesia*. Convinced, that is, by so palpable a divine presence in the assembly. Whereas the world, void of that divine presence, has nothing but emptiness in itself.

'If I go not away, the Comforter will not come unto you: but if I depart, I will send him unto you. And when he is come, he will'—by no more than the fulness of his presence in the entire *ecclesia*, over against his total absence from the whole world—'he will reprove the world of sin, and of righteousness, and of judgment.'

'Of sin, because they believe not on me'. But the *ecclesia* believes on him, and the Spirit's powerful presence fills and indwells the *ecclesia*, clearly endorsing that belief. But he does not endorse the unbelieving world, which is altogether void of his presence.

But why not? Because they do not believe on the Christ, the Son of the living God.

'Of righteousness, because I go to my Father'. He goes, that is, having first brought in justifying righteousness by the shedding of his blood on behalf of all who believe, but of none who disbelieve. Thus it is that Christ goes to the Father, who sends the Spirit to the justified assembly, but denies him to the condemned world.

The Spirit fills the one, and leaves the other empty. This convinces the world of righteousness having been wrought on behalf of the Spirit-filled assembly, but not for the self-justifying world.

'Of judgment, because the prince of this world is judged'. The world denied the true Christ. The world hopes for another Christ—more compatible with its taste—yet to come. Thus the world denied not only the Son but the Father which sent him. The world owns—but in different forms, by various paths, in diverse ways—one god. But it was in the name of their one god, and for his service, that the world crucified the Son.

But the baptism of the Spirit was upon the *ecclesia*. Not upon the world. Then who was the god of this world?

Their god was the prince of this world, who had just been judged. That convinced them of judgment.

It was not so much what was preached. It was not so much the apostles' doctrine. It was the fulness of the presence of the Holy Ghost in the whole assembly, and his total absence from the whole world. That in itself convinced the world not only of sin, not only of righteousness, but of coming judgment on all the earth and on the spirit that was in it, besides every worldly system, religious, political, and social.

This sharp almost tangible difference between the assembly and the world will and must appear whenever and wherever Christ builds his assembly.

Otherwise, of what worth are his words?

But his words are invaluable, and hence, always come to pass. If they do not come to pass in the denominations, sects, organisations and assemblies of men, for all their presumptuous claims, theories and doctrines, there can be but one conclusion: *they* are the builders, and the builders of a dead, unendorsed religion.

As for him, *he* is the Stone which these builders rejected. And that rejection is the norm of this present day, in terms of the 'church'. Save for a few, very few, separated and gathered saints.

However, the more the truth is fearlessly held forth, the more the Spirit will baptize into one body, and the more we shall see by faith with our own eyes the result of the fact that Christ repeats this day these words from heaven 'Upon this rock I will build my *ecclesia*'.

From everlasting to everlasting the *ecclesia* abides a heavenly and divine concept, to which in time the assembly on earth, filled with the the Holy Ghost, conforms.

It was but one. It must be one. The *ecclesia* answered in unity as a body to the Head, as a bride to the Husband, as a household to the Father, as a city to the King, as a temple to the Holy Ghost. One assembly.

This was most clearly seen in the very beginning at Jerusalem. There was but one pool of light, it was the one *ecclesia*. Elsewhere all the world, every nation, all religion, to the ends of the earth, lay in thick darkness.

The whole world lay in wickedness, under the power of darkness, beneath the sentence of death. But out of the *ecclesia*, the perfection of beauty, God shined. This one place on earth, the assembly at Jerusalem, was full of light, life, and love, it was filled with heavenly glory radiating the divine presence of God, Father, Son, and Holy Ghost.

There was nothing else anywhere on earth. Nothing but darkness, blackness, deadness, and condemnation, throughout all nations, in all the world. All that there was, that was of God, existed in that one company at Jerusalem.

That was the *ecclesia*. If any were to be saved, they must be added to that. 'And the Lord added to the *ecclesia* daily such as should be saved.' As to every other creature under heaven, 'Of the rest durst no man join himself to them.'

Then came an apparent change, but it was not a real change. As the *ecclesia* increased by the going forth of the word of God, saints were gathered in other localities, too far from Jerusalem to meet with the assembly. A new thing occurred: *ecclesiai*. 'The assemblies'.

But this altered nothing in heaven. It made absolutely no difference to the heavenly concept. No difference to the Father. No difference to the Son. No difference to the Holy Ghost. No difference to Christ's *ecclesia*.

It was simply that the unity of that entity, that one heavenly concept, was now reflected in a manifold way: but it was still *that* which was reflected. It was, it is, and it ever shall be, but one *ecclesia*. The fact that the light of that one *ecclesia* shone forth in several assemblies altered nothing. The light remained just as one as the divine Person from whom it shone. No matter how many assemblies, there remained but one divine radiance.

The *concept* of the assembly appears always as one, no matter how many the assemblies. It continues that 'Upon this rock I will build my *ecclesia*', singular. The 'assemblies' do not alter that: they magnify it.

In fact the plural 'churches' does not occur until Acts 9:31. Thirty-six times the word is in the plural. Twice there is reference to 'every' assembly. Often 'the' *ecclesia* is used in the sense of one of the assemblies, as, 'the' *ecclesia* of the Thessalonians, 'the' assembly which is in Smyrna. Here the reference is to that particular one of the assemblies. But this does not alter the essential nature of the assembly of Christ as one assembly.

It *is* one assembly, irrespective of the multiplying of the testimony.

It is nothing other than the one assembly that is manifested by an assembly in such and such a place. It is *that* assembly in such and such a place.

Christ's *ecclesia* is ever one; indivisible. Wherever he should build his *ecclesia*, the *whole entity* is made manifest by his building in *that* place. It is *the* assembly that is seen there. 'The assembly of God which is at Corinth.' One God; one assembly. The assembly of God.

By the continuous disintegration of Protestantism into denominationalism, sectarianism, and independency—coupled with growing worldliness, indifference, and apathy—more than anything, the concept of the one assembly has been quite lost.

But when the apostle declared Christ to be 'Head over all things to *the* assembly', Eph. 1:22, here was no future ideal for the coming inheritance in glory. The apostle meant *now*.

What horror, then, would have taken hold upon Paul had he known that this precious doctrine was to be perverted into an empty theory for each division to rationalize as its own justification. A meaningless thought about which disobedient evangelicalism would utter its platitudes as it drifted even further into apostasy. The truth reveals that the *ecclesia* is a reality from which Protestantism, in its latter-day disobedience, has utterly departed.

In the beginning of the *ecclesia* the truth of Christ's Headship was actually realised in all the assemblies. Each assembly showed forth that one assembly over which Christ was Head.

Not merely to one of the assemblies, but to *the* assembly the following words of Paul are directed: 'To the intent that now' —not in eternity; not *only* at the beginning; *now*—'unto the principalities and powers in heavenly places might be known by the assembly the manifold wisdom of God', Eph. 3:10.

Now, although there were many assemblies, the assembly was but one, and the many assemblies were to show forth that oneness, and all heaven was to see it. Principalities and powers in heavenly places were to see it. To this end the assemblies on earth were to view themselves in a heavenly, not an earthly light. They were to see themselves as observed from heaven. For in the beginning they were not disobedient to the heavenly vision.

But this is a disobedient and gainsaying people, an evil generation, becoming the worse as the 'churches'—by which they mean their divided denominations—justify their unbelief and hardness of heart with a profession of Christ, and a veneer of scriptural quotations. Nevertheless all power is given to the Son, in heaven and on earth. And this, to the end of the age. The very end. So that in spite of all the working of man, we may boldly trust in that unchangeable word which shall stand even until the last day: 'I *will* build my assembly'!

And what could be more certain than the steadfast faithfulness of the Son of God, even to the very end, seeing that this fidelity springs from his everlasting love for his own *ecclesia*: 'Christ loved the assembly, and gave himself for it.'

This *ecclesia* or assembly of Christ is not some intangible fantasy of the disobedient 'evangelicals'—such as J.C. Ryle, an Anglican 'bishop' appointed by Disraeli, who believed nothing, to spite Gladstone, who was a high churchman—inventing an 'invisible church' with visible members permanently scattered among all denominations!

But still Christ builds his own *ecclesia*, which, though built spiritually, is built on earth. This is *the* assembly. Unscriptural philosophizing about 'the church militant', or 'the church triumphant', is wholly to be rejected. *The* assembly is the light which all the assemblies show forth, and with which each one is radiant. This light of the glory, shining in the face of

Jesus Christ, is that of one Head, one body, one *ecclesia*, dwelling in one Spirit, and indwelt by one God and Father.

This light—not talk about it—is what needs to be recovered in our day, and it is what should be looked for, and inwardly expected, by the faithful remnant. When these things are so, then the modern priests, scribes, Pharisees, lawyers, Herodians, Sadducees, doctors, rabbis—not to mention know-all Brethren, with their hard hearts, cold affections, and heads full of dead and self-righteous theories—will surely rage. Let them rage! Let them storm, slander, lie, persecute, do what they will. What care we for that? Nothing at all.

In the beginning each assembly answered to *the* assembly. And *the* assembly answered to each assembly. This is a heavenly vision: 'A glorious *ecclesia*'. Eph. 5:27.

This glorious assembly abides as one in heaven with the Lord, whilst one on earth in the midst of tears and tribulation. This oneness is shown forth in every single assembly, the oneness of heavenly union between Christ and his bride, the Head and the body. 'I speak concerning Christ and the assembly.' Each and every one of the assemblies shows forth *nothing less* than this whole, though it be by but two or three gathered in his name.

'He is the Head of the body, the *ecclesia*', Col. 1:18. I fulfil this ministry, said the apostle, 'for his body's sake, which is the *ecclesia*', Col. 1:24. Just as it was written of Jesus 'The zeal of thine house hath eaten me up'. So this same holy zeal consumed Paul.

How clear the apostle's vision! nothing less than all saints, every member of the body of Christ, the entire heavenly *ecclesia*. How fervent his love: in stripes, in imprisonments, in persecutions, in perils oft; yet his ardour remained unabated. How consuming was his ministry: day and night with tears, labouring in word and doctrine, Paul was indefatigable in this ministry 'for his body's sake'.

Never once was Paul's vision dimmed. Never once was his love quenched. Never once did he limit or constrain his ministry to a party. His ministry was 'for his body's sake, which is the *ecclesia.*'

The assembly, which is his body, is heavenly, it is one, it is in divine union, and *it* is seen and shown forth in all the assemblies gathered by Christ into the one assembly, the one fellowship of the mystery, and in none other.

This is the *ecclesia* as it was in the beginning. There is none other, there never will be any other, and there never will be the remotest shadow of turning from what was in the beginning, even to the very end, on the part of the heavenly Builder.

All the shadows, and all the turning, are on the part of the professions and confessions of Christ that fall short of the truth, or in the parties and divisions that miss the mark of the *ecclesia* built by Christ alone. All these have come in since the beginning. But there was no need for it. And there is even less need for it to continue now.

Whilst the history of the beginning of the *ecclesia* appears in the Acts of the Apostles, the doctrine is unfolded in the succeeding epistles.

It was by the apostolic ministry that Christ raised up the *ecclesia.*

Hence the book of Acts is called 'The Acts of the Apostles'. The book is not called 'The Acts of the Holy Ghost'. Nor even 'The Acts of Christ'. Though every divine work recorded in the Acts came from Christ on high by the Spirit below. But it came from him through the apostolic ministry below. He acted through the ministry of the apostles. Thus the record is called 'The Acts of the Apostles'.

It is true that the saints 'went everywhere preaching the word'. But it is equally true that this was neither their choice nor their doing, it was the result of the persecution. They did not initiate it, it happened to them. They fled the persecution. That was how they came to travel abroad. In consequence they testified. That is, they went everywhere preaching the *apostolic* word which they had been taught, and in which they had been nourished and brought up under the ministry.

Having gone forth as a result of the persecution, scattered by the providence of God, so the word sprang up among the Gentiles. In consequence the great apostle of the Gentiles was raised up and sent forth from Christ in heaven, with a unique ministry, to edify and build up the *ecclesia* among all nations.

This is hardly 'The Acts of the Brethren'. Such acts, springing as they do from the will of man which cannot stand being subordinate to the ministry, will never build up Christ's *ecclesia*. They will pull it down. Brethrenism is in the very teeth of scripture at the salient point of the ministry. The record refutes them: It is the Acts of the *Apostles*; it is not The Acts of the *Brethren*. Why not? Because Christ does not use brethren as such to build up his *ecclesia*, he uses the apostolic ministry. Then brethren are built up, and so God has ordained it, for thus the body is brought to the 'edification of itself in love'.

And, sending his ministers from heaven, as subject to the apostolic word, example, and doctrine, God continues the same acts in principle even until now. He never does, and he never will, vary from his own divine principles and terms. With him there is no variableness neither shadow of turning. Hence the saying, As it was in the beginning, is now, and ever shall be. Amen.

It goes without saying that the immutable divine principles and acts seen in the new testament scriptures are utterly different from all the humanly devised methods of subsequent ages. Never is this more true than of the ministry. The ministry of the new testament is clean contrary in principle to the hiring of some manufactured professional 'pastor' by a denominational, un-denominational, or inter-denominational organisation or congregation, which then has the impertinence to call him 'the minister' and themselves 'the church'.

No such thing existed in all the record of the new testament. None of the epistles addressed any such organisation, none addressed any such office, and none acknowledged any such system. Look and see.

In the beginning of the *ecclesia* God did something, not man. It was from heaven, not the earth. It was all of God's initiative, man had nothing to do with it. God wrought the work. The assembly and the assemblies were the result.

Unless today we come out of the division and confusion, the pretence and play acting, to be gathered as they were, under that ministry sent from heaven; or unless we will submit with meek penitence to being found in the way of it, calling upon God to work what we cannot; then we are at best little better than the foolish virgins with no oil in their vessels with their lamps, slumbering on in indifference. Then, like them, we shall surely awake at last to the dreadful reality, the reality which we refused to face as we trifled on in our journeying to that great and notable day of the Lord.

All that man builds, or can build, in a way of religion; all that he does, or can do, that conforms with scripture; all his reforming, reviving, renewing, is nothing to the point. *Christ built his own ecclesia.* From heaven. And he still does. Not man. '*I will build* my assembly.'

Man builds nothing but earthly vanity and human pretence, scorning to become as humble as a little child, obstinately refusing to submit to Christ's building. Why? Because *man* wants to be the builder. Such men are afraid—not without good cause—that if they submit to him, they will be nothing more than the least of all, which is what their vanity and self-esteem cannot stand.

Hired 'ministers' may speak from the scriptures to the congregations which form their sects, but the scriptures were not given by the Holy Ghost to them, their congregations, or their sects, that they should so speak. Nor did the Lord from heaven put one such word, by the Spirit, into their mouths.

If they deny this, then let them tell us why they went to bible school, to learn how to substitute what man can manufacture, for what, in the beginning, the Lord himself did from heaven without human aid? Tell us? But we know. The Lord has not done it with *them*, and that is what they cannot stand. For they will be first, and they will have the chief seats in the synagogue. Hence they must force themselves to turn to man's substitutionary system, to do for them what the Lord did not do, and would not do. This is Saul's offspring.

Neither were the epistles written to them, their sects, their denominations, or their divisions, each single one of which separately calls itself 'the church'! As if these many misnamed divisions were in the same position or on the same basis as was the one *ecclesia* in the beginning! They were not, and they are not. They must all come down, like Zacchaeus, if the Lord is to do the work. For he shall do all of the work, or none of the work. But climbing down is the very thing that they have never done, and that they never will do.

Incumbent hirelings may speak to their paying audiences out of texts from Romans to Revelation. As though there were any relation between *their* 'ministry', and the ministry of those Spirit-filled, God-taught, divinely called ministers whom Christ sends from heaven! Or as if there were any comparison between *their* 'building', and the *ecclesia* built by Christ in the beginning!

The scriptures pertain neither to them, nor to their congregations. Neither does Christ put his word from heaven into the mouth of the one, nor write it upon the heart of the other, at any time. They should cease from fantasy, and admit reality. But they have not the humility.

The *ecclesia* in Acts was formed by the Holy Ghost from heaven, and the apostles in Acts were sent from the Lord in glory. And all this without the hand or work of man once appearing. Indeed, should the flesh have shown itself, immediately it would have been discerned, judged, and rejected. All was of God, first and last. And it still is. Nothing has happened that makes the least difference to anything that really matters.

The *ecclesia* in the beginning was supernatural: it was past the power of man to mimic. Men could not copy it, nor could they 'pattern' their religious organisations upon it. It was the assembly of God, for the very reason that God formed it for himself by himself as his own peculiar dwelling.

The fear of God rested upon this assembly. The power of God filled it. And there was a great fear of grieving, or in any way marring, the mighty power, influence, glory, and presence of the Holy Ghost from heaven, whose indwelling life was more tangible to them, and much more important, than their own existence.

Once given the descent of the Holy Ghost, and his Person filling the assembly, the power of union was present, uniting the saints in one body. The saints were then to be taught by the living ministry all the words of this life.

In consequence the saints hung on the apostles' doctrine in order to be nourished up in the life of the one body. All outside was barren: they needed to be fed within. All around was dark: they needed light in the way. All about was danger: they needed the trumpet blast of warning.

Baptized by one Spirit into one body, the saints sought earnestly for spiritual communion in the apostles' doctrine and fellowship, according to the anointing of the Holy One, concerning the common life of the members of that one body. Moreover, having been brought into the habitation of God through the Spirit, they must needs learn how to behave themselves in the house of God, which is the assembly of the living God, the pillar and ground of the truth.

The saints had been begotten by the incorruptible seed of the word of God. Then, as newborn babes, they craved with the earnest desire of life itself for that nourishment and admonition, chastisement and scourging, tribulation and patience, experience and hope, which would bring their newborn life to fulfilment; to attain to the maturity of sonship; to develop priestly discernment; and to have their senses exercised to discern both good and evil. Nothing but the heaven-sent apostolic ministry could provide for these deep-seated desires.

The record of this provision from on high may be found in the epistles. But these epistles were certainly not written to divided sects and denominations, with dead and worldly congregations, presided over by some salaried hireling. They were written by holy men of God to the *ecclesia* of the living God, gathered by the power and unity of the Spirit into one body.

The very idea that these epistles should have been appropriated by papists, Anglicans, and other denominational missions and sects—each to 'support' his own system!—as if any of them bore the least resemblance to the original recipients, would have filled the writers with horror.

And to this very day, such writings apply only to those gatherings which have the same character and distinctiveness as the one *ecclesia* to which they were addressed in the beginning.

The apostolic epistles were addressed to Christ's *ecclesia*, and to Christ's *ecclesia* alone, wherever that one body was represented locally. Such local assemblies never lost sight of *the* assembly, of which each was the one divine manifestation in that given locality. Neither did the saints ever lose sight of the ministry sent down from the one heavenly Head on high in the glory, to minister to the whole assembly filled by the one Person of the Spirit on earth below.

For the variously divided but uneasily confederate—though suspiciously jealous—'ministers' and 'pastors' of the denominations, sects and independencies, to use these epistles for their hire, why, this is to steal God's words indeed. It is to make trade of God's words—though they belong neither to them nor their employers—and it shall surely be required at the hand of every one of them in the last day.

For these are of the sort in whose mouth the Spirit did not put a single word at any one time. And their sects are those which the Spirit never gathered in any single instance.

Therefore, to speak of any of the epistles, from Romans to Revelation, as having the least bearing upon or relevance to the denominated and partial, not to mention worldly and carnal, sectarian gatherings—in divisions which they misname 'churches'—is nothing short of ridiculous.

Each epistle was written to Christ's *ecclesia*, with words which the Holy Ghost gave, framed from the lips of the Lord in glory, attested by the everlasting God, and set down by the pen of holy, faithful, and sent ministers. Unless men are in the light, life and power, that these ministers were, what have such words to do either with them, or with the divisions which hire them?

Heart-broken and penitent, with weeping and mourning, the saints are to be gathered out of all the sects and divisions, and from under all the dead hirelings. For these deny the unity of the body of Christ, shaming the Head of the *ecclesia*, stealing his names and words to describe themselves, when such names and words have nothing to do either with them or with their systems.

These things being so—and so late in the age—now, therefore, it is time to remember that the blessing rests upon such as the poor in spirit; upon those that mourn; upon the meek; upon all who hunger and thirst after righteousness. Such as these.

It is time to recall that of the many 'woes' pronounced by Christ, the 'woe' that he fastened upon the religious was against the 'rich', for they should be sent empty away; against the 'full', for want shall come upon them as an armed man; against the 'laughing', for there shall be weeping and gnashing of teeth; against those 'of whom all men speak well', for they shall hear the words, Depart from me, ye cursed.

Then it is time to heed the midnight cry, Behold, the bridegroom cometh! For the night is far spent. 'Behold, the bridegroom cometh, go ye out to meet him.' It is time to awake out of sleep. It is time to put on sackcloth and ashes. It is time to be poor; to hunger; to weep; to be hated of men; to be separated from their company; to be reproached of men; to have one's name cast out as evil, for the Son of man's sake. It is high time.

High time to repent. To become as little children. To mourn every one by himself apart. Surely this becomes us in these last days. For there are still conditions upon which the blessing is pronounced. These abide. They are the conditions to which the power of the Spirit is assured. 'For he saith, I have heard thee in a time accepted, and in the day of salvation have I succoured thee: behold, now is the accepted time; now is the day of salvation.'

With those in just such conditions, that is, from the Lord's poor, Christ builds his *ecclesia.* Why from those? Because in them already there is made manifest that prior work of God, which shall surely be followed by the revelation of his Son from heaven.

'Hear the word of the LORD, ye that tremble at his word; Your brethren that hated you, that cast you out for my name's sake, said, Let the LORD be glorified: but he shall appear to your joy, and they shall be ashamed.' Now, of those whom these hypocrites cast out, Christ shall build his *ecclesia.*

When Jesus had given sight to the man born blind, the Pharisees—these hypocrites—cast him out of their assembly. 'And Jesus heard that they had cast him out'—mark that, he heard it—'and when he had found him'—mark that also: he found him—'he said unto him, Dost thou believe on the Son of God? He answered and said, Who is he, Lord, that I might believe on him? And Jesus said unto him, Thou hast both seen him, and it is he that talketh with thee. And he said, Lord, I believe. And he worshipped him.' Now, that is revelation. But the poor man knew his blindness first, and that by long and bitter experience.

'Thus saith the LORD, To this man will I look, even to him that is poor and of a contrite spirit, and trembleth at my word.' 'The sacrifices of God are a broken spirit: a broken and a contrite heart, O God, thou wilt not despise.'

'For thus saith the high and lofty One that inhabiteth eternity, whose name is Holy; I dwell in the high and holy place, with him also that is of a contrite and humble spirit, to revive the spirit of the humble, and to revive the heart of the contrite ones. For I will not contend for ever, neither will I be always wroth.'

This consciousness of being born blind; this broken and contrite heart; this humble spirit; precede sonship. It is that by which sonship is ushered in. All who are of this spirit are in the secret. All these Christ shall take and build into his *ecclesia.* None other. For these he calls 'babes', and, of a truth, to them the Father reveals his Son from heaven. It is upon them that the LORD commands the blessing, even life for evermore.

This is that people, previously cut to and pricked in their heart, of whom one reads in the Acts. Upon all of these, having first received and been convicted under John's ministry, thereafter having followed Jesus, the Spirit was poured out. This is the beginning of the *ecclesia.* It was the *ecclesia* in the beginning. And it is the *ecclesia* now. As it was in the beginning, is now, and ever shall be. Amen.

THE END

INDEX

TO OTHER PUBLICATIONS

PSALMS, HYMNS AND SPIRITUAL SONGS

THE PSALMS
OF THE
OLD TESTAMENT

The Psalms of the Old Testament, the result of years of painstaking labour, is an original translation into verse from the Authorised Version, which seeks to present the Psalms in the purest scriptural form possible for singing. Here, for the first time, divine names are rendered as and when they occur in the scripture, the distinction between LORD and Lord has been preserved, and every essential point of doctrine and experience appears with unique perception and fidelity.

The Psalms of the Old Testament is the first part of a trilogy written by John Metcalfe, the second part of which is entitled *Spiritual Songs from the Gospels*, and the last, *The Hymns of the New Testament*. These titles provide unique and accurate metrical versions of passages from the psalms, the gospels and the new testament epistles respectively, and are intended to be used together in the worship of God.

Price £2.50 *(postage extra)*
(hard-case binding, dust-jacket)
ISBN 0 9506366 7 3

SPIRITUAL SONGS

FROM

THE GOSPELS

The *Spiritual Songs from the Gospels*, the result of years of painstaking labour, is an original translation into verse from the Authorised Version, which seeks to present essential parts of the gospels in the purest scriptural form possible for singing. The careful selection from Matthew, Mark, Luke and John, set forth in metrical verse of the highest integrity, enables the singer to sing 'the word of Christ' as if from the scripture itself, 'richly and in all wisdom'; and, above all, in a way that facilitates worship in song of unprecedented fidelity.

The *Spiritual Songs from the Gospels* is the central part of a trilogy written by John Metcalfe, the first part of which is entitled *The Psalms of the Old Testament*, and the last, *The Hymns of the New Testament.* These titles provide unique and accurate metrical versions of passages from the psalms, the gospels and the new testament epistles respectively, and are intended to be used together in the worship of God.

Price £2.50 *(postage extra)*
(hard-case binding, dust-jacket)
ISBN 0 9506366 8 1

THE HYMNS

OF THE

NEW TESTAMENT

The *Hymns of the New Testament*,. the result of years of painstaking labour, is an original translation into verse from the Authorised Version, which presents essential parts of the new testament epistles in the purest scriptural form possible for singing. The careful selection from the book of Acts to that of Revelation, set forth in metrical verse of the highest integrity, enables the singer to sing 'the word of Christ' as if from the scripture itself, 'richly and in all wisdom'; and, above all, in a way that facilitates worship in song of unprecedented fidelity.

The *Hymns of the New Testament* is the last part of a trilogy written by John Metcalfe, the first part of which is entitled *The Psalms of the Old Testament*, and the next, *Spiritual Songs from the Gospels*. These titles provide unique and accurate metrical versions of passages from the psalms, the gospels and the new testament epistles respectively, and are intended to be used together in the worship of God.

Price £2.50 *(postage extra)*
(hard-case binding, dust-jacket)
ISBN 0 9506366 9 X

‘THE APOSTOLIC FOUNDATION OF THE CHRISTIAN CHURCH’ SERIES

FOUNDATIONS UNCOVERED

THE APOSTOLIC FOUNDATION
OF THE
CHRISTIAN CHURCH

Volume I

Foundations Uncovered is a small book of some 37 pages. This is the introduction to the major series: 'The Apostolic Foundation of the Christian Church'.

Rich in truth, the Introduction deals comprehensively with the foundation of the apostolic faith under the descriptive titles: The Word, The Doctrine, The Truth, The Gospel, The Faith, The New Testament, and The Foundation.

The contents of the book reveal: The Fact of the Foundation; The Foundation Uncovered; What the Foundation is not; How the Foundation is Described; and, Being Built upon the Foundation.

'This book comes with the freshness of a new Reformation.'

Price 30p *(postage extra)*
(Laminated cover)
ISBN 0 9506366 5 7

THE BIRTH OF JESUS CHRIST

THE APOSTOLIC FOUNDATION
OF THE
CHRISTIAN CHURCH

Volume II

'The very spirit of adoration and worship rings through the pages of *The Birth of Jesus Christ.*

'The author expresses with great clarity the truths revealed to him in his study of holy scriptures at depth. We are presented here with a totally lofty view of the Incarnation.

'John Metcalfe is to be classed amongst the foremost expositors of our age; and his writings have about them that quality of timelessness that makes me sure they will one day take their place among the heritage of truly great Christian works.'

From a review by Rev. David Catterson.

'Uncompromisingly faithful to scripture ... has much to offer which is worth serious consideration ... deeply moving.'

The Expository Times.

Price 95p *(postage extra)*
(Laminated Cover)
ISBN 0 9502515 5 0

THE MESSIAH

THE APOSTOLIC FOUNDATION
OF THE
CHRISTIAN CHURCH

Volume III

The Messiah is a spiritually penetrating and entirely original exposition of Matthew chapter one to chapter seven from the trenchant pen of John Metcalfe.

Matthew Chapters One to Seven

GENEALOGY · BIRTH · STAR OF BETHLEHEM
HEROD · FLIGHT TO EGYPT · NAZARETH
JOHN THE BAPTIST · THE BAPTIST'S MINISTRY
JESUS' BAPTISM · ALL RIGHTEOUSNESS FULFILLED
HEAVEN OPENED · THE SPIRIT'S DESCENT
THE TEMPTATION OF JESUS IN THE WILDERNESS
JESUS' MANIFESTATION · THE CALLING · THE TRUE DISCIPLES
THE BEATITUDES · THE SERMON ON THE MOUNT

'Something of the fire of the ancient Hebrew prophet .... Metcalfe has spiritual and expository potentials of a high order.'

The Life of Faith.

Price £2.45 *(postage extra)*
(425 pages, Laminated Cover)
ISBN 0 9502515 8 5

THE SON OF GOD AND SEED OF DAVID

THE APOSTOLIC FOUNDATION
OF THE
CHRISTIAN CHURCH

Volume IV

The Son of God and Seed of David is the fourth volume in the major work entitled 'The Apostolic Foundation of the Christian Church.'

'The author proceeds to open and allege that Jesus Christ is and ever was *The Son of God.* This greatest of subjects, this most profound of all mysteries, is handled with reverence and with outstanding perception.

'The second part considers *The Seed of David.* What is meant precisely by 'the seed'? And why 'of David'? With prophetic insight the author expounds these essential verities.'

Price £6.95 *(postage extra)*
Hardback 250 pages
Laminated bookjacket
ISBN 1 870039 16 5

CHRIST CRUCIFIED

THE APOSTOLIC FOUNDATION OF THE CHRISTIAN CHURCH

Volume V

Christ Crucified the definitive work on the crucifixion, the blood, and the cross of Jesus Christ.

The crucifixion of Jesus Christ witnessed in the Gospels: the gospel according to Matthew; Mark; Luke; John.

The blood of Jesus Christ declared in the Epistles: the shed blood; the blood of purchase; redemption through his blood; the blood of sprinkling; the blood of the covenant.

The doctrine of the cross revealed in the apostolic foundation of the Christian church: the doctrine of the cross; the cross and the body of sin; the cross and the carnal mind; the cross and the law; the offence of the cross; the cross of our Lord Jesus Christ.

Price £6.95 *(postage extra)*
Hardback 300 pages
Laminated bookjacket
ISBN 1 870039 08 4

JUSTIFICATION BY FAITH

THE APOSTOLIC FOUNDATION OF THE CHRISTIAN CHURCH

Volume VI

THE HEART OF THE GOSPEL · THE FOUNDATION OF THE CHURCH
THE ISSUE OF ETERNITY
CLEARLY, ORIGINALLY AND POWERFULLY OPENED

The basis · The righteousness of the law
The righteousness of God · The atonement · Justification
Traditional views considered · Righteousness imputed to faith
Faith counted for righteousness · Justification by Faith

'And it came to pass, when Jesus had ended these sayings, the people were astonished at his doctrine: for he taught them as one having authority, and not as the scribes.' Matthew 7:28,29.

Price £7.50 *(postage extra)*
Hardback 375 pages
Laminated bookjacket
ISBN 1870039 11 4

Newly Published

THE CHURCH: WHAT IS IT?

THE APOSTOLIC FOUNDATION
OF THE
CHRISTIAN CHURCH

Volume VII

The answer to this question proceeds first from the lips of Jesus himself, Mt. 16:18, later to be expounded by the words of the apostles whom he sent.

Neither fear of man nor favour from the world remotely affect the answer.

Here is the truth, the whole truth, and nothing but the truth.

The complete originality, the vast range, and the total fearlessness of this book command the attention in a way that is unique.

Read this book: you will never read another like it.

Outspokenly devastating yet devastatingly constructive.

Price £7.75 *(postage extra)*
Hardback 400 pages
Laminated bookjacket
ISBN 1 870039 23 8

OTHER TITLES

NOAH AND THE FLOOD

Noah and the Flood expounds with vital urgency the man and the message that heralded the end of the old world. The description of the flood itself is vividly realistic. The whole work has an unmistakable ring of authority, and speaks as 'Thus saith the Lord'.

'Mr. Metcalfe makes a skilful use of persuasive eloquence as he challenges the reality of one's profession of faith ... he gives a rousing call to a searching self-examination and evaluation of one's spiritual experience.'

The Monthly Record of the Free Church of Scotland.

Price £1.90 *(postage extra)*
(Laminated Cover)
ISBN 1 870039 22 X

DIVINE FOOTSTEPS

Divine Footsteps traces the pathway of the feet of the Son of man from the very beginning in the prophetic figures of the true in the old testament through the reality in the new; doing so in a way of experimental spirituality. At the last a glimpse of the coming glory is beheld as his feet are viewed as standing at the latter day upon the earth.

Price 95p *(postage extra)*
(Laminated Cover)
ISBN 1 870039 21 1

THE RED HEIFER

The Red Heifer was the name given to a sacrifice used by the children of Israel in the Old Testament—as recorded in Numbers 19—in which a heifer was slain and burned. Cedar wood, hyssop and scarlet were cast into the burning, and the ashes were mingled with running water and put in a vessel. It was kept for the children of Israel for a water of separation: it was a purification for sin.

In this unusual book the sacrifice is brought up to date and its relevance to the church today is shown.

Price 75p *(postage extra)*
ISBN 0 9502515 4 2

THE WELLS OF SALVATION

The Wells of Salvation is written from a series of seven powerful addresses preached at Tylers Green. It is a forthright and experimental exposition of Isaiah 12:3, 'Therefore with joy shall ye draw water out of the wells of salvation.'

Price £1.50 *(postage extra)*
(Laminated Cover)
ISBN 0 9502515 6 9

OF GOD OR MAN?

LIGHT FROM GALATIANS

The Epistle to the Galatians contends for deliverance from the law and from carnal ministry.

The Apostle opens his matter in two ways:

Firstly, Paul vindicates himself and his ministry against those that came not from God above, but from Jerusalem below.

Secondly, he defends the Gospel and evangelical liberty against legal perversions and bondage to the flesh.

Price £1.45 *(postage extra)*
(Laminated Cover)
ISBN 0 9506366 3 0

A QUESTION FOR POPE JOHN PAUL II

As a consequence of his many years spent apart in prayer, lonely vigil, and painstaking study of the scripture, John Metcalfe asks a question and looks for an answer from Pope John Paul II.

Price £1.25. *(postage extra)*
(Laminated Cover)
ISBN 0 9506366 4 9

THE BOOK OF RUTH

The Book of Ruth is set against the farming background of old testament Israel at the time of the Judges, the narrative—unfolding the work of God in redemption—being marked by a series of agricultural events.

These events—the famine; the barley harvest; the wheat harvest; the winnowing—possessed a hidden spiritual significance to that community, but, much more, they speak in figure directly to our own times, as the book reveals.

Equally contemporary appear the characters of Ruth, Naomi, Boaz, and the first kinsman, drawn with spiritual perception greatly to the profit of the reader.

Price £4.95 *(postage extra)*
Hardback 200 pages
Laminated bookjacket
ISBN 1 870039 17 3

'TRACT FOR THE TIMES' SERIES

THE GOSPEL OF GOD

'TRACT FOR THE TIMES' SERIES

The Gospel of God. Beautifully designed, this tract positively describes the gospel under the following headings: The Gospel is of God; The Gospel is Entirely of God; The Gospel is Entire in Itself; The Gospel is Preached; The Gospel Imparts Christ; and, Nothing But the Gospel Imparts Christ.

Price 25p *(postage extra)*
(Laminated Cover)
No. 1 in the Series

THE STRAIT GATE

'TRACT FOR THE TIMES' SERIES

The Strait Gate. Exceptionally well made, this booklet consists of extracts from 'The Messiah', compiled in such a way as to challenge the shallowness of much of today's 'easy-believism', whilst positively pointing to the strait gate.

Price 25p *(postage extra)*
(Laminated Cover)
No. 2 in the Series

ETERNAL SONSHIP AND TAYLOR BRETHREN

'TRACT FOR THE TIMES' SERIES

Eternal Sonship and Taylor Brethren. This booklet is highly recommended, particularly for those perplexed by James Taylor's teaching against the eternal sonship of Christ.

Price 25p *(postage extra)*
(Laminated Cover)
No. 3 in the Series

MARKS OF THE NEW TESTAMENT CHURCH

'TRACT FOR THE TIMES' SERIES

Marks of the New Testament Church. This exposition from Acts 2:42 declares what were, and what were not, the abiding marks of the church. The apostles' doctrine, fellowship and ordinances are lucidly explained.

Price 25p *(postage extra)*
(Laminated Cover)
No. 4 in the Series

THE CHARISMATIC DELUSION

'TRACT FOR THE TIMES' SERIES

The Charismatic Delusion. A prophetic message revealing the fundamental error of this movement which has swept away so many in the tide of its popularity. Here the delusion is dispelled.

Price 25p *(postage extra)*
(Laminated Cover)
No. 5 in the Series

PREMILLENNIALISM EXPOSED

'TRACT FOR THE TIMES' SERIES

Premillennialism Exposed. Well received evangelically, particularly through the influence of J.N. Darby, the Schofield bible, and the Plymouth Brethren, Premillennialism has assumed the cloak of orthodoxy. In this tract the cloak is removed, and the unorthodoxy of this system is exposed. A remarkable revelation.

Price 25p *(postage extra)*
(Laminated Cover)
No. 6 in the Series

JUSTIFICATION AND PEACE

'TRACT FOR THE TIMES' SERIES

Justification and Peace. This tract is taken from a message preached in December 1984 at Penang Hill, Malaysia. In this well-known address, peace with God is seen to be based upon nothing save justification by faith. No one should miss this tract.

Price 25p *(postage extra)*
(Laminated Cover)
No. 7 in the Series

FAITH OR PRESUMPTION?

'TRACT FOR THE TIMES' SERIES

Faith or presumption? The eighth tract in this vital series exposes the difference between faith and presumption, showing that faith is not of the law, neither is is apart from the work of God, nor is it of man. The work of God in man that precedes saving faith is opened generally and particularly, and the tract goes on to reveal positively the nature of saving faith. Belief and 'easy-believism' are contrasted, making clear the difference between the two, as the system of presumption—called easy-believism—is clearly shown, and the way of true belief pointed out with lucid clarity.

Price 25p *(postage extra)*
(Laminated Cover)
No. 8 in the Series

THE ELECT UNDECEIVED

'TRACT FOR THE TIMES' SERIES

The Elect undeceived, the ninth Tract for the Times, earnestly contends for 'the faith once delivered to the saints' in a way that is spiritually edifying, positive, and subject to the Lord Jesus Christ according to the scriptures.

The Tract is a response to the pamphlet 'Salvation and the Church' published jointly by the Catholic Truth Society and Church House Publishing, in which the Anglican and Roman Catholic Commissioners agree together about JUSTIFICATION. The pamphlet shows how they have agreed.

Price 25p *(postage extra)*
(Laminated Cover)
No. 9 in the Series

JUSTIFYING RIGHTEOUSNESS

'TRACT FOR THE TIMES' SERIES

Justifying Righteousness. Was it wrought by the law of Moses or by the blood of Christ? Written not in the language of dead theology but that of the living God, here is the vital and experimental doctrine of the new testament. Part of the book 'Justification by Faith', nevertheless this tract has a message in itself essential to those who would know and understand the truth.

Price 25p *(postage extra)*
(Laminated Cover)
No. 10 in the Series

RIGHTEOUSNESS IMPUTED

'TRACT FOR THE TIMES' SERIES

Righteousness Imputed. The truth of the gospel and the fallacy of tradition. Here the gospel trumpet of the jubilee is sounded in no uncertain terms, as on the one hand that truth essential to be believed for salvation is opened from holy scripture, and on the other the errors of Brethrenism are brought to light in a unique and enlightening way. This tract is taken from the book 'Justification by Faith', but in itself it conveys a message of great penetration and clarity.

Price 25p *(postage extra)*
(Laminated Cover)
No. 11 in the Series

THE GREAT DECEPTION

'TRACT FOR THE TIMES' SERIES

The Great Deception. The erosion of Justification by faith. All ministers, every Christian, and each assembly ought not only to possess but to read and reread this prophetic message as the word of the Lord to this generation, set in the context of the age. This tract is part of the book 'Justification by Faith' but contains within itself a message which is at once vital and authoritative.

Price 25p *(postage extra)*
(Laminated Cover)
No. 12 in the Series

A FAMINE IN THE LAND

'TRACT FOR THE TIMES' SERIES

A Famine in the Land. Taken from the Book of Ruth, with telling forcefulness this tract opens conditions exactly parallel to those of our own times. 'Behold, the days come, saith the Lord GOD, that I will send a famine in the land, not a famine of bread, nor a thirst for water, but of hearing the words of the LORD: and they shall wander from sea to sea, and from the north even to the east, they shall run to and fro to seek the word of the LORD, and shall not find it.'

Price 25p *(postage extra)*
(Laminated Cover)
No. 13 in the Series

BLOOD AND WATER

'TRACT FOR THE TIMES' SERIES

Blood and Water. Of the four gospels, only John reveals the truth that blood was shed at the cross. When it was shed, Jesus was dead already. With the blood there came forth water. But what do these things mean? With devastating present-day application, this tract tells you what they mean.

Price 25p *(postage extra)*
(Laminated Cover)
No. 14 in the Series

WOMEN BISHOPS?

'TRACT FOR THE TIMES' SERIES

Women Bishops? This is a question that has arisen in America, but should it have arisen at all?
Read this tract and find out the authoritative answer.

Price 25p *(postage extra)*
(Laminated Cover)
No. 15 in the Series

THE HEAVENLY VISION

'TRACT FOR THE TIMES' SERIES

The Heavenly Vision not only transformed the prophet himself, it became a savour of life unto life—or death unto death—to all the people.
'*Where there is no vision the people perish*', Proverbs 29:18. This is true. But where is the vision today? And what is the vision today? This tract answers those questions.

Price 25p *(Postage extra)*
(Laminated Cover)
No. 16 in the Series

EVANGELICAL TRACTS

EVANGELICAL TRACTS

1. *The Two Prayers of Elijah.* This tract, first printed in 1972, was reprinted in 1982. It shows the spiritual significance of the drought, the cloudburst, and the two prayers of Elijah.
Green card cover, price 10p.

2. *Wounded for our Transgressions.* An evangelical message taken from Isaiah 53. Declaring the salvation of God, this is a tract intended to help those seeking the Saviour and his work.
Gold card cover, price 10p.

3. *The Blood of Sprinkling.* Taken from Hebrews 12:24 this booklet expounds the things to which the people of God are not come, besides those to which they are come. Obvious from the context, this is striking in the exposition. The saving grace of God is clearly preached in this evangelical tract.
Red card cover, price 10p.

4. *The Grace of God that brings Salvation.* An evangelistic address from Titus 2:12—originally preached in South East Asia in 1985—which brings home to the heart the work of God in the salvation of the sinner.
Blue card cover, price 10p.

5. *The Name of Jesus.* First preached to a Chinese congregation in the Far East, this pamphlet declares the reason for and meaning of the name given to the Saviour: 'Thou shalt call his name JESUS: for he shall save his people from their sins.'
Rose card cover, price 10p.

These tracts may be ordered directly from the Trust, or through Bookshops. If money is sent with order, please add letter post allowance.

MINISTRY BY JOHN METCALFE

TAPE MINISTRY BY JOHN METCALFE
FROM ENGLAND AND THE FAR EAST
IS AVAILABLE.

In order to obtain this free recorded ministry, please send your blank cassette (C.90) and the cost of the return postage, including your name and address in block capitals, to the John Metcalfe Publishing Trust, Church Road, Tylers Green, Penn, Bucks, HP10 8LN. Tapelists are available on request.

Owing to the increased demand for the tape ministry, we are unable to supply more than two tapes per order, except in the case of meetings for the hearing of tapes, where a special arrangement can be made.

THE MINISTRY OF THE NEW TESTAMENT

The purpose of this substantial A4 gloss paper magazine is to provide spiritual and experimental ministry with sound doctrine which rightly and prophetically divides the Word of Truth.

Readers of our books will already know the high standards of our publications. They can be confident that these pages will maintain that quality, by giving access to enduring ministry from the past, much of which is derived from sources that are virtually unobtainable today, and publishing a living ministry from the present. Selected articles from the following writers have already been included:

Eli Ashdown · Abraham Booth · John Bunyan
John Burgon · John Calvin · Donald Cargill
John Cennick · J.N. Darby · George Fox
John Foxe · William Gadsby · William Huntington
William Kelly · John Kennedy · Hanserd Knollys
James Lewis · Martin Luther · Robert Murray McCheyne
John Metcalfe · Alexander—Sandy—Peden · J.C. Philpot
J.B. Stoney · Henry Tanner · John Vinall
John Welwood · George Whitefield · J.A. Wylie

Price £1.75 *(postage included)*
Issued Spring, Summer, Autumn, Winter.

Book Order Form

Please send to the address below:-

Title		Price	Quantity
A Question for Pope John Paul II		£1.25	......
Of God or Man?		£1.45	......
Noah and the Flood		£1.90	......
Divine Footsteps		£0.95	......
The Red Heifer		£0.75	......
The Wells of Salvation		£1.50	......
The Book of Ruth (Hardback edition)		£4.95	......
Psalms, Hymns & Spiritual Songs (Hardback edition)			
The Psalms of the Old Testament		£2.50	......
Spiritual Songs from the Gospels		£2.50	......
The Hymns of the New Testament		£2.50	......
'Apostolic Foundation of the Christian Church' series			
Foundations Uncovered	Vol.I	£0.30	......
The Birth of Jesus Christ	Vol.II	£0.95	......
The Messiah	Vol.III	£2.45	......
The Son of God and Seed of David (Hardback edition)	Vol.IV	£6.95	......
Christ Crucified (Hardback edition)	Vol.V	£6.95	......
Justification by Faith (Hardback edition)	Vol.VI	£7.50	......
The Church: What is it?	Vol.VII	£7.75	......
Tracts			
The Two Prayers of Elijah		£0.10	......
Wounded for our Transgressions		£0.10	......
The Blood of Sprinkling		£0.10	......
The Grace of God that Brings Salvation		£0.10	......
The Name of Jesus		£0.10	......
'Tract for the Times' series			
The Gospel of God	No.1	£0.25	......
The Strait Gate	No.2	£0.25	......
Eternal Sonship and Taylor Brethren	No.3	£0.25	......
Marks of the New Testament Church	No.4	£0.25	......
The Charismatic Delusion	No.5	£0.25	......
Premillennialism Exposed	No.6	£0.25	......
Justification and Peace	No.7	£0.25	......
Faith or presumption?	No.8	£0.25	......
The Elect undeceived	No.9	£0.25	......
Justifying Righteousness	No.10	£0.25	......
Righteousness Imputed	No.11	£0.25	......
The Great Deception	No.12	£0.25	......
A Famine in the Land	No.13	£0.25	......
Blood and Water	No.14	£0.25	......
Women Bishops?	No.15	£0.25	......
The Heavenly Vision	No.16	£0.25	......

Name and Address (in block capitals)

. . . .

. . . .

. . . .

If money is sent with order please allow for postage. Please address to:- The John Metcalfe Publishing Trust, Church Road, Tylers Green, Penn, Bucks, HP10 8LN.

Magazine Order Form

Name and Address (in block capitals)

. . . .

. . . .

. . . .

Please send me .... current copy/copies of The Ministry of the New Testament.

Please send me .... year/s subscription.

I enclose a cheque/postal order for £ ....

(Price: including postage, U.K. £1.75; Overseas £1.90)
(One year's subscription: Including postage, U.K. £7.00; Overseas £7.60)

Cheques should be made payable to The John Metcalfe Publishing Trust, and for overseas subscribers should be in pounds sterling drawn on a London Bank.

10 or more copies to one address will qualify for a 10% discount

Back numbers from Spring 1986 available.

Please send to The John Metcalfe Publishing Trust, Church Road, Tylers Green, Penn, Bucks, HP10 8LN

All Publications of the Trust are subsidised by the Publishers.